NEW LIGHT ON OLD LAMPS

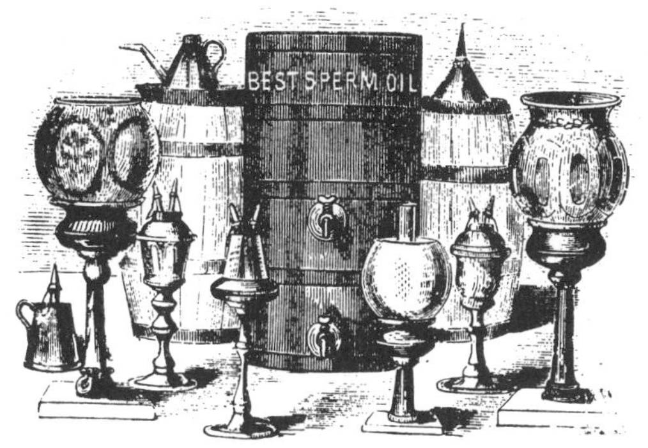

Does the Road Lead Upward Every Day?
Even for Everyone!
And Will There Be Help Upon the Way?
Yes, Lamps for All Who Come!

Larry Freeman

Library of Victorian Culture

How to Make and Restore Objets D'Art.

New Light on Old Lamps.

Victorian Silver: Holloware and Flatware.

Downing's Cottage Residences,
Landscapes Gardening, Rural Architecture.

Victorian Social & Political Satire.

Victorian Art Pottery.

Children's Picture Books,
Yesterday & Today.

Currier & Ives Victorian Battle Scenes.

Victorian Furnishings & Eastlake Design.

Victorian Poster Art.

Together with ten other promised titles, as suggested by the American Life Foundation's Study Institute.

NEW LIGHT ON OLD LAMPS

by Dr. Larry Freeman

Century House

Watkins Glen, N. Y.

Fancy Metal Goods

THE TURNER & SEYMOUR MFG. CO

TORRINGTON, CONN.

 See also our Collecting Old Lamps.

TABLE OF CONTENTS

EXTREMELY RARE EARLY AMERICAN HANGING LAMP

Eight spoked wooden wheel, with iron rim, supporting eight South Jersey glass hanging bowls for oil and wicks, these pressed to resemble pineapples. Three of translucent emerald-green, four of fine amber tone and one of beautiful amethyst. Four chains for suspension.

Diameter, 24 *inches; approximate height,* 38 *inches*

FOREWORD

If one has always heard, "The heart of America is the home," certainly to our Victorian grandparents, the **heart of every home** was the lamp. This is the story of the lamp's social development and the early collector items that are left behind. In those "dear, dead days beyond recall," mother quickly cleared away the supper dishes while father set a lighted lamp in the center of the table and the children brought out their toys and school books. Around this rosy glow the entire family now drew closely together. Mother went after her pile of mending, the children did lessons or played and father finished his daily paper. Then as the sandman approached, there would be reading from **Little Women, The Five Little Peppers** or **Pollyanna;** finally day clothes would be exchanged for night clothes, and tiny night-lights taken up to guide little sleepyheads to their nests upstairs. Thus did the lamp ever bring another day to its peaceful close.

Today people neither wish nor can recapture that period when the oil lamp was the center of the home; what they do want and can have is the object itself adapted to modern living. This fact alone will explain the truly amazing interest which collectors, dealers and decorators shower on all types of old lighting devices that have survived the ravages of time. Nineteenth century lamps of the kerosene-coal oil variety had their first rebirth of interest in the 1920's and '30's, those of candle, lard and rushlight days were rediscovered even earlier, while today's collectors are now busy with bygone gas and even early electric fixtures.

This comprehensive reference work on old lamps is a greatly expanded up-dated version of the author's original LIGHT ON OLD LAMPS (1944) written while serving as a Naval officer. One reviewer called it, "the only concise book in the field which names and illustrates the different types of lamps used in Eighteenth and Nineteenth century America, shows the constituent lamp parts, supplies a standard nomenclature, (very useful for describing items wanted or offered for sale), all the result of a prolonged search for old lamp catalogs, and very basic." Passing through 5 editions (the last in 1955) and having sold over 10,000 copies without benefit of bookstores or special advertising, one might be content just to repeat the old formula. The time has come, however, when a complete revision and enlargement of this entire field is required.

Part I covers domestic lighting from primitive times through the kerosene era (roughly to 1900). Part II begins with the gas light era (which started around 1870 and was practically blown out of existence when the Edison lamp began to make electric headway in the cities) and extends through the 1920's. In between (for both parts) more attention than formerly is given to previously neglected lamp-forms such as travel, coach and auto lights, street, store and yard lights, train, barn, signal and parade lanterns. In so far as possible, we have retained the spirit and pictures of old lamp catalogues which made the original issue so valuable. Part I adds several new chapters on early lighting, especially in the field of candle lamps and candelabra. The second part gives considerable space to the reassembly of old lamp parts. With the help of pictures from original catalogues, one can often find many accessories in today's junk shops. These together with the missing burners, chimneys, and bowls (still made by one or two surviving old lamp manufacturers) will enable the home handyman to recreate old lamps on his own. The number of lamp collectors and Mr. Fix-its in this field is legion!

In fact so many have written the author about their hobby, that in 1968 the American Life Foundation decided to have its Study Guide and Seminar No. 3 deal exclusively with "How to Make-Do with Old Lamp Parts." Only a number of invited experts in this field participated in the Seminar; but all collectors have the opportunity to purchase the results of the Seminar's ALF Study Guide, #3, price $4.50. The author wishes to thank his many friends whose interest and assistance have made the present book a reality. Unfortunately this number is so large, individual citation is all but impossible.

Larry Freeman

Watkins Glen, New York
Old Irelandville
May 1968

Part of American Life Foundation's Study Display.

Lamps of the early 1800's.

PARIS BRONZES.

THE great Candelabrum in the centre is the production of one of the most famous artistic establishments in Paris, that of Froment-Meurice; of the design we can only say that none but a French artist would probably have dared to put it in execution. This is the result of a whim, one of those daring fancies which can only be excused when carried out with that consummate skill here shown. It contrasts curiously, perhaps unfortunately, with its two companion figures.

The Tripod to the left is one of M. Barbédienne's charming works, designed after Greek models; it is the perfection of grace and lightness.

That on the other side is by another famous bronzist, M. Charpentier. Here again we have Greek types, but of a later style. The effect of the whole is very elegant, the Lamp extremely so, and the corona on the top of the stand to receive the Lamp is a happy notion.

BELGIAN, VENETIAN, AND FRENCH BRONZE WORK.

THE Chandelier in the centre was exhibited with many other metal works by an association of Belgian manufacturers at the International Exhibition at South Kensington in 1872: without any high claim to Art, the design of the work here represented is somewhat novel and light. The compound character of many Continental chandeliers, or lampadaires, as they might more properly be called—that is to say, with a shaded reading-lamp in the centre and lower than the others, and lamps with ground globes around—is a very useful one.

On the left hand is a very original Candelabrum, the work of a distinguished artistic manufacturer of Venice, Signor Joseph Michieli: this appears to be a kind of allegory of society, with the phases of innocence, activity, and crime, and it is carried out in faithful likeness of the old Venetian style.

The remaining example is as good a specimen in its special style as any we have given. The figure is exquisitely modelled, and the attitude easy and pleasant to regard—a great recommendation in a work of Art always present to the eye. The pedestal is remarkably elegant. The work was a contribution of the famous bronzist Charpentier, of Paris, to the International Exhibition of 1862.

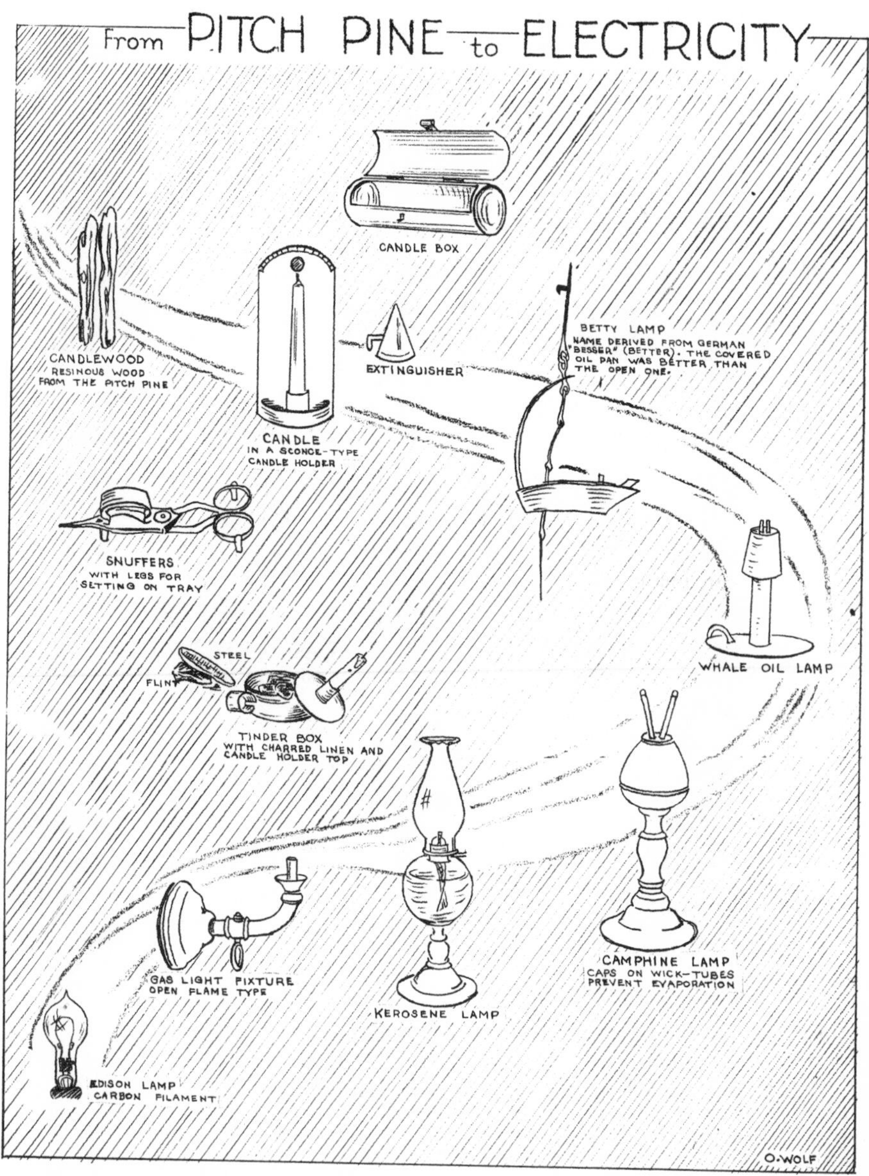

Primitive home lighting, of course, started with the **pine knots and splinters** from the resinous pine tree. The early Colonists called these splinters 'candlewood' and used them for illumination. The candlewood was placed in the corner of the fireplace on a flat stone and set afire.

Chapter I
INTRODUCTION

Lamps are one of the oldest accomplishments of human ingenuity. By arranging a wick in a container of grease, oil or other inflammable material man was first able to light his way about in the dark and so escape the nightly confinement of the primitive campfire. The history of the rise of western civilization is carried in the study of lamp developments. Most fascinating of all is the story of lighting as it unfolded in America. The primitive Rush lights and Betty lamps are a far cry from the fluorescent lighting of today. But collectors have long displayed avid interest in early lighting fixtures. Many of the old forms have been preserved and "adapted" to modern needs. This trend in decorative lighting has gone so far that many objects not intended to serve the function have been made into lamps by the dexterous use of electrical wiring and new shades. As an instance of the opposite trend, there are the "purists" who would never think of wiring an old lamp and who are content to use only the feeble beams as originally intended. Both "adapters'' and "purists" would admit however, that the study of early lighting is largely an adventure in guesswork.

The origin of the lamp is unknown. We have no certain information as to who first made lamps, but we do know they have been in use for over six thousand years. Excavations in Babylon and other early cities have revealed many specimens of open type lamps made of sun-baked clay. The development of the fine arts in Ancient Greece and Rome produced elaborate examples of the open type lamp and these were carried throughout the civilized world. Practically no fundamental improvement resulted in lamp design until late in the Eighteenth century, and so we find the colonists of early America using substantially the same type of lighting device as did the Romans, that is, a small handled oil container with a spout or slot at one end for wick. A Roman lamp of the first century and a Colonial "Betty" lamp seventeen hundred years later shows an astonishing similarity.

Major decorative interest in old lamps has always centered in those of the Victorian era. Possibly because so many varieties survive from that day and possibly because these are thought by many to be the most elegant types ever made. No end of critical opinions and research papers have been written about the difficulties and patent improvements in lighting. From A (Alabaster Sandwich lamps) to Z (Zesta replicas of the Glory lights) a host of domestic furbelows pass in review. Between early home lighting with pine knots, float or rush lights to the later developments with gas and electricity, one finds that Victorian coal-oil devices had many superior feaures. Recall the power failure and massive blackout of the entire eastern states a few years ago and one can appreciate how much a still functioning old kerosene lamp might be appreciated. Before spending major time with such Victorian artifacts, a brief study of the entire social history of domestic lamps is in order.

To understand the artistic development of domestic lighting fittings, one must consider both the technology of lamp developments and the application of materials and crafts as the centuries unfold. There was neither art nor craft in the flaming pine knots or burning fat in hollowed-out stones which primitive cave dwellers used to ward off the dangers of night's darkness—15,000 years ago. Not until 4,000 B.C. did that belt of civilization represented by Egypt and Sumeria develop a craft of lamp making based on consciously designed art-forms of metal or pottery which would burn oil in an open saucer with a fiber wick. Often called "float lamps" during these first thousand years, man's cry to "let there be light" conceived only this very simple device. Of the few notably artistic specimens that have survived, attention was first centered on a turned-over lip or wick channel to prevent oil spillage and which eventually became a lid or by the use of a thin alabaster, bell-shaped cover dome which would protect the feeble oil-flame's extinction and provide a warm translucent glow. Olive oil was in use by the time of the Exodus (1300 B.C.) but fish and animal grease were more common illuminants. Always the urge was to get the light up where it would do the most good; but not until Greek and Roman times do we find artistically integrated table and floor lamps which placed the flame in high solid containers which would not spill the oil or set the entire house afire.

So far nothing has been said about the use of candles; for it is doubtful if the use of a coating of tallow or pitch over a flax thread developed into anything remotely resembling the Eighteenth century candelabra before 200 A.D. In between, man had the rushlight, not true candles but essentially the pith of rushes dipped or soaked in fat and held in an iron stand by something like a pair of pliers which could be shifted forward as it burned.

For a long time the Medieval Church made prodigal use of sticky beeswax candles to increase the aura of lighted Godliness in its services. Spike or pricket candleholders standing as high as five feet from the floor were designed by the best craftsmen of the day with bronze as the most common material for both sacred and secular tables of power. Low folk had to be satisfied with the Betty or grease lamps.

Not until the Seventeenth century did molded hard-wax tallow candles make their appearance to be followed in the next century by crystal glass chandeliers in the home of the Lords. These were designed to "reflect the feeble glow from hundreds of individual tapers, surrounded by prisms to make a ballroom delightfully bright." Likewise there was no significant change in oil lamps as domestic illuminants until near the end of another century. Then there occurred two developments, one abroad and one in America, that revolutionized the history of lamp design. One, credited to Benjamin Franklin, gave us the whale oil burner—a stopper to be inserted in the top of a bottle-shaped lamp and holding two small ropelike wicks that extended into the fluid. The other and more important development is the creation by Aime Argand, a Swiss chemist and philosopher, of the cylindrical wick lamp which admitted air on both the inside and outside of the burner and so greatly increased the illumination. The development of a chimney to ward off drafts further increased the brilliancy and was used with both whale oil and Argand burners. From this time on there was steady improvement in all the factors making for a good strong light.

The cyclonic impact of kerosene on the domestic lighting field sparked that vast array of hand, table and ceiling lamps now known as Victorian. Kerosene replaced grease and whale oil. The proper draft principles were finally perfected in the famed "Rochester Burner" of the late Nineteenth century. Cotton wicks with strong capillary attraction replaced twisted rags and ropes. Late Victorian Parlor lamps took on a flambuoyance now immortalized in the "Gone With The Wind" movie sets. It was a dying gesture, however. The oil lamp could no longer compete with the little vacuum-sealed bulb that drew its source of illumination from a distant electric power plant. The Rochester Burner and the Aladdin gas-mantel type of lamp still held out for a while on the farms. But with the coming of rural electrification, here, too, the oil lamp found its way to the attic or back shelf of the cupboard.

As is usually the case, the end of one cycle coincides with the beginning of another. The period of the first World War marks not only the end of oil lighting as a commercially profitable venture, but also the beginning of interest in the use of old lamps for their decorative value .Adaptations to use of electricity were first made for the beautiful sandwich glass and astral lamps which antedate 1850. From then on interest has grown to include the products of the late Nineteenth century—and there is even an active demand for nickel plated Rochester burners, some of which are still being made. It is a joy to know that these old oil lamps will continue to light the way, even though they have changed their mode of illumination in their years of maturity.

Gas was considered an improvement over kerosene, partly because it was cheaper and partly because its illumination could be had anywhere in the house. Such gas lighting reached its peak around 1875. But by 1880, Edison had developed the incandescent lamp and we were on our way to the modern lamp era. It is interesting to point out that many of the first electric lamps for the home aped the candle and not the Gone With The Wind (GWW) type of kerosene parlor lamp of former days.

About 1664 Dr. John Clayton distilled gas from coal. In 1785-86,

Jean Minckelers distilled coal gas to light his lecture room. In 1792 William Murdock distilled gas from coal and lighted his home. In 1809 Sir Humphry Davy demonstrated the carbon arc lamp (and it stayed for years). The first public gas service company was formed in London in 1810. Natural gas use came next and in 1886 Dr. Carl Auer VonWelsbach developed the gas mantle. In 1879 Thomas Edison made the first filament lamp bulb and lighted it with electric current.

While the arc lamp had its use only in street lighting and gas-piped into the home was subject to pressure cut-outs and acetylene flair-ups, people sought a safe automatic domestic lighting service that would do away with the filling and tending of oil lamps not essentially different from the chores daily done by primitives. The answer came with the introduction of Edison's first practical household electric lamp. Starting slowly at first, by 1910 gas was being converted to electricity in the city homes and a whole new development of fixtures was well under way and with it all a hopelessly insufficient source of power. As this development is primarily the task of our second volume (with the need to sell this "Z" of automatic lighting to the public) let us reflect on the previous centuries of "A" lighting devices which preceded automation. Yes, there is still a place for decorative use of old lamps in the home; but the need for the original oil light-source is gone forever.

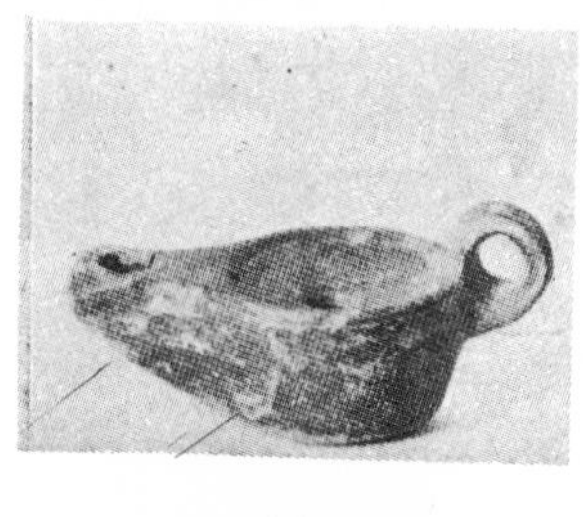

Primitive Float and Slut Lamps.

Chapter II
PRIMITIVE HOME LIGHTING

This has such ancient history, our subject is best covered by reference to specific early devices which have been used for artificial illumination in the home. Prehistoric man had only a flaming branch snatched from his campfire for a portable light. In the early Greek and Roman civilization, poor people used the 20,000 year old pan lamps (a saucer not over half an inch deep in which could be floated some oil with a piece of moss resting on the bottom); later on both Greece and Rome developed elaborate vessels of bronze and alabaster with oil pans placed on high standards so as to place its feeble flame where it would shed more light. Some devices are described for adjusting the wick of a saucer-type lamp automatically but, no satisfactory solution was given to supplying a more abundant flow of oil to the wick by some pressure means. Nor did the thousand years following the Fall of the Roman Empire make any substantial improvement. The substitution of animal fat for olive oil occurred in Nordic races, but so-called wick-supported grease lamps are little more than metal replicas of the simplest clay pans of early historic times, whether called Crusies, Pans, Betty's or Float lamps. Their common factor is that all have no loose or movable parts. With very slight improvement, their use extended throughout the Eighteenth century along with candles and night lights. Pictures of the Float lamps for the year 1,000 on are exremely rare. Benjamin Franklin, however, describes such a **Float lamp** which he made to read by while sailing for England. This brings us into our own Colonial times.

Lighting in Colonial America was accomplished by four means. There was, first of all, the great fireplace whose radiance was sufficient to enable the pioneers to carry out many of the tasks and pleasures incidental to long winter evenings. Secondly, there was the tallow candle, to be carried about in the hand candlestick, mounted by a chair on a candlestand, or placed in elaborate hanging chandeliers in the houses of quality folk. Thirdly, there were various crude substitutes for the tallow candle, especially the Rush Light, cut green from the marshes, soaked in grease and mounted in holders for burning. Finally, there were the early lamps, about which this chapter is especially concerned. We have termed all the lamp types to be described herein as "primitive." Some are not very early in origin, but all are "primitive" in the sense that they were used in pioneer homes and the "back country" rather than in places of elegance and distinction.

Slut Lamps. Of all the lamps developed to burn the grease and fat manufactured in the pioneer household, the slut type is probably the oldest!

Betty with trammel

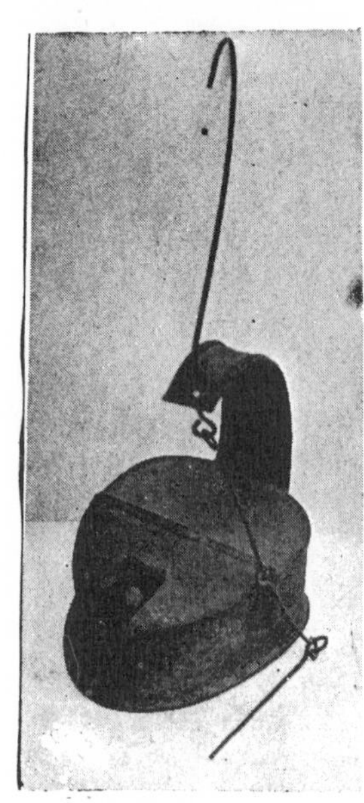

Three typical Betty lamps

To some collectors this term is regarded as a synonym for all grease lamps; but it usually stands for a distinct type of open lamp made of iron or pottery and with one or two spout-like protuberances over which a burning rag could be held away from the grease cup (see Figures). Lamps of this type were used by the earliest Pilgrim settlers, for an inventory of a Salem, Massachusetts shopkeeper who died in 1660 lists among other items, "1 slut L," valued at twelve pence. The term "slut" properly refers to "a piece of rag dipped in lard or fat and used as a light," and slut lamps were the containers for the tallow burning rag. Being open, the oil in the container could easily catch fire, and so one of the earliest and most obvious improvements placed a metal disc over the reservoir part of the lamp. Slut lamps of the latter type continued in use until well into the nineteenth century, particularly in the Middle West where pioneer conditions still persisted.

The Crusie. Relatively few of these lamps ever found their way to America, though they were common in England and on the continent. They may be described as a wrought iron open grease lamp, with an attached hook for hanging. In America an improvement called a **Phoebe lamp** is sometimes found, particularly in New England. Its distinct feature is a secondary wrought iron scoup container, set to catch the drippings which fell from the burning wick, due to the fact that grease fed through faster than it could be consumed (see Figures).

The Betty Lamp. The covered hanging grease lamp, known as the betty, was probably brought to America from seventeenth century England. Its distinctive feature is a slanting wrought iron wick support which suspends the wick above the nose of the lamp and thus permits the excess oil to run back into the reservoir. Unlike the crusie, this lamp is flat on the bottom and has flaring sides. The chain hook attached to late models was for rescuing the wick in case it dropped back into the oil reservoir. Most betty lamps are in iron, but a few of the type known as the **Ipswitch Betty** (see Figures) were made around 1800 of tin. Their distinct feature is the attachment of the betty lamp to a candlestand, making thereby a hand rather than a hanging lamp. The term betty is probably derived from the old English word, **beet,** or **bete,** meaning to kindle or make better. It certainly made a better light than the more primitive crusie, and its use continued in the back country until 1850. Figures also picture iron and tin betty lamps of the later "Pennsylvania" type. The use of these and other so called open lamps was not continued generally after 1820, or thereabouts when the closed or whale oil type of lamp came into prominence.

Spout lamps. Another primitive lamp, which attained considerable popularity in colonial America, is the spout lamp. In this the oil reservoir is mounted on a standard and a spout protrudes upward from the bottom of the vessel to hold a thick wick. Lamps of this type were apparently developed by the Dutch in the Middle Ages (see Figure). Certainly the

Spout and Saucer Lamps.

TIN LAMPS WITH WIDE, FLAT WICKS BURNED LARD OIL

finest types come from Holland and are made of brass with a removable reservoir and upward curving spout. These were brought to this country by the Dutch and German settlers; but soon the form was modified almost beyond recognition by our ingenious tinsmiths and ironsmiths. The easily congealing oil used by the fisher-folk of Cape Cod was probably responsible for the brazier type of tin spout lamp, in which the lower part was employed to heat the fluid in the reservoir above (see Figure). A very late type of tin spout lamp resembles a tiny pint oil measure and was carried as a miner's lamp until quite recently (not illustrated). Pennsylvania also provides us with pottery spout lamps of rather late vintage. That most frequently encountered closely resembles a teapot with a wick inserted appropriately.

The **pottery lamps** of Pennsylvania are a subject in themselves. It is known that over the century from 1770 to 1870 the potters of Chester, Montgomery and Bucks county copied all the varieties of early lighting devices including the betty lamp and slut lamp as well as the spout lamp.

The Saucer lamp. These lamps are very like the earlier slut lamps, except that their form is more finished. Handled heart shape saucer lamps of pottery were frequently given as marriage presents among the Pennsylvania Dutch. A hanging saucer lamp is occasionally seen still in use by Negroes and some of the Kentucky mountain folk (see Figure).

Lard Oil lamps. During the last half of the Nineteenth century, the majority of people were using kerosene lamps, complete with patented burners, shades and chimneys. But in a few places there was still a market for lamps to burn the crude lard oil that could be made right on the home premises. Lard oil is a heavy yellowish fluid, a product left over from the trying-out of leaf lard. In order to burn it for lighting purposes it is necessary to use a short and loosely woven wick. The two drawbacks to its use were its heavy consistency, particularly in cold weather, and its lack of good capillary action in the wick. This resulted in a number of patented improvements and a considerable variety in design (see Figure). First of these improvements was the **canting lamp.** In it the tin reservoir was mounted on bearings so that it tipped down toward the wick as the oil level was used up. The original canting is usually attributed to Woodward in 1841, and the last of these lamps was invented by Dexter Chambith in 1854. A rare and early broadside describing what was probably a lamp of this type is shown, (see Figure).

Among other patent lard-oil burners was that of Zuriel Swope of Lancaster, Pennsylvania. In March 13, 1860 he perfected a lamp in which a copper funnel above the flame collected heat and converted it downward into the barrel to warm the oil. The angular or wedge shape barrel is the invention of Delamar Kinnear (pat'd. Feb. 4, 1851) and was made by S. N. and H. C. Ufford, 113 Court St., Boston, Massachusetts. There was also a tin shaded type and several varieties with removable reservoirs.

EARLY TIN LAMPS — Dr. C. A. Q. Norton, Hartford, Connecticut

Probably the most ingenious is one with large and small cylinders set on a saucer base. The plunger in the large cylinder is used to force the lard oil into the small cylinder for burning. It is the invention of Ira Smith and John Stonesifer of Brownsboro, Maryland (pat'd. Aug. 8, 1854) and was produced under license by Tildon and Sleeper of Freemont, New Hampshire, (see Figures).

Interest in wick-supported oil lamps of the Colonial Period will always center around the Betty. Its roughly triangular iron basin with a half-round wick attached to the bottom and a covered bail over its top for hanging should be in every lamp collection. Memento of the best cheap lamp of its day and still a good one yet to have in a lighting emergency, it will burn salad oil, mineral oil or even candle ends and will not spill over. For such reasons, the Betty was probably the most popular cheap house lamp from the late Middle Ages to the 1850's in America. Lamps with vertical wick supports (i.e. whale oil, etc.) came in before that, but are not considered here.

Primitive home lighting, of course, started with the **pine knots and splinters** from the resinous pine tree. The early Colonists called these splinters 'candlewood' and used them for illumination. The candlewood was placed in the corner of the fireplace on a flat stone and set afire. Before primitive grease lamps and tallow came into common use, the price paid for such pitchy wood was greater than that paid for walnut; small wonder the next move was to the cheaper Rushlight and homemade candles.

Crusie on stand (Carleton Brown Collection)

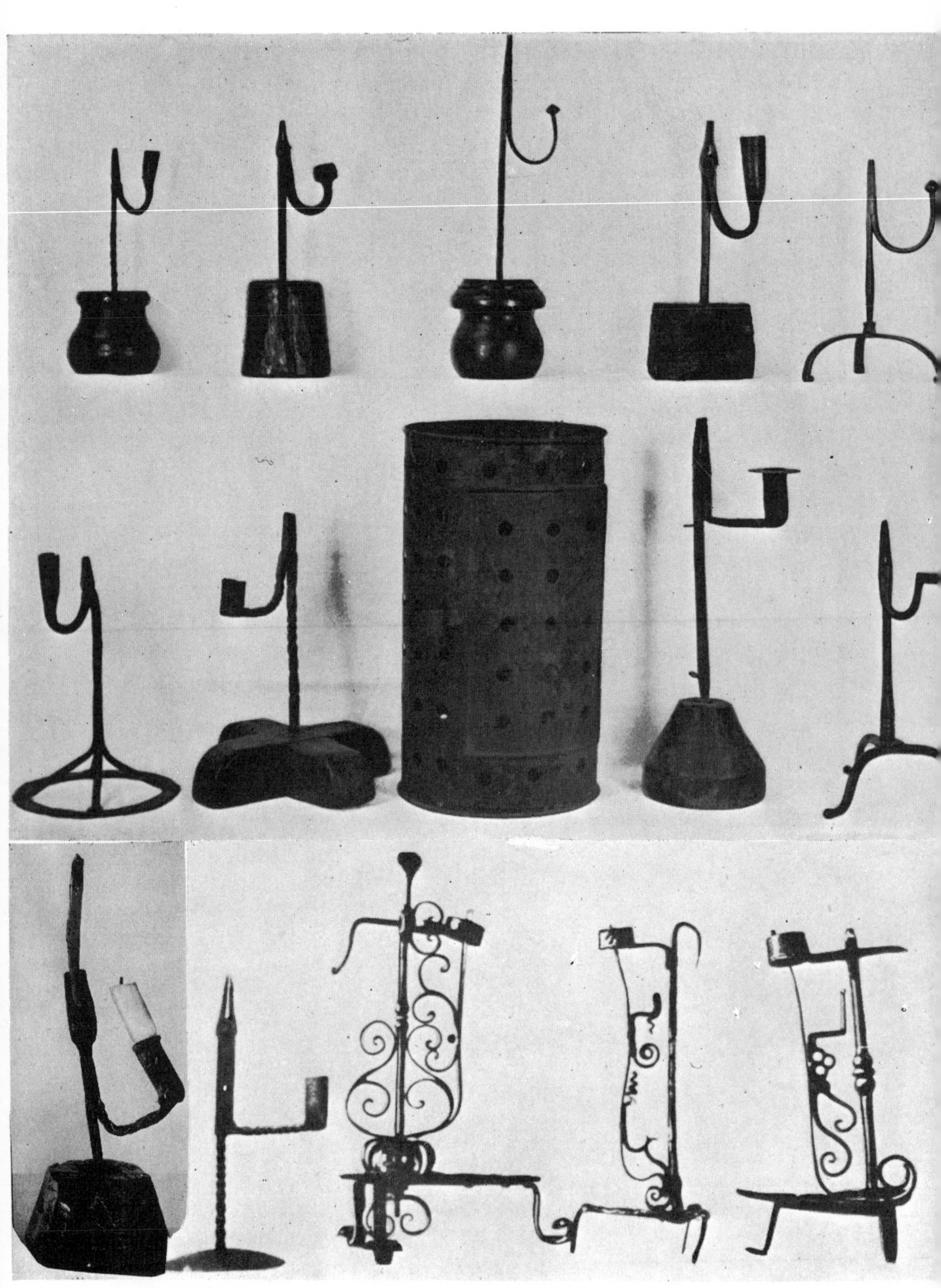

Rushlight holders and a rushlight shade (Carleton Brown Collection)

Chapter III

RUSHLIGHTS, CANDLES AND CANDELABRA

While early Americans used either Betty's and other wick supported lamps or Rushlights in their pioneer cabins, the affluent nabobs of the coastal cities preferred the expensive tallow-dipped candles held in wall sconces, silver candlesticks and Waterford crystal chandeliers. Actually, even the Rushlight is a type of non-lamp illuminant since it depends neither on oil nor on a wick. Any report on the candle begins there.

Rushlights are candle-like devices for domestic lighting made by dipping the pith of soft rush or cattails into melted fat which burns slowly in a semi-vertical position. Probably much older than true candles, and used in England as early as the Ninth century, it was not until 1788 that anyone described Rushlights and told how they were made. Later in the present century, the first American Association of Early Lighting Collectors called themselves the Rushlight Club. Dr. Rushford (a World War I veteran who wrote extensively on such devices) is largely responsible for what we now know as the candle counterpoint of the early American oil-lamp craze. Certainly Rushlights are the oldest candle-like devices to continue in home use, "unchanged well into the Ninteenth century." As late as 1850 some could be found in guest rooms of large country estates for use as night lights instead of oil or **candle (fairy) lamps.** Compared to these, the true candle (always highly taxed if made abroad) was a very complex device.

If **candles** were as simple as they appear on the surface, these would have been developed much earlier to their Eighteenth century perfection. Like all flame-type lighting devices, it is the burning gas that feeds the flame. All but the simplest float lamps have something to help gasify the oil; but candles start with solid fuel and require no outside attachment to accomplish this. The candlewick, however, is far from simple and although made of twisted cotton, it first gave off a very dim light and smoky flame unless constantly trimmed. About 1820 braiding the wick was found to improve combustion and to make for automatic snuffing. The other development in candlemaking came from refined components in the use of tallow, suet, bayberry, wax, beeswax and other animal fat. Candles were made either by dipping or molding and vast how-to-do literature is available to anyone wishing to make some. Here we would simply indicate that the best candles were never homemade but in Colonial times sent from abroad and subject to high tax. Old candle molds are still quite plentiful in the East and it is fair to assume that those for six to twelve molds were for domestic use whereas any large number were for the **candler,** which could mold as many as two hundred at one time in a wooden frame.

As a student of lighting, we are mainly concerned with the artistic de-

Candelabra and Chandeliers (Athenium)

vices that were used as sticks and candles (including wrought iron or brass for the wealthier class which are quite rare); **chafing balls** (i.e. heaters rather than lamps), the many portable types with saucer and hand-grip **prickets** which held the candle on a sharp spike are worth mention especially the crystal chandeliers or candelabras (many bracketed for table or religious functions).

Candelabra collectors of glass chandeliers of the Eighteenth century usually do not think of their expensive purchases so much in terms of lighting as in the decorative play of light on the prisms, bobesches, and assorted dingle-dongles which are draped about a central pole or attached to wall sconces. So called **Waterford crystals** are the most desired of these candelabras but evidence is that the glass was made in many other places. Everyone agrees that English glass chandeliers excel European rivals in artistic designs and the clarity of reflecting light effects. Very few of the original chandeliers and candelabras of the period still exist. Other than those which have remained in the home of Kings and nobility, it would be very difficult to say that a glass chandelier made in the Queen Anne period manner was not a fairly modern reproduction. Signed and dated early specimens are extremely rare. Until the Eighteenth century, brass chandeliers had arms radiating on all sides of the vertical shaft with a candle cup to hold each of the possibly hundred candles that made up the piece. At first, these chandeliers were elaborately decorated with cast ornaments, carefully placed so as to enrich the appearance of the chandelier and increase the lighting capacity by reflecting the tiny candle flames. Rock-crystal decorations were introduced during the Seventeenth century and added greatly to the brilliance of the display. Naturally, such lighting devices were found only in the courts. Intended primarily to give brilliance to a ballroom, drawing room or occasionally the Lord's supper table, an elaborate ritual of placing the candles so as to secure a minimum of guttering or dripping wax, was practiced. By the time of the Sun King (Louis XIV) glass had replaced rock crystal completely covering the entire brass fixture and producing a total reflecting surface which hung high above the head, brought the effects of lighting to bear upon the visitors below. Glass became preferred over all other types of chandeliers, not because it was cheap but because it could be molded to cover the entire lighting device and emphasize the sparkling multiplicity of candle light rays. Venetian glass drops and bobesches were blown in the extreme Rococo style and that is what people think about when they talk about candles and candelabras.

Candles. The first American candles, imported from England, cost five pence apiece and were not supposed to be made in the colonies. As soon as the colonists developed domestic animals, all tallow fat was saved and candle making began in the home. This was a cold-weather occupation which coincided with fall butchering. A wick was alternately dipped in hot tallow and cooled to make the candle. Some used rush, others loosely

FRENCH BRONZE WORK.

THE noble central figure is an admirable adaptation of the Oriental by the famous bronzist Barbédienne, of Paris. The manner in which the Eastern forms, interlaced work, and other elements are adapted to the intended purpose show the true artist in the designer. The work was probably produced for some Turkish or other Mohammedan grandee, as three interlaced crescents form the apex of the design. The centre is very effective.

On the left hand is a superb Candelabrum by another eminent bronzist, who is himself an artist, M. Ernest Royer, also of Paris. The style is essentially French, and the details all executed to perfection: this work was gilt, and was shown in 1867.

The remaining figure also represents the work of Parisian bronzists, Messrs. Schlossmacher & Co., who give their attention principally to table lamps, in the designs for which they employ much artistic talent and clever executive ability. The object before us is a compound of the Lampadaire and Candelabrum, and when the lamp is removed, as in the engraving, we have an elegant Tazza which might hold a glass of flowers. The scrolls are original, and the introduction of the acanthus leaf very effective.

FRENCH, ENGLISH, AND AUSTRIAN BRONZE AND SILVER-GILT WORK.

THE remarkable Chandelier which occupies the central place here is, or was, in the room known as the cabinet of Louis XVI., in the Château of Versailles. It is, of course, in keeping with the fittings and decorations of that gorgeous place, in the style of Louis XIV., but probably of later date: it is a remarkably fine example of its peculiar class.

Towards the left hand is a graceful Greek Candelabrum, the work of the eminent firm of Rennie and Adcock, of Birmingham. It is remarkable how much originality has been thrown into this charming adaptation of a well-known ancient type.

The third engraving represents an Austrian work, equally remarkable for originality of treatment; it is a Monstrance executed by Anton Raser, of Vienna, from the design of Professor Frederic Schmidt, cathedral architect. It is in silver-gilt, or, as called in France, *vermeil.*

GREEN'S PATENT

ARCTIC LAMPS

Take the place of unprotected Candles for the lighting of

DINNER-TABLES, BALL-ROOMS, &c.

WHAT THEY ARE!

The Arctic Lamps fill a long felt want wherever candles are now used. They are constructed on the same principle as a carriage or reading lamp, in which the candle is enclosed in a metal tube and forced up as it burns by means of a spiral spring inside. They fit in any candlestick and when in use exactly resemble wax candles.

WHAT THEY DO!

They prevent the risk of the candle-shades taking fire, the shade support being fixed. They entirely do away with all guttering candles. They ensure the candles always remaining the same height, however long they have been burning. The candles are extinguished instantly without smoke or smell.

WHAT THEY SAVE!

The candles are burned to the very end although in appearance they always look the same; the saving is considerable, so much so that the Arctic Lamps are being used wherever candles are burned frequently. Better shades can be used with safety, as there is no risk of their taking fire.

WHO THEY ARE FOR!

EVERYONE! whether residing in Palace or Cottage, as they simply take the place of ordinary candles. For Hotels, Clubs, Restaurants, where candles are largely used, they are invaluable. They are not affected by Draughts or Heat, so can be used with safety in India and the Tropics.

PRICE (COMPLETE WITH SHADE SUPPORTS).

	Brass Fittings.	Plated.	
6-in., size of 6's Wax Candles, for Small C'sticks, Pianos, &c.	**9/-**	**10/6**	pair.
8 „ „ 8's „ „ Tall „ „ „	**10/-**	**11/6**	„

ARCTIC LIGHTS.

Suitable Candles for burning in the Arctic Lamps. Highly recommended.

For 6-inch Lamp, burning about 4½ hours ..	**1/4**	per box of 12.
„ 8 „ „ „ „ 7 „ ..	**2/-**	„ „ 12.

Postage extra, according to weight.

Showing the Arctic Lamp fit[ted in] an ordinary candlestick, sho[wing] Shade-Support, and patent E[xtin]guisher attached.

No. 133.

The Arctic Lamp for dec[orative] purposes. White china f[lower] flower Holder. complete [with] Arctic Lamp and fancy Sh[ade]. **12s.** each; or by post, **9d.**

The Lamps, &c., can be obtained through any of the leading Silversmiths, Lamp Dealers, and Furnishing Ironmongers in the United Kingdom; they can be seen in use with a great variety of accessories for Table and Room Decoration at the Show-Rooms of

The ARCTIC LIGHT CO., 170, Regent Street, London.

CANDELABRA.

No. 1128. Candelabra.
Per Pair, $55.00
Silver or Barbedienne. Height, 20¼ inches.

No. 1110. Candelabra.
Per Pair, $55.00
Gilt or Silver. Height, 20 inches.

No. 1066. Candelabra.
Per Pair, $65.00
Gilt or Silver. Height, 22 inches.

No. 1062. Candelabra.
Per Pair, $30.00
Gilt or Silver. Height, 16¼ inches.

(*a*) PRICKET CANDLESTICKS

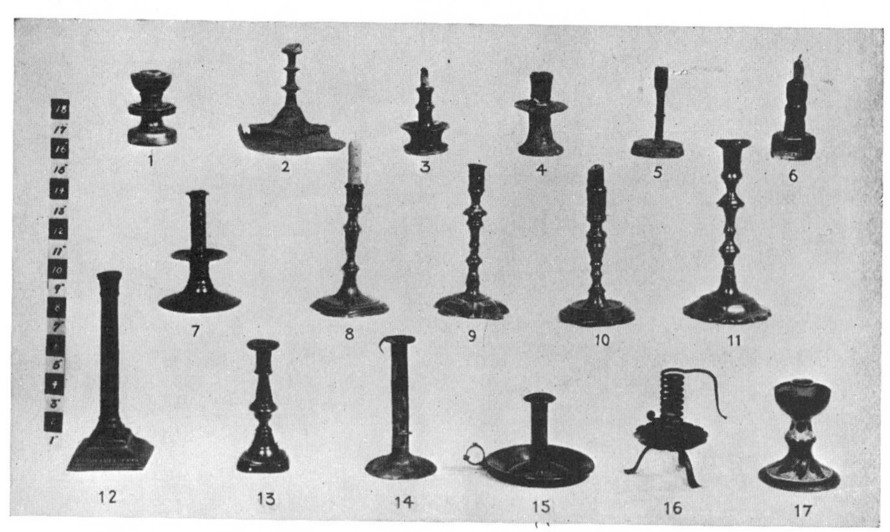

(*b*) SOCKET CANDLESTICKS

spun hemp cotton or milkweed silk to make the wick. Later (when molds became generally available), candles were poured (not dipped) and the results stored in covered metal "candle boxes" until needed. The Eighteenth century developed the itinerant professional candler who made 'runs' for the housewife from her drippings. Beeswax candles, made by pressing heated wax around the wick, were much more valuable because of their bright smoke-free flame. Many farmers kept hives of bees as much for the wax as for the honey. The spermaceti candles (using the fatty substance found in the head of the sperm whale) gave double the light of beeswax and tallow dips. Another type was made by boiling bayberries, skimming off the wax, and molding it around a candlewick. These candles gave a very pleasing odor and are still highly valued for use at Christmas.

Candle holders took many forms with rarely two pairs exactly alike (a fact which makes for a very interesting collection). However brass was the chief material used; many families have candlesticks which have come down through several generations. The sconce or reflector was often attached to the candle to improve the quality of light. From the Eighteenth century on a **sliding candlestick** was made in which a partly-used candle could be moved-up for longer service (also little wire **"savealls"**). After the Revolution, candle factories became numerous in New England with fat supplies imported from Russia. The advent of the kerosene lamp, of gas illumination and of electricity took candle making out of the home. Modern molding machines can produce as many as 10,000 candles a day with some still used for fairy or night-lights. While the Roman Catholic Church prescribes the use of beeswax for Mass, most modern candles are made from paraffin or stearin.

The candle group of lamps usually receives scant mention in any treatment of our subject. However, one finds them in use even today because of their soft lighting effects at the dinner table. The true candle has a wick surrounded by some form of wax and its purpose is to consume the fat, whereas cruder devices use a rope soaked in fat and the fat helps burn the wick. The oldest types of candles used a **pricket** or spoke on which the candle was stuck. Later devices as shown in our pictures, had a candle cup. **Candle molds** are not a special study for this chapter but holding devices such as those used for rush lights, tapers and candles require some attention. **Rushlights** and tapers have to be gripped by something resembling a sissor or pair of pliers. Mostly such taper holders were used by the wealthy classes to hold a candle while melting sealing wax with which one would affix his seal. Very few of such taper holders are found, most of them were in silver. Rush stands or **rush** holders have to be held at an angle in order for the rush to burn, hence most **rush** or splint holders take the form of inverted pinchers. Most **Rushlight** holders either came from England and Scotland or were developed in early America. Among the candle holders one finds few early ones of the birdcage type in which

COLLECTION OF VERY EARLY LANTERNS, OF WHICH THE MOST NOTABLE IS THE PIERCED "PAUL REVERE" TYPE

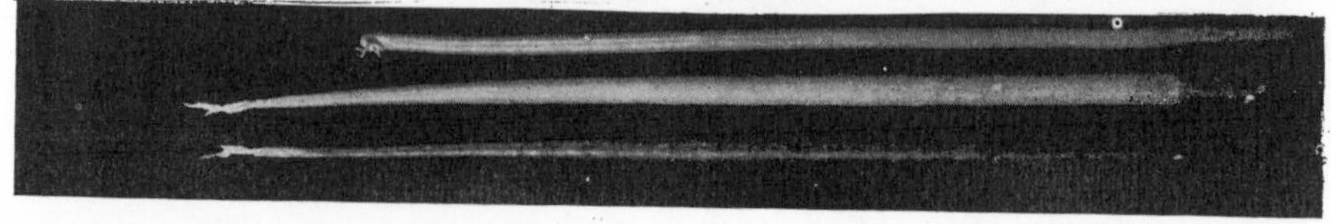

wire would keep the rush from falling over, whereas prickets hold a candle on a sharp spike, the candlestick has a cup above a saucer which will hold the bottom of the candle away from the table. One can argue as to whether a candlestick was made to be carried about or always left in one spot. Apparently the early Seventeenth century candlesticks remained fairly stationary whereas later types might have a saucer and a handle for inserting the finger. Candle accessories include such things as snuffers, pickwicks, and conical extinguishers. The latter were commonly made of cheap iron or brass for extinguishing the flambeau and the candle-chandelier which hung so high above the head, that one would have to push a stick there. While on the subject of candle parts, one might also mention the water lenses often held between the lighted candle (or lighted lamp) and the work which the person was doing. An illustration shows one of these as a part of the lace maker's equipment, in which the water filled globe magnified the light of the single candle upon intricate hand weaving of lace. Sometimes cobblers used water lenses and certainly scholars of the Sixteenth century used them as a means of getting more light from a candle and to the book they were trying to read.

Far more common than the glass chandelier of high society were brass and tin candlesticks of students also the iron and **tin candle lanterns** which have become prime collector targets. On accompanying pages are shown a variety of these devices, everything from the so-called **Paul Revere lantern of pierced tin to bulls-eye searchlights, railroad lanterns and on down to the barn lanterns** of the kerosene era. In this chapter we have dealt only with the candlestick and candle lighted devices. They are of quite a different character technologically from the oil lamp which precede and follow the use of the candle. Today, many of the early candlesticks and candelabras have been modernized to use electricity. Near the dawn of the electric light era and on into the late 1920's, one finds a whole series of floorlamps and wall sconces designed to look like candles. The era of massed candlelight from candelabras has now passed. Restaurants and homes which use a true candle for dining place it near the table surface, rather than as a blaze of light from the ceiling or wall. Thus we are at least back with the candle to where it originally started.

(By the courtesy of Mr. Julius Daniels)

Making wax candles (Diderot) Rolling, pouring, the long taper

Making tallow candles (Diderot) Melting, wick twisting, dipping, casting

Chapter IV

WHALE OIL AND VERTICAL WICK LAMPS

Even though the vertical wick lamp was a great improvement over the Bettys, its actual lighting and wick tending was of considerable trouble for early Americans. If a going fireplace was not around, one had to resort to the patience-trying tinder box which might require half an hour to get a light. Early matches were clumsy affairs; to get a flame one had to dip them in acid before they could be struck to make a light. Once lighted, a grease or fish oil lamp burned with a smoky ill smelling flame and required constant attention. Cod-liver oil was the common illuminant until whale oil provided a brighter light which was less smelly. Lamps made of brass or pewter first had a single wick tube. Later Benjamin Franklin found that two tubes placed side by side gave more light than two lamps with single tubes. When it was found that turpentine could be mixed with alcohol to make things even brighter, this gave our forefathers their first white light. It was highly dangerous, causing frequent explosions and burning down many houses. Thus until coal-oil or petroleum was distilled to make kerosene, did we have a fuel which afforded a clear light which could be enjoyed with any comfort and safety. A whole new industry then developed trying to get a chimney that would not break and a ventilated burner. Glass was discovered only accidentally as the ideal material for a chimney when the bottom of a bottle a workman was heating cracked off over the flame and the light source became more steady. Whole issues of the Scientific American were given over to such inventions (see Bibliography). Many Patents, of course, were never utilized in the home.

It is difficult to give a strict chronological account of lamp development, and at the same time deal with the various types. From one point of view, the lard oil lamps described at the end of the second chapter belong with the closed lamp types which are now to be described. The last of the "primitives," these lamps actually came into use slightly after whale oil and fluid types had had their hey day. They were used, however, not to supplant the latter, but as an improvement over the open type "Betty" lamps still in use in the pioneer districts.

The development of the closed fluid container is more or less indigenous to this country, and certainly the whale oil type is wholly American. An early writer states that "the use of whale-oil necessitated the introduction of lamps of a form peculiar to the country." Who invented these lamps with their distinctive burners will probably never be known. Popular tradition attributes the invention to Benjamin Franklin. It would be like this early American statesman and philosopher to interest himself in lamp improvement. But all we know from actual records is that Franklin did

GREAT IMPROVEMENT

EXTRA SPECIAL NOTICE.

TO THE ECONOMIST....ALL WHO WISH FOR

LIGHT!

AT ONE HALF THE USUAL EXPENSE,

are respectfully invited to examine Jones' new and

VALUABLE LAMPS!

Tallow, Grease or Oil, of the very poorest quality, will burn in them equally as well as the best.

Mechanics, who want a good brilliant light to work by, through the long winter evenings; we most earnestly invite you to try them. We guarantee that 25 cents worth of the poorest Tallow, Grease or Oil, will last as long, and give as

BRILLIANT LIGHT IN ONE OF THOSE LAMPS,

as 50 cents worth of the best Oil used in any other Lamp.

Farmers try it, and we are sure you will say with us, that they are decidedly the best Lamp ever invented. They may be seen in operation at

WHERE THEY ARE LEFT FOR SALE.

The subscribers have purchased of the patentee the exclusive right of the above Lamp, for the State of New Hampshire, and shall hold all persons responsible who may infringe upon said right.

CRESSEY & HANSON.

September **1845.**

invent a square type lantern for lighting the streets of Philadelphia; also that he once mentioned the advantage of using two wick tubes, rather than one in whale oil lamps. Even if the basic wick principle was developed in England by Miles as some claim, the knowledge did not reach America at this period. It is generally agreed that a few blown glass closed fluid lamps were produced by Richard Wistar, a friend and neighbor of Franklin's who made the glass tubes for his electrical experiments and the glass panes for his street lantern. Consequently, it would be very reasonable to assume, as have many writers, that the whale-oil had its origin in a cork stopper holding a wick placed in a bottle by Benjamin Franklin, then taken to Wistar who developed a blown glass handled lamp such as the early types pictured.

We do know that the cork wick holder antedates those of tin, pewter and brass and that in the 1770's Wistar is reported to have made a number of glass lamps of the closed whale-oil type. The progress of this development was halted by the Revolution and the death of Wistar in 1781. Not until after the war of 1812, when glass manufacture was revived in New England, do we see the reappearance of the glass lamp. In the interim, with supplies of imported lamps and oils cut off, even the homes of quality folk were dependent upon whale oil for lighting, and so pewter lamps are presumed to have then made their appearance.

The **whale-oil lamp** derived its name, of course, from the fluid it burned. Whale oil was extracted from the blubber of the North Atlantic whale and its price ranged from 35 cents a gallon in 1835 to 50 cents a gallon in 1850. The more desirable "sperm" oil came from a cavity in the head of the sperm whale and cost from 85 cents a gallon in 1835 to one dollar and 25 cents in 1850. It gave a more brilliant light than did whale oil, but because of its greater cost, was not in general use. Pewter and glass lamps of the whale-oil type continued to be popular until shortly after the middle of the Nineteenth century, when kerosene lighting made its appearance. It will be noted that in practically no instance did these lamps employ a chimney or globe to shade the flame.

Burner Developments. The whale oil burner is a distinctive American invention. It was never used with any other type of lamp. Probably the first burner of this type had a cotton rag or wick inserted in a cork and plugged into a blown glass oil reservoir. Soon a small tin cylinder was inserted in the cork to hold the wick erect and away from the fluid and two tin discs were placed on each side of the cork. Next the cork was replaced by a pewter burner that screwed into a pewter collar fastened to the lamp bowl. These burners and collars of tin and brass were made and a hole placed in the wick cylinder so a pick could be inserted to raise the wick as it burned away. Finally, with the development of camphene and other burning fluids, there came the distinctive splayed and capped burners of brass which mark the last of the whale oil type of lamp

Whale Oils;

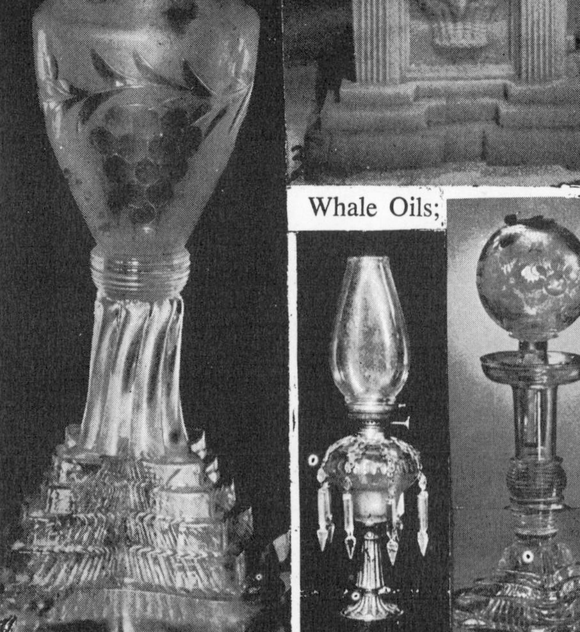

(see Figures).

Pewter lamps. It is generally believed that pewter lamps were in use during the latter part of the Eighteenth century, but no evidence of such lamps has been discovered among the products of pewterers who marked their wares until 1825. This period coincides with the great upsurge of American manufacture, particularly in New England. Pewterers had to compete with the mass production methods of the newly invented pressed glass machine, and so pewter lamps are more rare than are some of their contemporaries in glass.

Two names stand out in the manufacture of pewter lamps. These are Freeman Porter and Rufus Dunham, both of Stevens Plains in Maine. Porter's wares were produced between the years 1835 to 1850 and are of two types, the saucer-footed handled type and a smaller type. The typical Dunham lamp is also shown and is the most common variety to be found today. These three lamps measure in height six, three and eight inches respectively (see Figures).

It is interesting to note how these pewter lamps were made. The metal was a compound of tin, copper, antimony and bismuth melted in a pot and cast into molds. After that it was turned on lathes which were powered, first by hand and later by horses. Parts were soldered together and the finished product laid aside, later to find its way, via the peddler's pack, to usefulness in some household. Pewter lamps that have brass collars and burner screws were the last type to be made. Occasionally one runs onto a low handled pewter lamp of late vintage, but the typical product of the era will be found to accord with lamps shown.

Blown-Molded lamps. Aside from an occasional very early one, glass lamp making begins in the blown-molded type, with a blown bowl attached to a pressed glass base (see Figure). Lamps of this type are among the earliest products of the Sandwich Glass Works, and also of their competitor, The New England Glass Company. The earliest is slightly higher than three inches and has the characteristic waterfall base. It is attributed to the 1825-1830 period of American glass making. Figures show a typical blown-molded lamp of the 1830 period. It measures almost six inches in height and its pear shaped molded bowl is fused with a pressed base. A pair of lamps shown measure about 8 inches in height and were made presumably around 1840, when the blown bowl was supplanted by the pressed bowl. Occasionally one of these blown-molded lamps is found with a pressed base in some Lacy Sandwich pattern. A few small, low handled lamps may also be attributed to the 1825-1840 period.

Pressed Glass Lamps. The whale-oil lamp reached its highest development from the standpoint of artistry with the all-pressed glass lamp. This is the period when Sandwich was turning out its beautiful candlesticks, vases and lamps in both colored and clear glass and was experimenting widely with shapes and patterns. It is beyond the scope of this book to

Pattern Glass
and
Early Sandwich Lamps

Part of American Life Foundation's
Study Display.

picture and list every known variety. Rather, the typical colored glass lamps are assembled in one figure and the typical clear glass lamps in another. Pairs of some of the colored examples are now unbelievably rare, and since this type of lamp lends itself readily to conversion for modern lighting, the demand will always exceed the supply. Among the colored varieties, attention is invited to the very popular "Achanthus" pattern which is found in milk white and also in blue and white combinations. There is also a "Waffle" and a "block" pattern which are found in yellow and amethyst glass. The clear glass lamps include the fairly common "Sweetheart" pattern, the "Bull's Eye & Fleur de Lys" pattern and the "Diamond Point" pattern. Other early patterns in pressed glass tableware were reproduced in lamps; particularly in the lamp bowls of the later kerosene burners. It should be noted that the characteristic feature of these early whale-oil lamps is an elongated bowl. The height of most of these lamps is 10¼ inches. The Sweetheart lamps are usually found in the 8¼ inch size, but a taller variety was also made, (see Figures).

Camphene and Fluid Lamps. Almost as soon as whale oil began to be used for lighting, people sought to improve the quality of illumination by introduction of new fluids. Oil of turpentine was tried, but the smoke from its rosin made its use impractical. In 1834, J. Porter of Boston discovered that by adding quicklime to oil of turpentine and distilling the mixture several times, the rosin could be eliminated and the resulting fluid made to burn more brightly than whale oil and without smoke. This fluid, and its subsequent improvements by addition of alcohol were marketed under patent as "Porter's Burning Fluid" for a period of twenty-five years. Because of its white and brilliant light, Porter's Fluid rapidly came into general use. The majority of people however, tried to use this fluid in the old whale-oil lights and some had disastrous results. For one thing the fluid was highly inflammable and gas generated in the lamp bowl was often ignited. Fires from this cause became so frequent that in the 1850's many New England fire insurance companies inserted a clause in the policies forbidding the use of burning fluid, except when a special premium was paid. The great brilliance of the flames produced by Porter's fluid and by camphene (refined turpentine without the addition of alcohol) led to many attempts to improve the safety features of such lighting. Finally, a new type of burner, as is shown, was perfected. From a metal base, threaded to fit the lamp bowl, there projected two wick tubes which narrowed at the top and which could be covered by attached caps. Wicks made by weaving loose cotton yarn through the round opening of a wooden spool were fixed tightly in the burners so that the flame would not get down to the gas generated in the oil bowl. But this was not extremely successful and the accumulation of heated gas in the large and long bowls of the whale-oil lamps sometimes exploded. The only solution here was the introduction of smaller lamp bowls, and the true fluid lamp has a small rounded

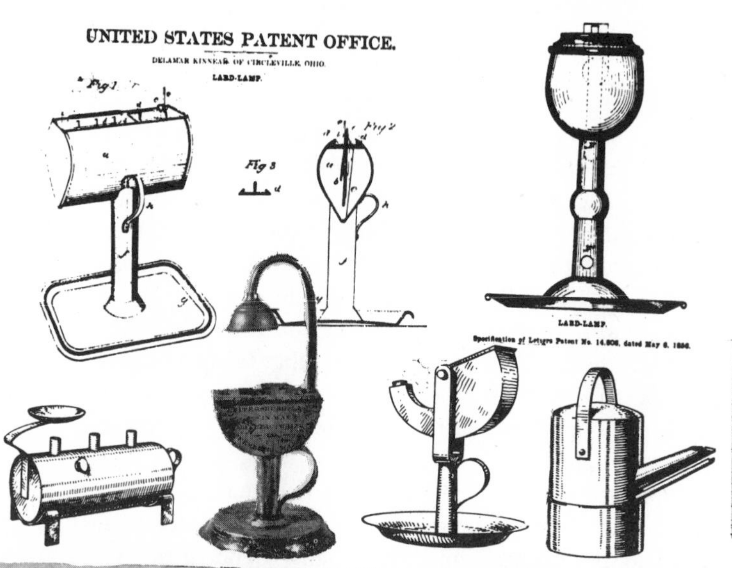

New-conſtructed Lamps.

LAMPS of various kinds, that will conſume their own Smoke, and at the option of the Buyer, can be made to give a light equal to three, ſix, or one hundred Candles; Made and Sold by

Joſeph Howe,

TIN-PLATE Worker, near the Mill-Bridge,

N. B. All other kinds of TIN-WARE, made in the beſt manner.

J. F. DODGE,

Manufacturer of and Dealer in

BURNING FLUID,

CAMPHENE, LAMPS,

CHANDELIERS, GIRANDOLES, GLASSES,

WICKS, &c.

15 Union Street, near Dock Square,

BOSTON.

Lamps, Chandeliers, and Brass Work of all kinds, Altered Repaired, and Re-lackered in Bronze or Ormolu.

All kinds of OIL LAMPS FITTED to burn the Fluid.

CANDLES IN THESE HOLDERS COULD BE RAISED

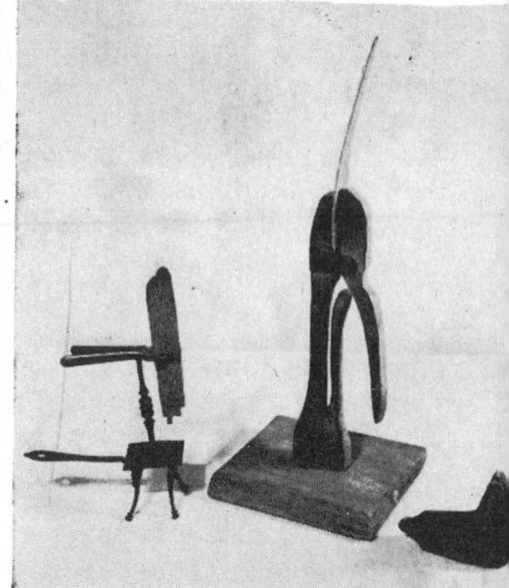

ODD HOLDERS FOR BURNING SPLINT

ADDED TO THE GEORGE L. BALL WHALE-OIL AND CAMPHENE LAMPS OF PEWTER AND GLA

Hitchcock lamps showing two types of blowers

Pewter whale oil; 1810 Bullseye; 1852 Boston.

Lace Maker's Lamps.

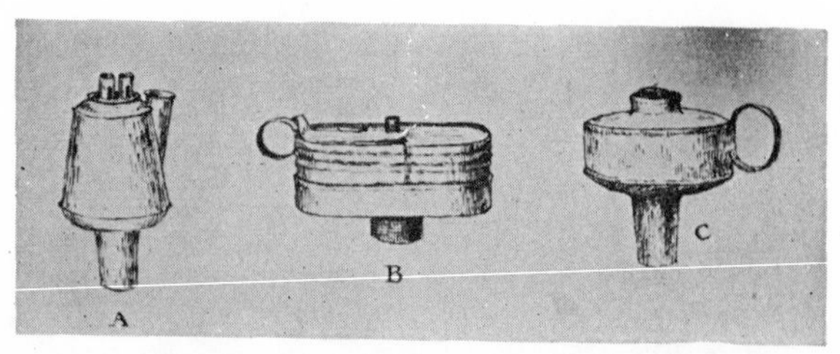

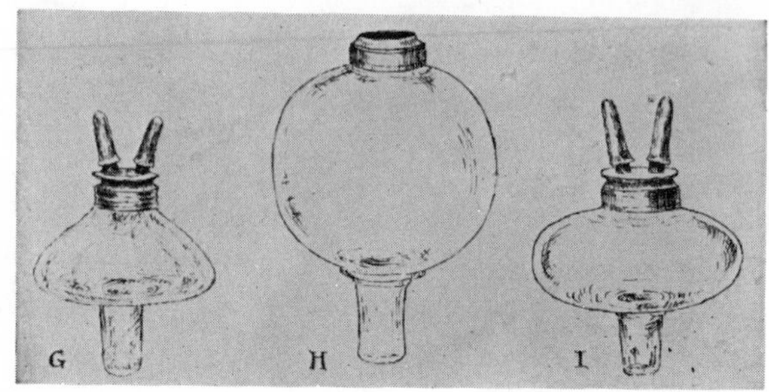

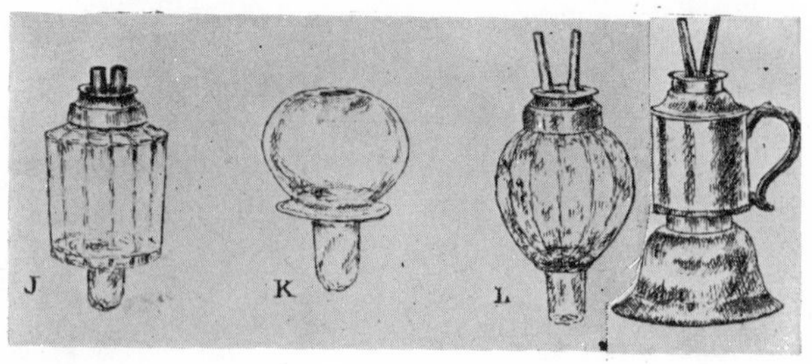

Peg lamps (Sketches by Arthur Hayward, from *The Rushlight*)

bowl very similar to some of those we associate with kerosene lighting. One "safety lamp" developed by J. Newell in 1853 provided a wire gauze cylinder extending from the collar to the bottom of the lamp bowl, and the wick came down into this cylinder, (see Figure). It was claimed that the heat from the burning wick would be absorbed by the wire mesh and so not explode the inflammable gas in the bowl. Another safety lamp was "Dyott's Patent Camphene Solar Lamp" of 1852, described as being able to burn dry with a short wick. Sanford and Kinne's Patent Hydro-carbon Vapor Lamp of 1860 purported to mix the fluid with gas for brighter burning. The far more common type of early fluid lamp, however, was the peg lamp described below.

Peg Lamps. The thrifty folk of the early Republic were loath to discard their silver, pewter and glass candlesticks, even though they could see the advantages of lighting with whale oil or camphene. This thriftiness undoubtedly is the reason for the creation of the peg lamp. Bowls of pewter, tin and glass were easily made with a peg on the bottom for insertion into candlesticks or other holders, (see Figure). They seem to have been especially useful in connection with the burning of Porter's fluid, and many small tin peg lamps survive from that era. Many peg bowls were later made to connect with the brass, iron and marble bases of kerosene lamps.

Agitable Lamps. Our chapter on the closed whale-oil type of lamp ends, quite properly, with the description of a lamp, first perfected in England, that some believe is the forerunner of all whale-oil types. The British Registry of Patents shows that on February 18, 1787, a John Miles of Birmingham announced his patent for an agitable lamp that would "give perfect light though ever so much agitated." Its essential features were the whale-oil burner previously discussed, a rounded oil bowl or reservoir running down to a narrow peg or "bottom basin." Lamps developed from this patent appear to have reached America around 1800 and were much used for carriages, hearses, aboard ship and everywhere that an "unspillable, agitable construction" was desired. They are at once the genesis of both the oil carriage light and the peg lantern. A number of examples from the 1850 period survive, but earlier samples are indeed rare.

One popular lamp that should be included in any study of agitable lamps is named after Count Rumford, a Tory contemporary of Benjamin Franklin who died in France in 1814. Though never patented, his device greatly aided the Argand type burner (see next chapter) by constructing a special illuminator around the flame. This lamp became extremely popular because it was cheaper than the Argand and gave more light than the simple whale oils.

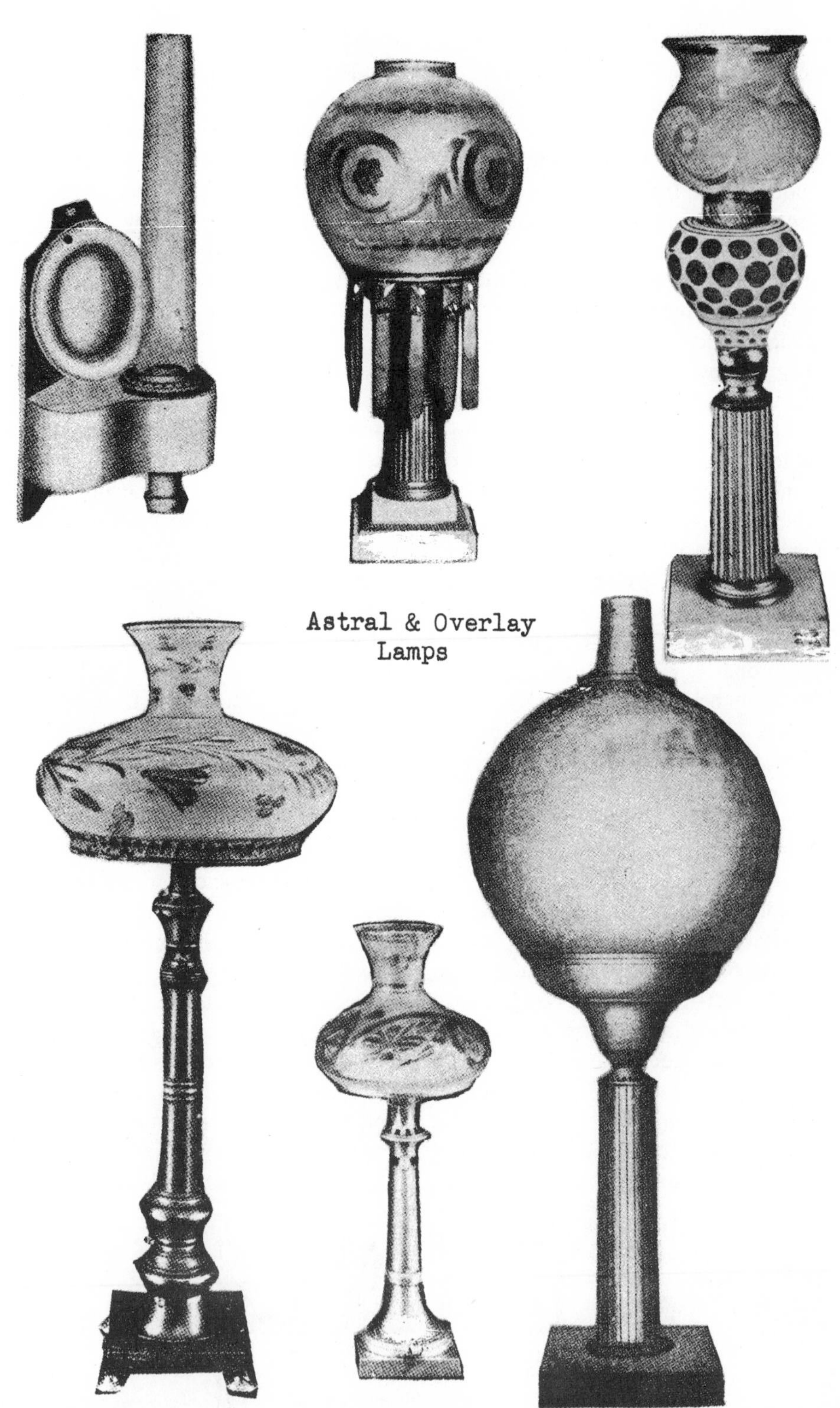

Astral & Overlay
Lamps

Chapter V

ARGAND BURNERS AND ASTRAL LAMPS

With this chapter we enter a territory where European and American interest coalesced and where the European influences led the way. Those citizens of the early Republic who patterned their household equipment after the latest thing from abroad and who could afford the high import duties, availed themselves of a type of lamp far superior to any described in previous pages. The astral lamps from England and the various continental oil lamps with patented Argand circular wick—central draft burners were never brought to this country in large numbers. It was not until in the 1850's that the large brass pillar lamps with their important looking astral globes and crystal pendants were made in any quantity in America. In the development of these lamps, the names of Argand of Paris and Cornelius of Philadelphia are linked across a century and an ocean.

The Argand Burner. The greatest single invention in the history of oil lighting is due to Aimee Argand, a Swiss chemist and philosopher who lived from 1755 to 1803. It was in Paris between the years 1780 and 1783, that he perfected the circular wick set between concentric cylinders of brass. When his burner was inserted into an oil reservoir and the flaming wick shaded from drafts by a chimney, a light of great brilliance resulted. It took several years of experimentation to bring the Argand burner to a deserving excellence to circular woven wick (through and around which air could be fed) required a gravity feed to the oil and this dictated new artistic features in lighting designs. Other necessities for increasing the amount of light given off were a circular **glass chimney,** a clockwork pump for turgid colza oil and other heavy lubricants, special wicks and burner fluids for camphene and other patent illuminants. The glass chimney had been invented before, but was being used to cut off all air drafts rather than only those above the flame. The burner had to be provided with openings to permit air to come in below the flame and on both sides of the circular wick, and the chimney had to be attached at a height sufficient to provide the right upward draft of the heated air. After these refinements, the case was by no means won, for it took a long period of time before the lamp gained any widespread acceptance and use. Argand's competitors in the field of lamp making would not pay for the use of his patent and were very jealous of his success. The burner seems to have crossed the Channel slightly before 1800 and was extensively used in the homes of nobility for mantle lamps, and also for some of the astral or reading type.

Argand Hand Lamps. When the Argand burner was taken up by the English, one of the first developments was a hand lamp made of pewter,

Mantel Lamps (National Gallery).

Lamps of the early 1800's.

French Vase Carcels

Astral Lamps

brass or sheffield plate. Thomas Jefferson once owned a pair of these hand-lamps, made at Sheffield in graceful Adam design. They were probably made before 1800, since the wick is elevated in the burner by means of the early lever arrangement, and not by the button turning device, patented in 1803 by George Penton. In Europe most of these lamps burned a type of vegetable oil, called colza, rather than the whale oil which lighted the American home. These early hand lamps are extremely rare, since during the early 1800's candles were more often carried about from room to room, while the newly perfected oil lamps remained fixed on the mantle or library table.

Mantle Lamps. Elaborate and expensive lamps of the Argand type were constructed in pairs for the mantle. Their use was not confined to England, where the type appears to have developed, but were to be found in the homes of wealthy American merchants along the Atlantic seaboard as well. Their characteristic style is shown, (see Figure). The oil reservoir has now been moved to one side, in most cases, and the Argand burner is fed by gravity through a tube. The entire lamp is highly ornamental and often includes cut crystal shades, prisms and special mounts of Bristol glass, Wedgewood pottery or Lapis Lazuli.

Some idea of the original price of these mantle lamps and their period of popularity was unearthed by a collector who found the account book kept by a Philadelphia merchant in the 1830's. It would appear that Astral lamp globes were blown, cut and etched by the Union Glass Company of that city and sold for as high as $25.00 each. The smaller size Astral shades cost $1.25 each and the "long French chimney" $1.50 per dozen. Some of the mantle lamps were purchased from abroad, but the great firm of Cornelius and Company was just getting underway, and the account book shows that pairs of Astral lamps with "simple furniture" wholesaled for $10.00 to $32.00 the pair. The more elaborate Mantle lamps with prisms and patterns inserts were never cheap, as testified by the fact that such a set cost the retailer $54.00 for the metal work alone. A complete hanging Astral lamp cost the dealer around $35.00.

Cornelius Table Lamps. There is little doubt but that several American firms went into the manufacture of the brass columned lamps. John Leadbeater and Son was one such firm, Thomas Hay another. But by far the best known and largest establishment was that carried on by Christian Cornelius, his son and another partner. In the 1830's he had a lamp manufacturing establishment located to turn out fine brass and copper font lamps for over a quarter of a century. His fountain mantle lamps with "cut glass stand and "drops" were very popular in Philadelphia and in the town houses of the early Republic. It is possible that some of the lamps illustrated were of a Cornelius make. The type of lamp that we associate chiefly with Cornelius is the table-type "astral," pictured. This type of lamp was patented April 1, 1843 by Cornelius and Company,

Sinumbra, Astral, Double and Single Action.

and is practically always marked with a nameplate on the brass oil font. There were many variants of this lamp. Some have the figure base as shown. A few were equipped with sperm-oil burners, but the great majority are now found equipped for kerosene or some vegetable oil burning fluid. The Cornelius type table lamp typically employed the tulip shaped shade with turned over lip. The large globular shade is also authentic on many types. Late models had inner chimneys and outer globes very much like 6 inch gas shades. A late and rare Cornelius and Baker double table lamp is shown in (see Figure). By placing the oil font above the flame and by use of a newly patented "spread burner" this lamp achieved the advantages of the true Astral type whose description follows, and also anticipated the design of the kerosene student lamp.

The Astral Lamp. It is common to refer to all lamps of the types already described as Astrals. But it appears that the true astral is a table lamp with a special patent ringlike reservoir and special ventilating system. In some accounts these lamps may have also been called "sinumbrals." In England, it apears they were often referred to as **"solar" lamps.** Three representative samples are shown. The oil reservoir surrounds the wick and feeds into it through a gravity system. Bordeau Marcet, brother-in-law of Aime Argand is credited with first developing the annular reservoir of the astral to minimize alterations in the oil level and to eliminate the shadow caused by the usual reservoir. The great advantage claimed for this type of lamp was that the illumination was thrown directly downward on the reading and writing table. The relative merit of the astral and the Argand burners was debated in publications on both sides of the Atlantic. A London editor in 1841, first came out against the "solar astral" as "too difficult to manage." Later he retracted and recommended it for a reading lamp in preference to the Argand burner.

There were several makers of astral lamps in America, among them the firm of Cornelius and Cornelius and Baker. The typical pinched top shade is sometimes found replaced by a substitute of later vintage. Prisms were not as common on these astrals as on the mantle and "Cornelius type" table lamps.

French Vase Lamps. During the second empire period, a number of vase lamps were made in France and imported by America. The beautiful porcelain vases were placed on brass mounts. The lamp part itself was of the "moderator type," so named because of the refined wick action developed for the Argand type burner. A more complicated type, known as the Carcel lamp, forced oil into the wick by the action of a clockwork pump. A sample lamp of this type is illustrated. Most vase lamps now offered for sale are simply electrical adaptations from vases, lustres and other old ornaments not originally intended for lighting purposes.

Care of Astral Lamps. Although the fine new lamps of the 1840's were a great improvement over the candles and early lighting devices that they

Lamps of the early 1800's.

supplanted, their care was a considerable chore. This is shown in the attention given to the subject by writers of the period. We quote from three of these to indicate how much thought was being given to improvement of home lighting 100 years ago:

From "New Leslie's Homebook" (Philadelphia 1840) buyers of astral lamps for the table are advised to "choose the shades of plain ground glass, as they give the clearest and steadiest light, and are best for the eyes. The fashion of having shades decorated with flowers or other devices, cut on the glass and left transparent is also on the decline, though it may do well for mantle lamps and lustres. To buy table astral lamps of inferior size, is by no means advisable. They only give light in proportion to their magnitude; and when they are small and low, the effort of seeing by them is so teasing to the optic nerve that the eyes seldom fail to become weak in consequence."

Added work on "Management of Astral Lamps" are: "Keep a distinct oil for the parlor lamp. Choose firm, light, sharp scissors or it will be impossible to trim the wick properly. Clean out every morning the cup or candlestick part that catches the drippings.

"When you light it (the lamp), remove the shade and the chimney, and ignite the wick with a paper match, a supply of which should always be kept in some convenient place. When you wish to extinguish the lamp entirely turn the screw to the left as far as it will go. When all your lamps (mantle, etc.) have been in use for company they should next morning be emptied completely of oil and the wick washed with luke-warm pearl-ash or water. The oil that is removed from these lamps should be put into a can and saved for use in the kitchen. On the day of your next company, (and not till then) replenish them anew. Unless a lamp is used nightly, no oil and wick should be left in it, even for a single day.

"After the large entry lamp is extinguished on the family going to bed, a small brass lamp should be kept burning all night, on a table in the passage, or landing place of the lower stairs. When visitors are expected place a lamp on a shelf fixed for the purpose, in the fan-light over the front door. Hall lamps of stained glass are very elegant, their colors throwing a beautiful tint on the walls and floors."

In 1847, Catherine E. Beecher, sister of Harriet Beecher Stowe, stated in her Treatise of Domestic Economy that, "The care of lamps requires so much attention and discretion that many ladies choose to do this work themselves, rather than trust it to domestics. If everything, after being used, is cleaned from oil and then kept neatly, it will not be so unpleasant a task, as it usually is, to take care of lamps.

"Weak eyes should always be shaded from the lights. Small screens made for the purpose should be kept at hand. Provide small, one-wicked lamps, to carry about; and broad-bottomed lamps for the kitchen, as those are not easily upset. A good night lamp is made with a small one-wick

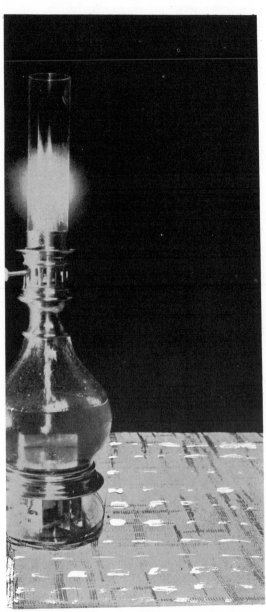

Moderator lamps (*Left*. Science Museum, London) *Right:* Glass Carcel lamp

lamp and a roll of tin to set over it.Cheap lights are made by dipping rushes in tallow."

In 1869, Harriet Beecher Stowe, in the "American Woman's Home" states: "Professor Phin, of the "Manufacturer and Builder," has kindly given us some late information on this important topic of lights which will be found valuable:

In choosing the source of our light, the great points to be considered are, first, the influence on the eyes, and secondly, economy. It is poor economy to use a bad light. Modern houses in cities, and even in large villages, are furnished with gas; where gas is not used, sperm-oil, kerosene or coal-oil, and candles are employed. Gas is the cheapest, (or ought to be); and if properly used, is as good as any. Good sperm-oil burned in an Argand lamp—that is, a lamp with a circular wick as the Astral lamp and others—is perfect."

Few lamps with Argand burners are so named today; often called a French vase lamp by decorators, it is the burner which counts, not the vase. Nearly all later Argands are known by the name of the inventor who improved the oil delivery system or gave it some descriptive or place name (i.e. The Rochester burner). Early English models were very expensive and the oil used was too heavy for efficiency. They were never in general use even among those who could afford the silver font employed. **Sinumbra** lamps date from 1820; **Solars** were common up to 1850 especially the Cornelius model patented in 1843. **Moderators** were a late and costly pre-kerosene development. They are so named because the flow of the oil to the wick was controlled by a small moderating tube; the oil was forced into the tube by a large spring at the base of the oil piston. **Carcel lamps,** patented in France in 1800 had a spring driven pump to force the oil flow up to the burner; this method was even used in the first kerosene oil lamp when early petroleum was too heavy to flow smoothly up the circle. The New York Gas Company at one time used the Moderator to develop a steady gas flow. Rochester burners are really descendants of the **English type Argand lamp.** They use a rack and pinion wick raiser and have a flame spreader as the major technical improvement. Most desirable collectors items of course are the Astral with Waterford prism drops and hand etched globular shades.

THE

EXCELSIOR

ttachment for Filling Lamps
the BURNER or CHIMNEY

Can be applie
ALL LAMPS

LAMP FILLER

Chapter VI
KEROSENE AND OIL LAMPS

When Edwin L. Drake drilled the first petroleum well in Pennsylvania in 1859, few people realized this would revolutionize the lamps of the whole world. An early product of such petroleum was kerosene, quickly followed by a new type of glass table lamp so much sought now by collectors. Prior to the Civil War, the whale oil lamp and the dim tallow candles were the primary sources of illuminating homes when there was any light at all. Many people went to bed with the sun and used a candle or small night-light to find their way in and out of bed. By the middle of the century, whale oil had become scarce and expensive; its substitutes in the form of camphene (alcohol mixed with turpentine) were far from safe. Even though a glass chimney or jar was placed over the flame, such lamps burned very feebly as very little air entered to help fan the flame which sucked the fluid up the wick. Around 1850 a Scotsman patented a method for getting liquid hyro-carbon from coal or shale and just before the Civil War, around thirty U.S. plants were using adaptations of his process for making "coal oil," as kerosene was first called when burned in lamps. Coal oil promised attractive rewards if one could find a more ready and inexpensive source of kerosene. This happened with the discovery that petroleum could be easily refined to make kerosene. Within four years after this discovery, American 'coal-oil' was lighting homes and palaces as far away as Palestine. Though kerosene was the first dominant product and used largely for lamps, the coming of the automobile, steam ship and airplane required even cheaper more efficient liquid fuel, for which was developed gasoline and related gases.

People found in Kerosene, or "Coal oil" a burning fluid which was far safer than camphene, gave as good light and cost far less. Most of the earlier types of lamps could be used with coal oil. At the same time, two contemporary developments resulted in a lamp form, usually now identified with the burning of kerosene. The first was the turnip shape oil reservoir, which was replacing the elongated type after mid-century. The second was the introduction of the flat-wick burner in the early 1860's. The burner was arranged so that a clear glass lamp chimney could be attached. The burner could be easily unscrewed from the oil font for filling and cleansing. These burners were practically fool-proof and non-explosive, consequently there was a great demand for the new lamps. Glass manufacturers throughout the country turned to the quantity production of table and hand lamps. Prices dropped within reach of the average purse and the slogan, "A lamp in every room" was actually realized in many places. The golden era of the table lamp was rapidly approaching.

PITTSBURGH LAMPS (1868).

Peg Bowl Lamps. First popular type of kerosene lamp was the Peg lamp so-called because its turnip or melon-shaped bowl was pegged to the glass or marble base. It had a glass chimney and from early in its career, a flat-wick burner, which made it safe from explosion and easy to clean and refill. Kerosene peg lamps were made in enormous quantities. Many in pressed glass copied popular tableware patterns. More elegant lamps of the 1860's were made of overlay glass. Common varieties made in great quantities had plain turnip and melon shaped bowls." Some of these "pegs" of course were made in the early Nineteenth century for insertion into candle sockets. To the purist, these early examples are the only true peg lamps; he likes to find them mounted in the pewter or brass candlesticks that originally held them and pays a considerable premium for the type. At the same time, the peg lamp developed by the pressed glass industry for insertion into special lamp mounts, is very like the early type in general form. Both are distinguished by a glass "peg" attached to the bottom of the oil reservoir for anchorage and insertion into a mounting. The first special (non-candle) mountings appear to have been the brass type attached to a marble base. The next type of base mount was a glass base, a brass collar being used to unite it to the oil font. One of these collars bears the patent date of 1870 and was often used by Hobbs, Bocunier & Co. to affix glass peg bowls on milk glass bases of the Blackberry pattern. Cast iron base mounts for peg lamps came very late in the century. Peg bowl lamps came in three sizes, small (6 to 8 inches high), medium (10 to 12 inches high and large (12 to 16 inches from base to burner). Examples of each type are shown.

Pattern Glass Lamps. Pressed glass lamps in great abundance were manufactured by such firms as Adams, Atterbury, Bryce, McKee & Co. and Sandwich. The Mount Washington Glass Works at New Bedford, Massachusetts specialized in lamp globes. The Excelsior Flint Glass Company of Pittsburgh made table lamps. Many glasshouses used the mold patterns of the popular tablewares for lamps. Pattern glass lamps are found in such early patterns as Bellflower, Honeycomb, Prism, Ivy, Argus, Diamond Point, Sawtooth, Horn of Plenty and Bull's Eye with Fleur de Lys, as well as in many later patterns. The pattern bowl is found pegged to brass bases and also attached to a matching or harmonizing base of glass. A rare type in pressed glass is the **Marriage Lamp** with double bowls, central match holder, on pedestal. Pattern lamps in which both bowl and base are poured in the same mold, are also shown. Unless they are of the elongated bowl whale-oil types, these lamps are of relatively late vintage. Plain glass table lamps were still being made for the trade in the 1920's.

Many patterns have appeared in pressed glass lamps which cannot be identified by a particular name. The identification of all the existent patterns is beyond the scope of a general survey. Their period of popularity ran from 1860 to 1890.

CATALOGUE OF PETROLEUM OR KEROSENE OIL LAMPS & CHANDELIERS.

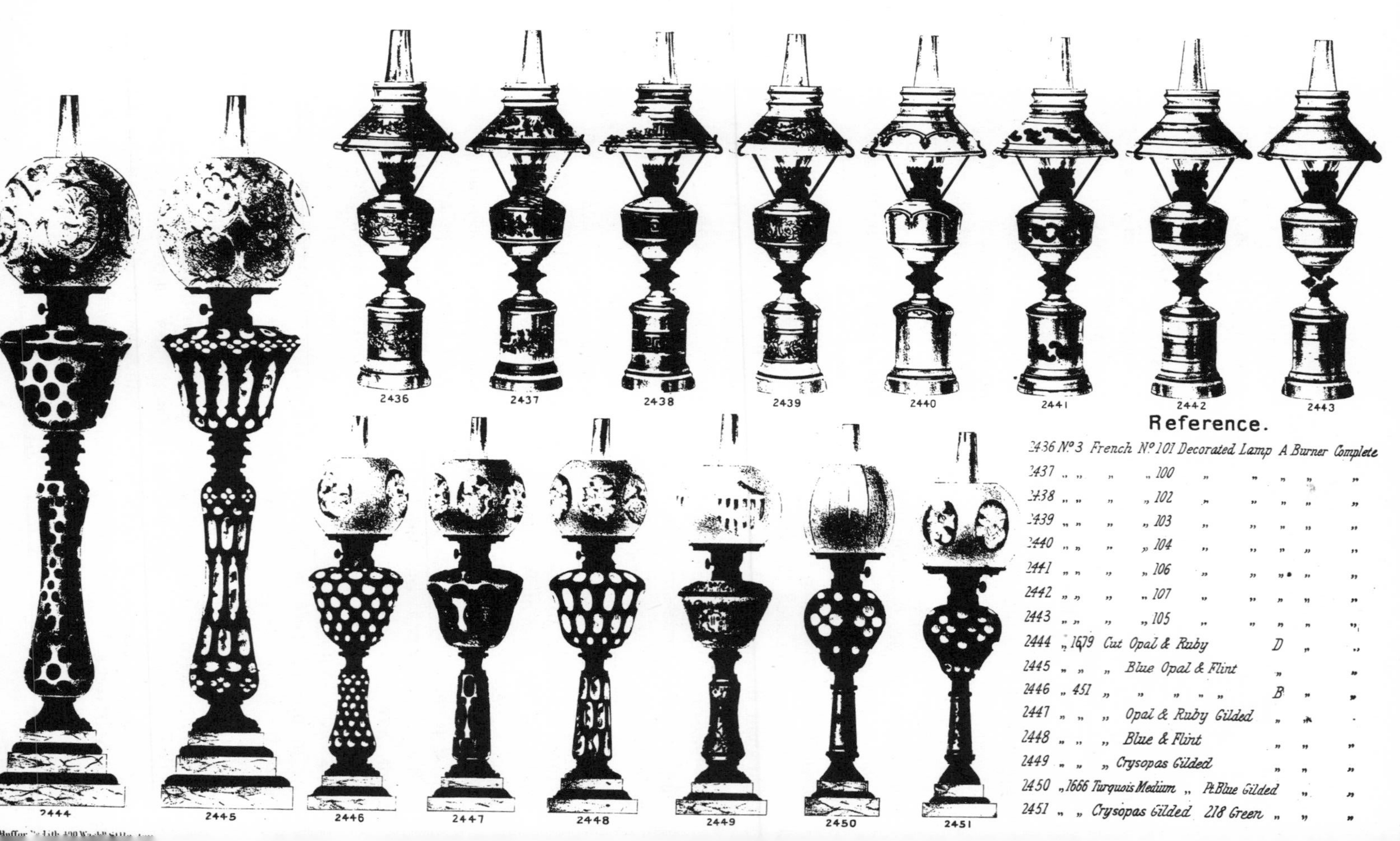

Reference.

2436 Nº 3 French Nº 101 Decorated Lamp A Burner Complete
2437 „ „ „ „ 100 „ „ „ „ „
2438 „ „ „ „ 102 „ „ „ „ „
2439 „ „ „ „ 103 „ „ „ „ „
2440 „ „ „ „ 104 „ „ „ „ „
2441 „ „ „ „ 106 „ „ „ „ „
2442 „ „ „ „ 107 „ „ „ „ „
2443 „ „ „ „ 105 „ „ „ „ „
2444 „ 1679 Cut Opal & Ruby D „ „
2445 „ „ „ Blue Opal & Flint „ „
2446 „ 451 „ „ „ „ „ B „ „
2447 „ „ „ Opal & Ruby Gilded „ „ „
2448 „ „ „ Blue & Flint „ „ „
2449 „ „ „ Crysopas Gilded „ „ „
2450 „ 1666 Turquois Medium „ Pt. Blue Gilded „ „
2451 „ „ Crysopas Gilded 218 Green „ „ „

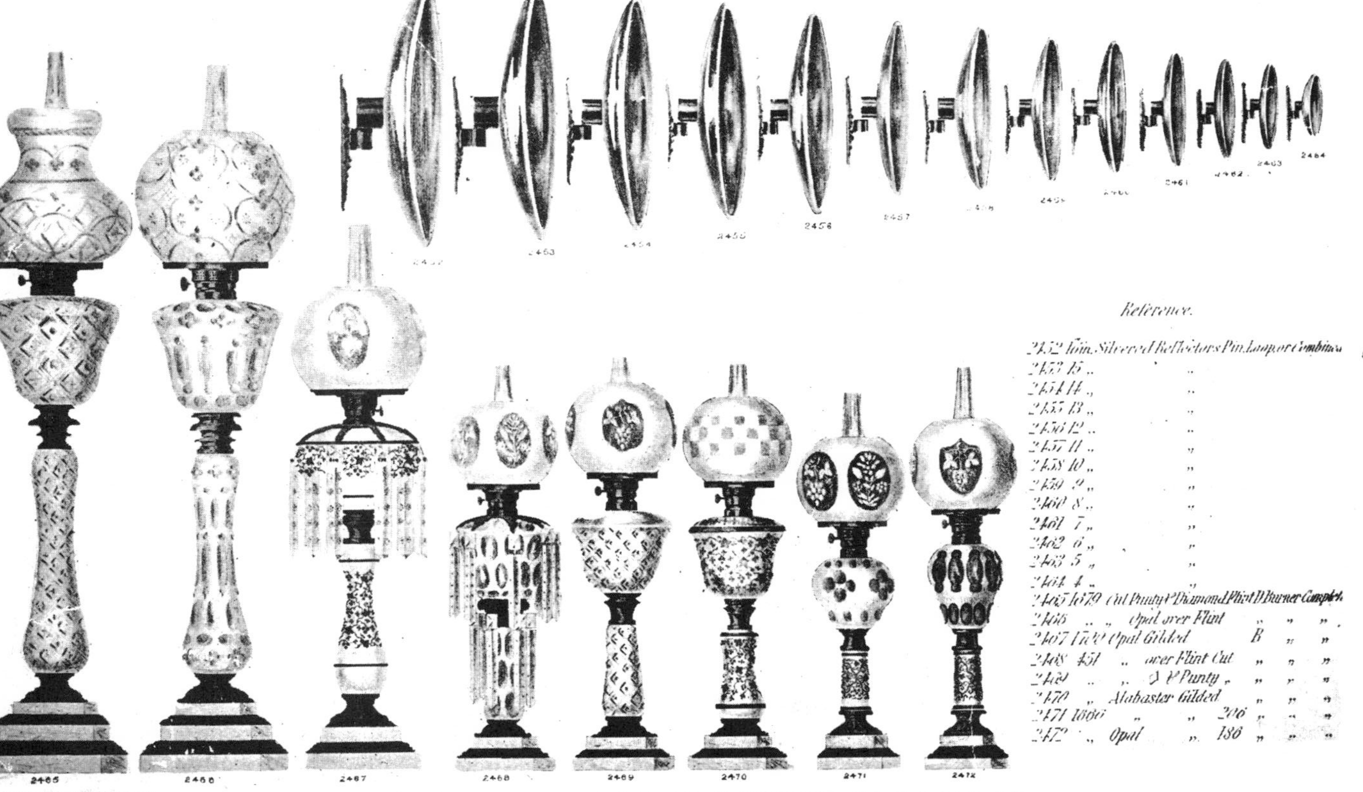

Reference.

2452 16in. Silvered Reflectors Pin Lamp or Combina
2453 15 „ „
2454 14 „ „
2455 13 „ „
2456 12 „ „
2457 11 „ „
2458 10 „ „
2459 9 „ „
2460 8 „ „
2461 7 „ „
2462 6 „ „
2463 5 „ „
2464 4 „ „
2465 1679 Cut Punty & Diamond Pl'st D Burner Complete
2466 „ „ Opal over Flint „ „ „
2467 1700 Opal Gilded B „ „
2468 451 „ over Flint Cut „ „ „
2469 „ „ D & Punty „ „ „ „
2470 „ Alabaster Gilded „ „ „
2471 1666 „ „ 206 „ „ „
2472 „ Opal „ 186 „ „ „

MANUFACTURED BY THE BOSTON & SANDWICH GLASS CO.

NIGHT LAMPS

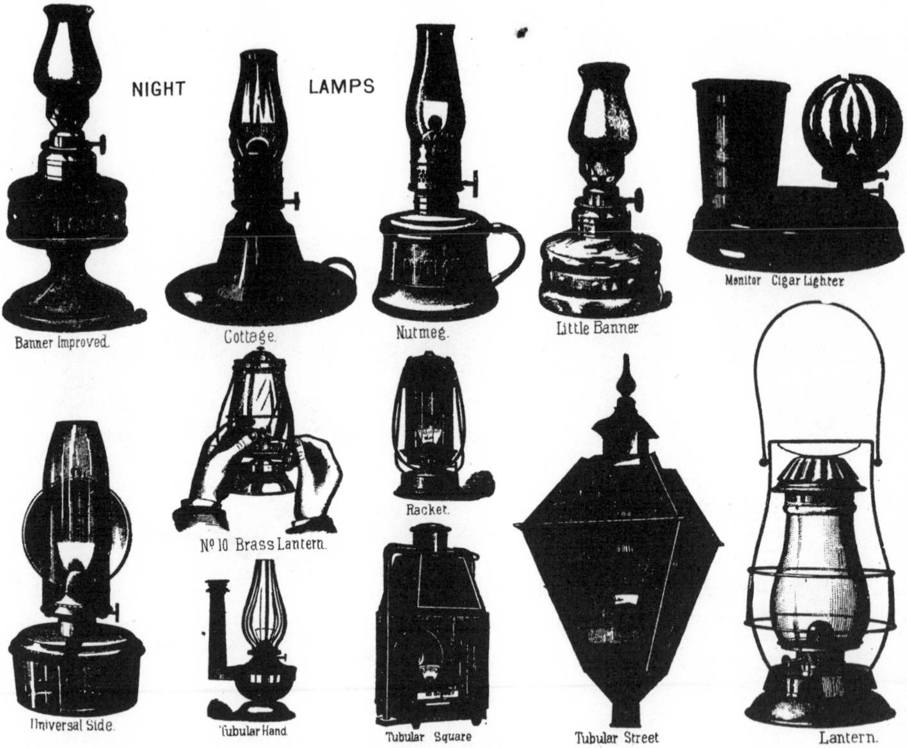

Banner Improved.

Cottage.

Nutmeg.

Little Banner

Monitor Cigar Lighter

No 10 Brass Lantern.

Racket.

Universal Side.

Tubular Hand

Tubular Square

Tubular Street

Lantern.

Candle Lanterns and other types.

No. 109. Metal Side Lamp.
A and B Collar.

No. 108. Bracket. Folding.
B Ring. Projects 6 inches.

No. 110. Metal Side Bracket.
A and B Ring.

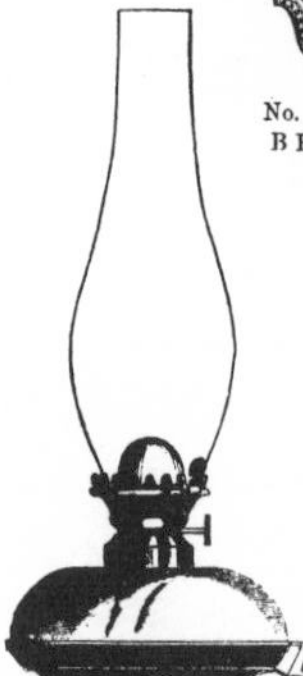

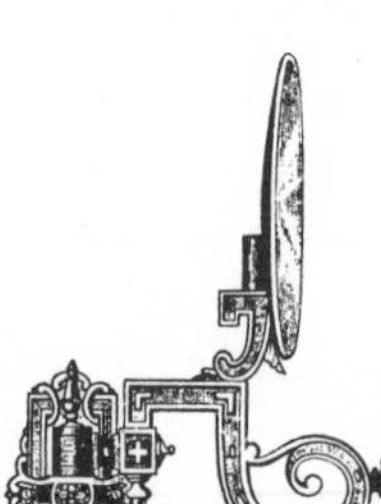

Overlay Lamps. We come now to an elegant type of lamp, very popular in the 1850's and 1860's among the more pretentious homes. Overlay is cased glass with the over layers cut away in spots to show the color of the base layer. Lamps appear with brass and glass bowls and overlay stems, with overlay bowls and brass stems and with overlay for both bowl and stem. Some overlay was imported from abroad and some was made by such American glass houses as Sandwich and New England. Cornelius of Philadelphia combined overlay columns with brass oil fonts and so did Holmes, Booth and Haydens of Boston. A type of simulated "fleck overlay" in which flecks of white opal glass were cast upon a colored base appears in small hand and table lamps with a square bowl. The base is usually clear glass. Such lamps are believed to have been made at Martin's Ferry, Ohio in the middle of the Nineteenth century. Overlay lamps were among the first to appreciate in value with the interest in antiques that developed after World War I. Demand soon exceeded supply, and as a result many reproduction overlay bowls were imported from Czechoslovakia and placed on old marble bases with brass fittings. It is extremely difficult to spot some of these late reproductions. Overlay lamps new or old are very scarce. In any contemplated purchase the fittings should be examined with great care, (see Figures).

Hand Lamps. In the 1870's and thereafter, improvement in burning fluid and burners had reached the stage where it was safe to carry a lighted lamp about from room to room. Small handled lamps now made their appearance in great numbers. Some glass ones were footed and some were not. Brass hand lamps were also made; all usually carried the flare-top sun-ray chimney and no other shade. They were primarily utility lamps, not designed for beauty. And yet some of the footed variety, collected in pairs, make exceptionally fine dressing table lamps. **Squatty** hand lamps in such pressed glass patterns as Peacock Eye, Cabbage Rose and Thousand Eye are prized by glass collectors for rounding out a table setting in these patterns. Originally such hand lamps were set out on a tray at night, and as various members of the family retired for bed a lamp would be lighted and carried to the chamber.

Bracket Lamps. A close relative of the hand lamp, but of slightly later vintage, is the bracket lamp. Made of glass or metal and arranged to set in a swinging iron frame attached to the wall, these lamps dispersed light from a good angle and were much in favor in the kitchen and bedroom. They were sold both with and without reflectors of mercury glass and tin. Those intended for bedroom and passageway sometimes had an auxiliary frosted glass open umbrella shade added for decorative value. All-tin lamps (reflector, font and bracket) are sometimes discovered. These find a ready market with collectors of "primitives" as they harmonize well with the crude mode of these furnishings. The New England brass and tin manufacturers were the chief fabricators of such lamps. Three firms whose

950 A. Hand.
5 in. High,

No. 300. Night Lamp.
9 in. High.

858. D. No. 1 or 2 G

WORLD'S FAIR LAMP

in Amber, Blue, Crystal

No.14

No.108 Hand Lamp.

D. New York, No. 2.

Footed Hand Lamp.

841 ½ A.

No.190 Fairy Night Lamp, Complete
6 ½ in. High;

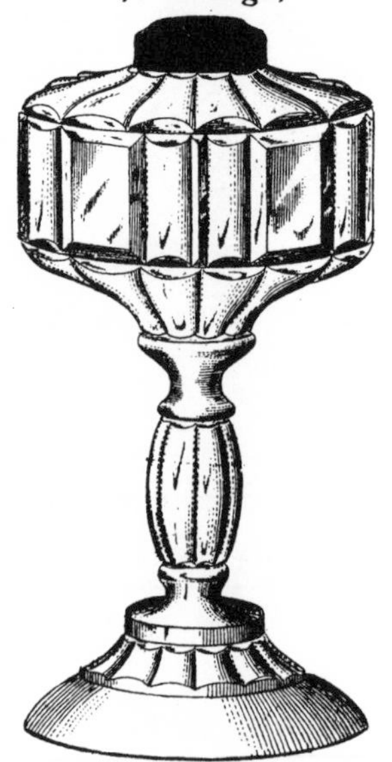

No.150 ½ A.

810 A.
5 in. High.

Nº 1.
Nº 2.
Nº 2 Squat Fount Handled.
Nº 6 Lamp. Patent Groove Top.
Pat. July. 1872
Foot Pat. Aug. 1875.
Nº 7 Lamp. Patent Groove Top.
Pat. July 1872
Foot Pat. Aug. 1875.
Groove Top Fount with Feeder.
without "
Nº 8.
Nº 9.
Nº 10.

NO. 47 ASSORTMENT.

Twelve Lamps. Two Each of the Six Patterns Illustrated on this Page.

B Collar. Glass Founts. Decorated Centers. Assorted Decorations. Black Bases. Polished Brass Trimmings.

No. 1—47
Height, 11½ inches.

No. 2—47.
Height, 11½ inches.

No. 3—47.
Height, 11½ inches.

No. 4—47.
Height, 12 inches.

No. 5—47.
Height, 11½ inches.

No. 6—47.
Height, 11¾ inches.

Priced WITHOUT Trimmings.

SOLD ONLY IN ASSORTMENTS.

THE BRADLEY & HUBBARD MFG. CO.

products are easily identified are the Plume and Atwood Company of Waterbury, Connecticut, the Miller Company of Meridian, Connecticut and the Bristol (Connecticut) Brass & Clock Company, (see Figures).

China Stem Lamps. During the 1880's popular tastes tended toward ornateness and color in lamps. The plain and pattern glass table lamps began to be superseded by a new type of lamp whose parts could be assembled in various ways to give individuality and uniqueness to each creation. The lamps had as a common feature a frosted pressed glass oil font, a black iron or stone base, assorted decorated stems and polished brass fittings. The first type of decorated stem that we mention is the china stem. As shown in the catalog page reproduced, such lamps were sold in "assortments" for the dealer and his customers to assemble as they wished. The lamps illustrated were sold by Bradley and Hubbard, an old New England manufacturing concern. Such lamps are in increasing demand today, as their stems add a warm note of color to a room, (see Figures).

Figure Stem Lamps. Lamps very similar to those just described and contemporaneous in time, use figures in place of the china stems. The figure stems (heads, children, animals) are of cast metal and were originally gilded. When found today, the gilding may be worn off. Smart decorators are painting these figures in light colors to resemble bisque. So treated they make a very amusing lamp. A few figure stem lamps are here shown. One figure stem lamp is frequently referred to by dealers as "Queen Eugenia," but we have found no real authentication for this designation. Figure stem lamps have not risen in value as rapidly as have the china stem lamps. It is believed that they have very distinct decorative possibilities and that their value will rapidly appreciate as soon as this is sensed more generally. Bases and fonts are the same as china stem lamps, (see Figure).

Glass Stem Lamps. The third group of lamps in the assembled lamp category are distinguished by a glass stem connecting the frosted oil font to the black iron base. This hollow glass stem usually has a small lithograph flower decoration pressed on the inside, and then the rest of the inside is painted in some bright and gay color. The patent drawing of a glass stem lamp arranged to be decorated in luminous paint is shown. From the distance these lamps look exactly like the china stem lamps. Many will prefer them to the china stem lamps, as the decoration is more restrained. Like china and figure stem lamps, the overall height runs to 12 inches. Such lamps look well with an opal white or tinted glass 7 inch shade, or with one made of chintz on a wire frame. It is difficult to say where all these lamps were made. Glass companies seem to have produced the fonts in many instances for lamp companies which specialized in assembly of the iron, glass and brass parts.

Rochester Burners. On July 21, 1888 Henry E. Shaffer was granted a patent on an improved central draft burner, which he promptly assigned to the Rochester Burner Company, of Rochester, N. Y. This company in-

No. 73 B. Height, 12¼ inches.
With Side Ornaments.

No. 74 B.
Height, 11 inches.

No. 75 B.
Height, 11 inches.

No. 76 B.
Height, 11 inches.

R. P. WALLACE & CO.=PITTSBURGH, PA.

No. 77 B.
Height, 11 inches.

No. 78 B.
Height, 12 inches.

No. 79 B.
Height, 12 inches.

No. 80 B.
Height, 11 inches.

No. 61 B.
Height, 9¼ inches.

No. 62 A.
Height, 8½ inches.

No. 63 B.
Height, 12 inches.

No. 64 B.
Height, 8 inches.

No. 81 B. K Base. Height, 14¼ inches.

No. 82 B. K Base. Height, 14¼ inches.

No. 83 B. K Base. Height, 14¼ inches.

No. 84 B. K Base. Height, 14¼ inches.

Naugatuck Table Lamps

Take No. 2 Royal Chimney and Wick.

No. 2110. No. 2. Plain.

No. 1995. No. 2, Embossed.

Packed 1 doz. in a case with 10-inch Tripods.

12 ins. high to top of Flame Spreader.

Order	Packed	Gro. Weight.	Net Weight.	Per Dozen. Brass.	Per Dozen. Nickel.
No. 2110.	1 dozen in a case—5cubic feet.	49 lbs.	29½ lbs.	$26.35	$27.90
" 1995.	1 " " " —5 " "	49 "	29½ "	25.60	27.15

Price does not include Glassware.

No. 2 Royal Table Lamps

These Lamps have Cast Bas[e] and Handles.

Take No. 2 Royal Chimney and Wick.

No. 1014. Plain.

No. 1032. Embossed.

Packed 1 dozen in a case with 10-inch Tripods.

12 ins. to top of Flame Spreader.

Order	Packed	Gro. Weight.	Net Weight.	Per D[ozen] Brass.
No. 1014.	1 dozen in a case—5 cubic feet.	52 lbs.	31 lbs.	$41.10
" 1032.	1 " " " —5 " "	52 "	31 "	41.10

Improved Little Royal Lamps, Fount and Hand Lamp

Improved Little Royal Lamps and Founts have screw attachment for raising and lowering wick.

A Fine Lamp for General Use.

Gives a light equal to a Gas Burner.

Packed 2 doz. in a case with 6 in. Tripods.

No. 1279 Lamp, Plain.
8½ ins. to top of Flame Spreader.

No. 1286 Lamp, Embossed.
8½ ins. to top of Flame Spreader.

Take Little Royal Chimney and Wick.

Packed 2 doz. in a case.

No. 1357 Fount, Embossed.
Height, 6¾ in.

No. 1299 Hand Lamp, Embossed
Height, 6¾ in.

No. 2 Royal Stand Lamps

With Cast Base.

Take No. 2 Royal Chimney and Wick.

Packed 1 dozen in a case with 10-inch Tripods.

12 inches hig[h] to top of Flame Sp[reader]

No. 1515. Plain.

No. 936. Embossed.

No. 1942. Plain

No. 2 Royal Stand Lamps

With Spun Base
Take No. 2 Royal Chimney and Wick.

12 inches high
to top of Flame Spreader.

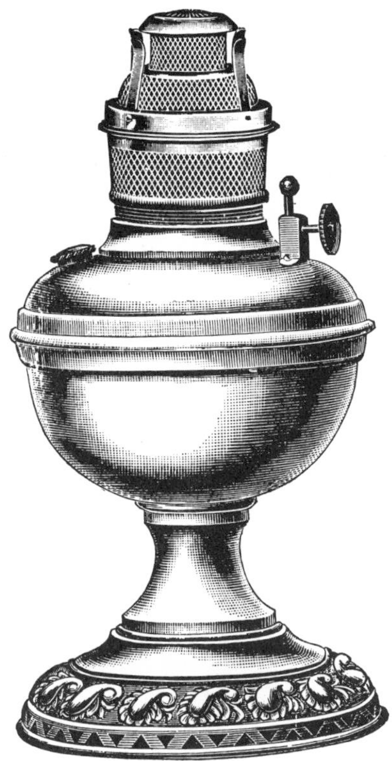

No. 1095. Plain.

Packed 1 dozen in a case
with 10-inch Tripods.

No. 1177. Embossed.

Order	Packed	Gro. Weight.	Net Weight.	Per Doz. Brass.	Per Doz. Nickel.
No. 1095.	1 dozen in a case—5 cubic feet.	45 lbs.	25½ lbs.	$28.70	$30.25
" 1177.	1 " " " —5 " "	45 "	25½ "	28.70	30.25

For Harps for above Lamps see page 66.

"Miller" Center Draught Parlor Lamps.

No. 1 Miller Parlor Lamp.

No. 1 Miller Parlor Lamp.

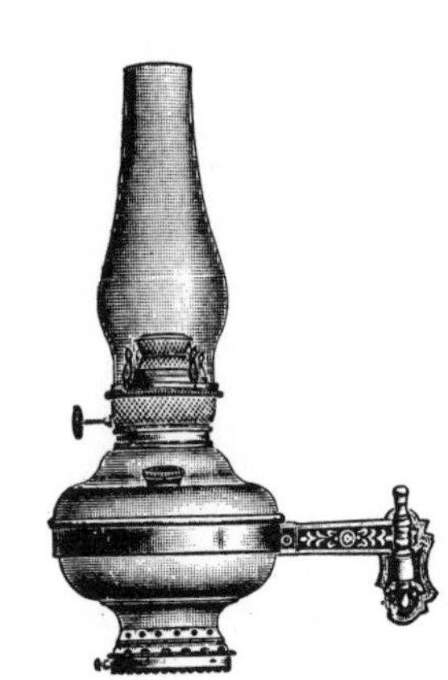

No. 217 Bracket Lamp.

No. 01 Miller Parlor Lamp.

No 2 "MILLER"

No. 104 Bracket Lamp.

No.02 "MILLER"

No. 7543 Bracket Lamp

No. 98 Glass Hand Lamp.

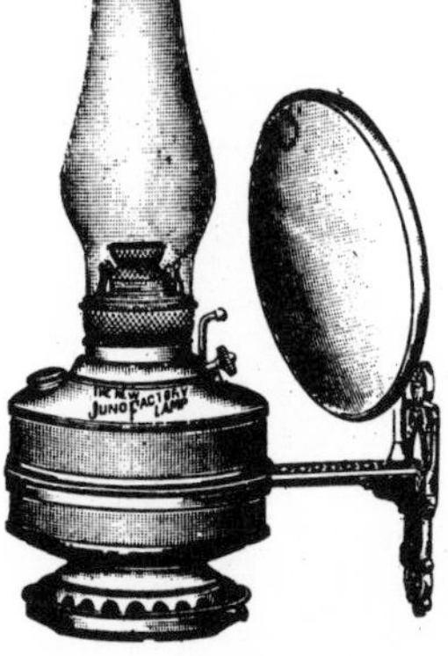

No. 102 Bracket Lamp.

No. 449 B Table Lamp.

With B Collar.
Thread Diameter, $1\frac{3}{16}$ in.
Height, 8¼ in.
50 Lamps in a case.
Made of Brass.
Polished Brass or Nickel Plated.

No. 445 B Table Lamp.

Base of Iron. Has B Collar
Brass Fount. Fount screws on to
Stand. Fits ⅜ in. Nipple.
Height, 10¼ in.
Fount in Polished Brass or Nickel Plated, with Bronzed Iron Stand.

No. 713 Dandy Candle Lamp.

Height to top of Holder,
10½ in.
Diameter of Base, 3¾ in.
Equipped with removable,
bayonet lock Globe Holder,
Hollow Base, and inside spring
for raising Candle as it
is consumed.
Base can be filled with sand
or other material for weight.
With 2 x 5½ in. Globe,
complete except Candle.
Nickel Plated.

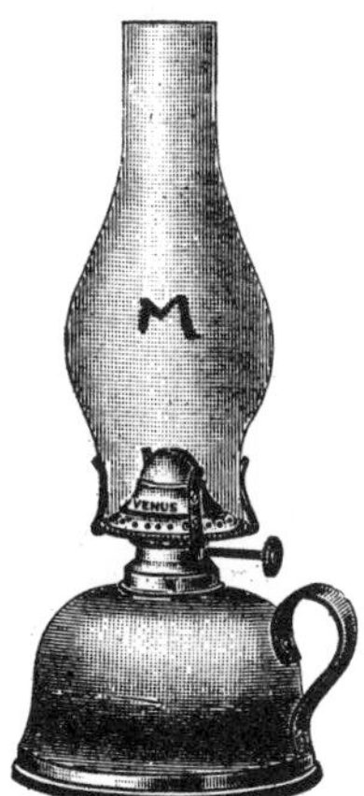

No. 20 Brass Hand Lamp.

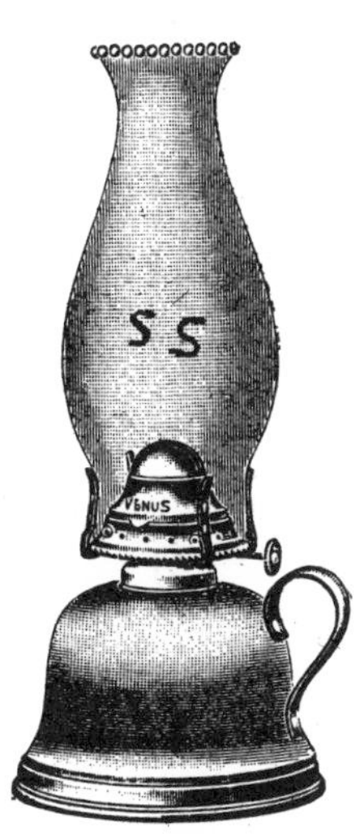

No. 25 Brass Hand Lamp.

No. 49 Kitchen Lamp.

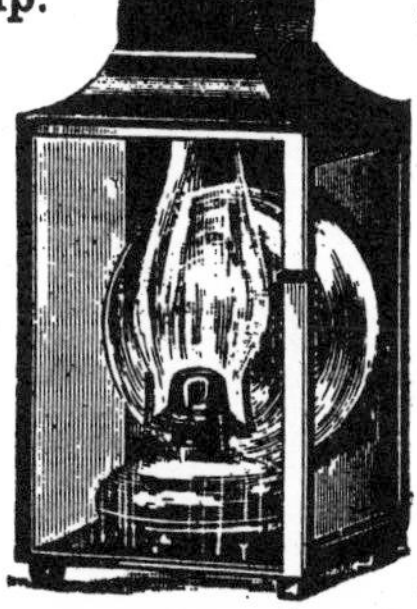

Portable or Wall Lantern.

No. 48 Bracket Lamp.

No. 180 Bracket Lamp.

Furnished complete with No. 0 Tiny Fount, No. 0 Miller Wick and Chimney, 6 inch Tripod and Plain Opal Dome Shade.

No. 144 Bracket Lamp

All Brass.

Furnished complete with No. 030 Vestal Fount. Wick and No. 2 Miller Chimney;

No. 350 Juno Reflector Lamp.

Furnished complete with No. 0 Juno Screw Thread Lift Burner, No. 0 Miller Chimney and Wick, 7 inch corrugated Tin Reflector.
Height to top of Burner, 6½ in.
Holds, 1⅓ pints. Burns, 8 hours.

Made of Tin, Brass or Nickel Plated

Packed 2 dozen in a case.
Weight, Gross, 50 lbs.; Net, 25 lbs.
Cubic measurements, 4 ft., 7 in.

NIGHT LAMPS

No. 193 Bracket Lamp.

Furnished complete with No. 02 Miller Fount, No. 2 Miller Wick and Chimney; 5 inch Shade Ring and Crown Etched Globe

Bracket made of Iron with Steel Band

No. 351 Juno Home Bracket Lamp.

Furnished complete with No. 0 Miller Wick and Chimney.
Made of Tin.

No. 0 Juno Home Lamp.

Furnished complete with No. 0 Miller Wick and Chimney.

LAMP FOUNTS

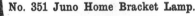

corporated the burner into a unique lamp design which came to be known throughout the world as a Rochester Burner lamp. Actually, this lamp type, with brass or nickeled brass base, tall chimney and white dome shade set on an iron tripod, was made by many other companies besides that at Rochester. Miller of Meriden, Plume and Atwood of Waterbury, made such lamps in great quantities until the early 1920's. The Miller, Vestal and Juno styles are shown in illustrations reproduced from one of their old catalogs. The Aladdin Company, which perfected a gas mantle burner for gasoline lamps also made Rochester's. The last maker of these lamps in America was forced to close down because of World War II and more vital war work. Now, 25 years later the form is again being made. However, they have disappeared from their role in the Sears-Roebuck catalogue as standard equipment for the farm home without electricity and are finding a new place in the antique shop. When the nickeled plate is stripped off these brass lamps prove to have highly decorative value in electrical adaptations. The baby "0" size makes a fine dressing table lamp and should be equipped with a 6-inch opal glass shade. The No. 1 size takes a 7-inch opal student lamp shade. The No. 2 size takes a 10-inch opal dome shade.

Lamp Parts. In the hey day of old lighting (1870-1900) manufacturers vied with each other in trying to capture popular fancy with a new style or "improvement." Patents were granted profusely for burners, chimneys, shade holders and other lamp parts.

Swan and Whitehead, the American Lamp and Brass Company of Trenton, New Jersey, The Manhattan Brass Co. and the Automatic Lighting Company of Meriden, Connecticut competed for the market in patent brass lamps. Often the only changes were in the way of outside novelty, for the fundamental principle of the central draft burner had been known since the time of Argand. Rather than trace the history of all these late patents, we have collected on four pages typical examples of lamp parts that are needed today to complete and reassemble old kerosene oil lamps. The four-inch shade holder is needed for "Gone With the Wind" ball shades, the ring shade holder for 10-inch and 7-inch student lamp globes, the tripod fixtures for Rochester burner lamps, etc. It is hoped that the inclusion of these pictures will help dealers and collectors to find and sell odd and missing lamp parts. To complete the picture, mention should be made of two items not illustrated. The 7, 10 and 14-inch shades with straight sloping sides are known as "cone" type shades. The proper chimney for a student lamp is straight sided, with an enlargement at the lower end. The other two types of chimney, "Macbeth" and "Sun Slip" are also shown.

Development in Burners, Chimneys and Globes. From the 1870's on kerosene lamps came in an increasing number of styles: some glass—some metal. Hand lamps made of brass and equipped with a handle also came into use in the 1870's. Improvement in burner design made it safe to

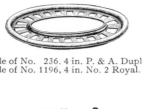

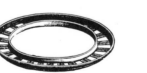

Globe Rings (Flat)

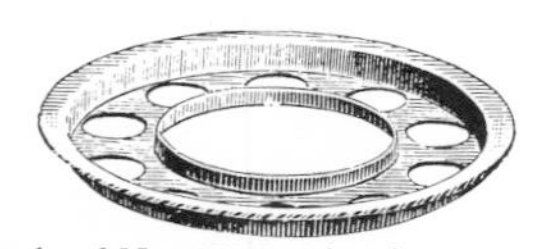

Style of No. 1092, 2 in. Acorn.
Style of No. 1531, 2 in. Nutmeg.

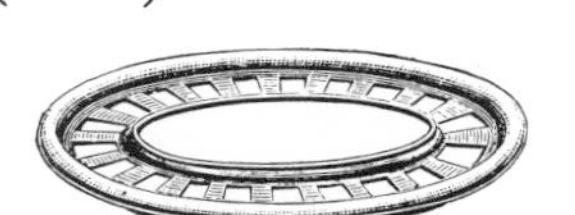

Style of No. 236, 4 in. P. & A. Dupl
Style of No. 1196, 4 in. No. 2 Royal.

No. 230. 4 in. Universal.
No. 373. 5 in. Universal.
For Fireside, Banner, Sun Hinge and Unique Burners.

No. 431. 5 in. Fireside.
For No. 2 Banner Lamps, American Duplex and No. 3 Climax Burners.

No. 764. 4 in. Climax.
For No. 3 Climax and American Duplex Burners.

No. 989. 4 in.
For No. 2 Royal Lamps and Oil

Feeder Caps and Collars

No. 189.

No. 1419.

No. 338.

No. 2445.

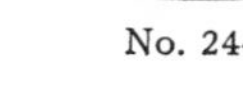

No. 188.

No. 415.

No. 2446.

No. 454.

No. 851.

No. 298.

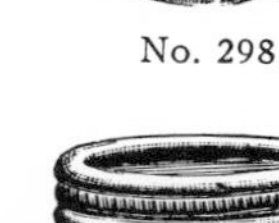

No. 2189.

No. 1896.

No. 938.

carry lamps from room to room. Bracket lamps, sometimes with a tin or mirror reflector were set in holders on bedroom and kitchen walls. Novelties of the 1880's were assembled lamps. These permitted dealers or their customers to put together lamps to suit their own taste from parts supplied by manufacturers. All assembled lamps had in comomn a frosted pressed glass oil font, stone or black iron base and brass fittings. Stems were offered in a choice of decorated china, glass and gilded metal cast in figures. Elaborately styled banquet and parlor lamps were very much in evidence in the 1880's and 1890's. Their most striking features were globular, hand-painted china shades and bulbous or tall columnar bases which are also applied to today's Gone With The Wind (GWW) lamps. Best known of all kerosene lamps is the Rochester burner, introduced in 1888. Its great merit lay in its improved central draft burner, which was attached to a brass or nickeled brass base.

The wide variety of burners, lamp chimneys and globes which one finds used with kerosene lamps almost defies description. Some burners spread the flame, some try to make a circular type wick work without a pump feature; some burners are round, some are oblong and triangular. Different types of chimneys, usually in glass, were developed to fit different types of burners. Around the chimney and the burner (as lamps became more ornate) various types of globes were introduced. These range all the way from open flair shades in pressed or cut glass, hand and acid-etched shades, even a few pure china or pottery shades. Catalogs of this period are used herein to indicate what types of burners, shades and chimneys are appropriate to the kerosene lamp. The author has discovered nearly 100 different patented types in the course of his researches. Not all are shown herein, but a look through the bibliography will indicate where the student of burner and shade development can find more detailed descriptions.

Look especially at S. E. Southland's **Catalogues and Wholesale Price List of Jones' Improved Patent Lamps** "for burning the various hydrocarbon oils such as Kerosene, Columbian, Albertine, Carbon and all other good coal oils. Kerosene, Coal and Carbon oils had at first imperfect and exceedingly disagreeable odors. This oil has at length been deodorized and brought to a state of perfection, hardly anticipated by the most sanguine. To make success certain, two things are indispensible—good oil and a good lamp. The heavy cheap oils do not burn well in a poor lamp!" Directions:

"Remove the cap and trim the wick even with the tube, replace the cap, turn the wick up through the opening, light it, and turn it down below the opening, adjust the chimney, and allow it to burn low for a few moments so as to prevent charring:—Breaking of the chimney is avoided by turning the blaze on gradually. To use as a night lamp, retrim, as the crusted wick prevents perfect combustion. Our lamps include sidewall brackets, chandeliers, hanging harp and shop lamps, side wall hanging chain lamps and stand lamps (prices on marble onyx, 3½″ (blue or ruby bowl) $18 doz.)

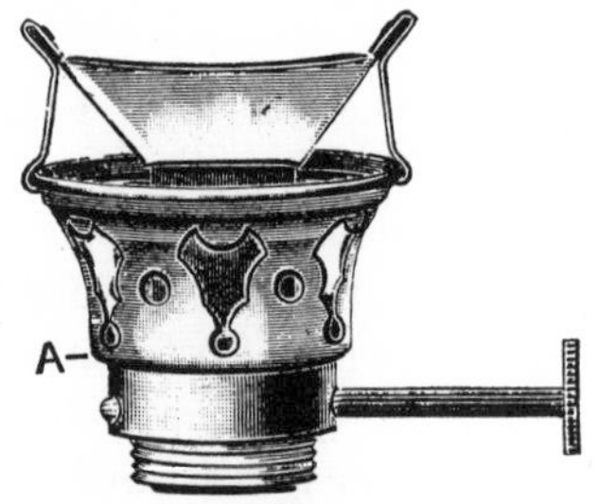

No. 1 (A) Signal
No Chimney Burner.
Made of Steel. Brass Plated.
For Kerosene or Coal Oil.
An Ideal Burner for Switch Lamps.

No. 1 Solar Burner.
All Brass. With Gas Tube.

No. 30 Burner and No. 3 Guide Ring.
For Incubators and Brooders.
Fits No. 3 (D) Collar.
Diameter of Thread, $1\frac{3}{4}$ in.
Diameter of Cone, $3\frac{7}{16}$ in.
Takes No. 3 (D) Wick.
Polished Brass.

No. 32 Incubator Burner.
No. 35 is same as No. 32 except it has Wide Blaze Hole.
Polished Brass.

Excelsior Sun Hinge Burners.

Heavy Oil Burner.
For Railroad and Steamboat use.

No. 2 (B) Dual Burner.
Has two Wick Tubes and two Springs. Fits No. 2 (B) Collar. Takes No. 2 (B) Wicks and Dual Lip Chimney.
Polished Brass.

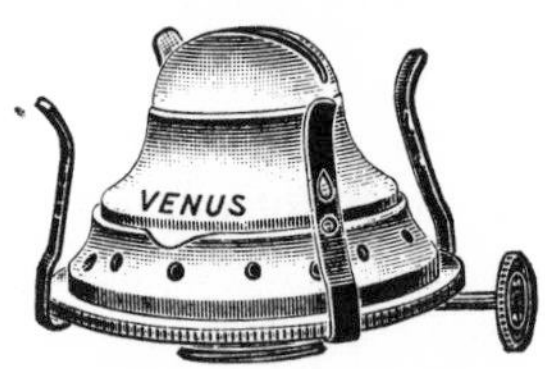

Venus Burners.
All Brass. With Gas Tube.
THE OLD STANDARD.

No.	Diam. of Thread.	Diam. of Body.
0 (E)	$\frac{7}{8}$ in.	$2\frac{3}{16}$ in.
1 (A)	$\frac{7}{8}$ "	$2\frac{1}{2}$ "
2 (B)	$1\frac{3}{16}$ "	3 "

Polished Brass.

Zenith No Chimney Burners.
With Gas Tube.
For Kerosene or Coal Oil.
Good for Incubators.
Polished Brass.

No. 3 (D) "E. M Duplex" Burner.

Duplex Burner Trimmings.

For "E. M. Duplex" Burner.

No. 2 Kerosene Blank Screw.

No. 54 Incubator Collar.

10 inch Duplex Tripod.

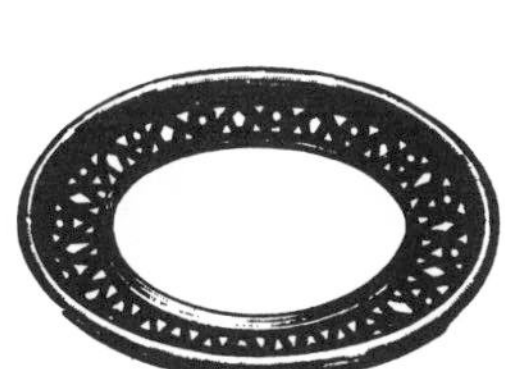

4 inch Duplex Globe Holder.

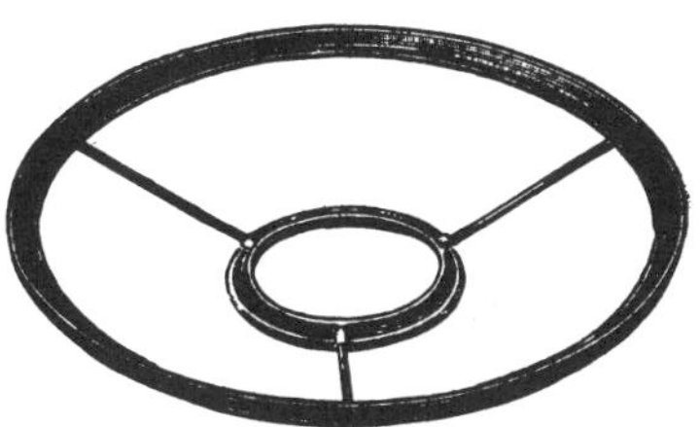

10 inch Duplex Shade Ring.

Above Trimmings furnished in Old Brass. Japanese or Nickel at slight advance in price.

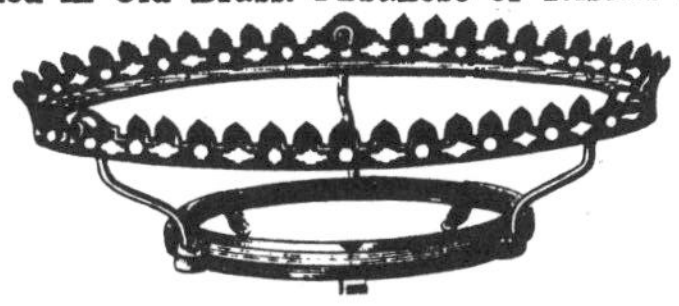

5 inch Combination

Apollo Duplex Burner Trimmings.

4 inch Apollo Duplex Globe Holder.

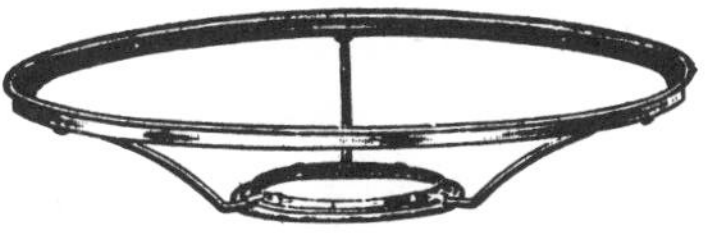

10 inch Apollo Duplex Shade Ring.

7 or 10 inch Combination Tripod.

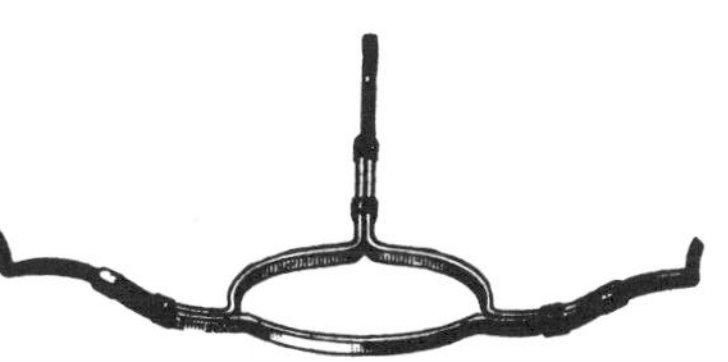

10 inch Adjustable Tripod. Bright Brass.

No. 00 Slip or Nobby Burner.

Polished Brass.

Fits No. 4 Collar.
Takes Nobby Chimney and Wick.
Diameter of Thread, 11/16 in.
Diameter of Body, 1¼ in.
50 dozen in a case.
Gross, 43 lbs.; Net, 29 lbs.
Cubic measurements, 2 ft., 1 in.

Victor Burners.

All Brass. Nos. 1 and 2 Have Gas Tubes.

No.	Diam. of Thread.	Diam. of Body.
0 (E)	⅞ in.	2 3/16 in.
1 (A)	⅞ in.	2½ in.
2 (B)	1 3/16 in.	3 in.

Polished Brass.

They take Sun Chimneys and regular Flat Wicks. No. 2 (B) takes Combination Shade Holders.

No.	In Case.	Gross.	Net.	Cubic Meas.
0 (E)	50 doz.	69 lbs.	43 lbs.	4 ft., 11 in.
1 (A)	50 "	80 "	50 "	5 " 4 "
2 (B)	25 "	66 "	41 "	4 " 6 "

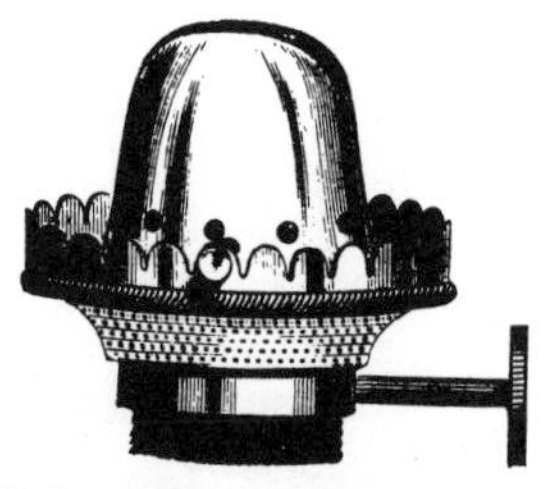

Light Hinge Burners.

Take Lip Chimneys.

No.	Diam. of Thread.	Diam. of Cone.	Extreme Lgth. Shaft.
1 (A)	⅞	1¾ in.	1⅞ in.
2 (B)	1 3/16	2 3/16 "	2¼ "

Polished Brass.

No. 1 fits No. 1 (A) Collar.
" 2 " " 2 (B) "

No.	In Case.	Gross.	Net.	Cubic Meas.
1 (A)	100 doz.	97 lbs.	71 lbs.	5 ft. 6 in.
2 (B)	50 "	72 "	55 "	5 " 0 "

No. 0 (E) Stellar Burner.

Takes Little Gem Chimney and No. 0 Flat Wick.
Diameter of Thread, ⅞ in.
Diameter of Body, 1⅝ in.

Polished Brass.

50 dozen in a case.
Gross, 44 lbs.; Net, 28 lbs.
Cubic measurements, 2 ft., 11 in.

Victor Burners.

Nos. 0 (E), 1 (A), 2 (B).

Heavy Hinge Burners.

Marcy's Patent.

Take Lip Chimneys.

No.	Diam. of Thread.	Diam. of Cone.	Extreme Lgth. Shaft.
1 (A)	⅞ in.	1¾ in.	1⅞ in.
2 (B)	1 3/16 "	2 3/16 "	2¼ "

Polished Brass.

No. 1 fits No. 1 (A) Collar.
" 2 " " 2 (B) "

No.	In Case.	Gross.	Net.	Cubic Meas.
1 (A)	100 dz.	150 lbs.	112 lbs.	6 ft. 11 in.
2 (B)	50 "	119 "	86 "	5 " 8 "

6 inch Opal Dome Shade.

For Lamps with No. 0 Burner.
Weight per dozen, about 6 lbs. net.

7 inch Opal Dome Shade.

For Lamps with No. 1 Burner.
Weight per dozen, about 10 lbs. net.

For Lamps with No. 2 Burner

10 inch Shade.

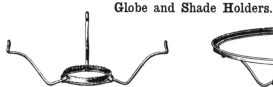

10 inch Plain Opal Dome Shade.

14 inch Plain Opal Dome Shades.

Globe and Shade Holders.

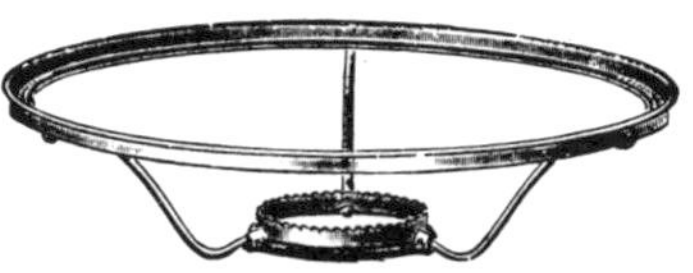

Tripods, 6, 7, 10 inch.

Fit Collars of Lamps.

6 inch,	for Lamps	with No.	0	Burners,
7 "	"	"	0	"
7 "	"	"	1 or 2	"
10 "	"	"	1 or 2	"

"Miller" Center Draught Burners.

Furnished in the following sizes.

		Diam. of Burner Body.
No. 0	for Small Lamps, . .	1¾ in.
" 1	" Medium Size Lamps, .	2¼ "
" 2	" Regular Size Table Lamps,	3 "
" 3	" Mammoth Founts, . .	4¼ "

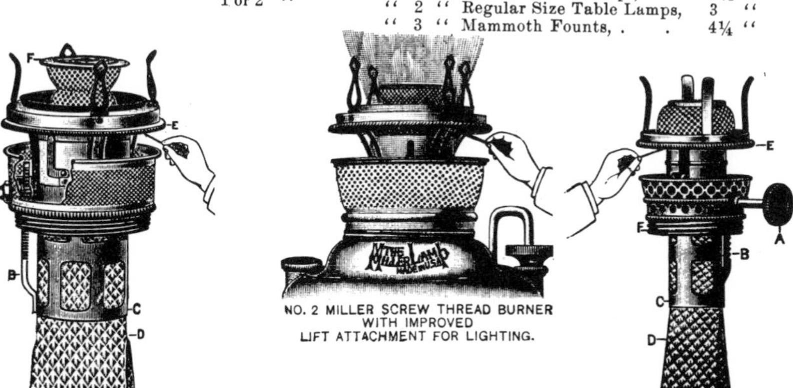

NO. 2 MILLER SCREW THREAD BURNER
WITH IMPROVED
LIFT ATTACHMENT FOR LIGHTING.

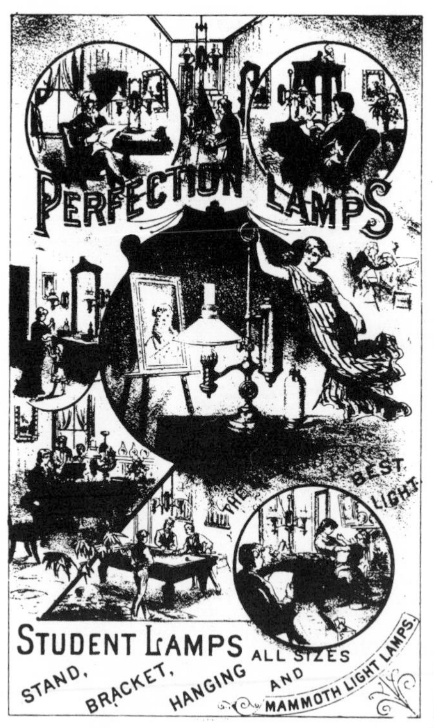

PERFECTION LAMPS
THE BEST LIGHT.
STUDENT LAMPS
STAND, BRACKET, HANGING
ALL SIZES AND MAMMOTH LIGHT LAMPS.

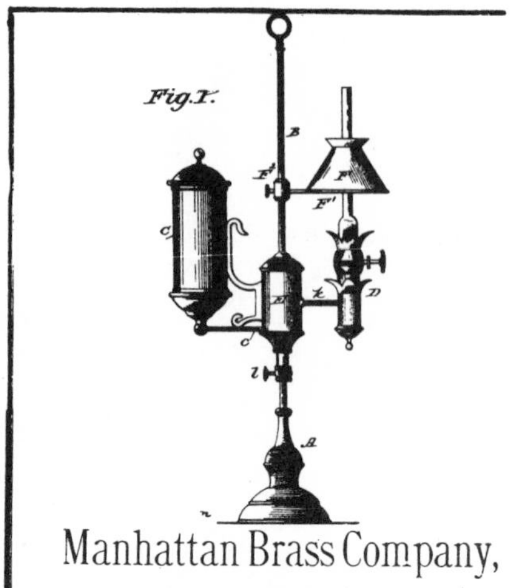

Manhattan Brass Company,

Sheet Brass, Wire & Tube Works,

—MANUFACTURERS—

LAMPS AND LAMP GOODS,

1st Avenue 27th to 28th Streets,

NEW YORK.

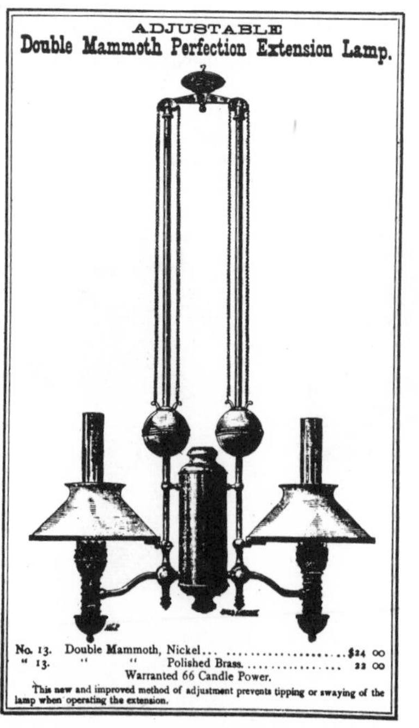

ADJUSTABLE
Double Mammoth Perfection Extension Lamp.
No. 13. Double Mammoth, Nickel.......................$24 00
" 13. " " Polished Brass................ 22 00
Warranted 66 Candle Power.
This new and improved method of adjustment prevents tipping or swaying of the lamp when operating the extension.

Perfection Lamps

are guaranteed to give the BEST and CHEAPEST LIGHT in the world.

THE STUDENT LAMP

is the heaviest and largest made, gives the most light, and is the least liable to get out of order. Each part is produced by machinery expressly constructed for the purpose, and can be replaced at a minimum of cost.

The New **Glass Fount** Student Lamp combines the one thing needed to make the absolutely perfect Lamp; its merits over all Student Lamps heretofore made are seen at a glance. *See page 6.*

Few persons realize the cheapness of light obtained by these Lamps; the smallest size lamp will give a light equal to twenty candles, or equivalent to four ordinary gas burners, at a cost of less than one cent per evening. The MAMMOTH size, which gives the largest light produced by kerosene, is 33 candle power, considerable more than the Argand gas burner, and a better and steadier flame—entirely free from the flicker and unsteadiness of gas, and at a cost not exceeding 50 cents a month per lamp.

These lamps are made in great variety, suitable for any place and purpose for which good light may be desired, and are warranted to be as represented and to give satisfaction in every respect.

Chapter VII
STUDENT AND PATENT LAMPS

The last quarter of the Nineteenth century saw the development of a number of patent and novelty lamps in America and abroad. The most famous of these is the so-called "student" lamp. Others include the Angle lamp, Spice lamp, Time lamp, Tumbler lamp and a host of adaptations of the lantern.

The Student Lamp. The origin of this lamp, now so much in demand, has been difficult to unravel. The author's old professor who studied in Germany in the 1870's, is an authority for the statement that these lamps were developed in Germany and brought back into this country by the returning students who favored their superior light at the reading table. Further study reveals a brass student lamp patented here in 1871, but this may well have been taken from a European model. A very similar model, adapted for colza oil, appeared in England in the early 1880's; hence the lamp may go back that far. Whatever its origin, the student reading light gained widespread popularity only from 1875 to 1900. An adaptation, the Argand burner for kerosene, the distinctive feature of the student light is a detachable oil font that feeds oil through a tube to a burner part so arranged on an arm that no shadow will be cast by the lamp upon the table surface. In these respects there is a similarity between the student lamp and the astral mantle lamp. But the student lamp is a much more utilitarian affair. It is a streamlined functural product, equipped to do a good lighting job with a minimum of furbelow. Oil font and burner arms revolve on an upright stand and for correct placement of the light. The base is heavily weighted so that the lamp will not be easily overturned. The chimney and shade are firmly attached and the wick is arranged for rapid and efficient care. So superior were these lamps for reading and study purposes that several colleges ordered their dormatories to be completely equipped with them. Harvard was one of the colleges to get such equipment, and this probably accounts for a student lamp type being known in some circles as the "Harvard."

Single Student Lamps. The single student lamp antidates the double variety. The author has a rare small type with an elongated burner bowl and six-inch shade which bears the date 1877. It is thought that this is the student lamp "improvement" patented by J. Kirby in 1877 and assigned to Post and Company for manufacture. The earliest student lamp patent was taken out in this country in 1871 by Schneidler, a citizen of the German Empire; a related type was registered by an American inventor, A. M. Blake, in the same year. Many student lamps of German manufacture were imported into this country by Hindricks & Company; as late

Perfection Mammoth Lamp.

No. 9—Perfection Mammoth—33 Candle Power.

Nickel Plated, ... $9 00 | Polished Brass.......... $8 00

Price Without Glass.

This Lamp gives the largest light that has ever been obtained from kerosene. It is superior to any Gas Argand Burner, much steadier flame, and costs about one-tenth that of gas.

EXTRA SIZE
Perfection Student Lamp,

For 10 in Shade,

TO BURN SEVENTEEN HOURS.

No. 5—For 10 in. Shade.—Perfection Extra.
20 Candle Power.

Nickel Plated.. $6 50
Polished Brass... 5 75

Price Without Glass.

This is a very desirable size for all Office and Desk use. Is made extra strong, with heavy base. The Strongest and Best Student Lamp made.

Perfection Double Student.

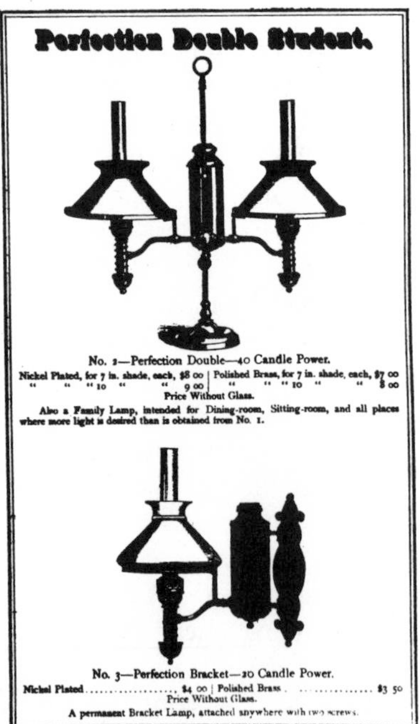

No. 2—Perfection Double—40 Candle Power.

Nickel Plated, for 7 in. shade, each, $8 00	Polished Brass, for 7 in. shade, each, $7 00
" " " 10 " " 9 00	" " " 10 " " 8 00

Price Without Glass.

Also a Family Lamp, intended for Dining-room, Sitting-room, and all places where more light is desired than is obtained from No. 1.

No. 3—Perfection Bracket—20 Candle Power.

Nickel Plated.................... $4 00 | Polished Brass.................... $3 50

Price Without Glass.

A permanent Bracket Lamp, attached anywhere with two screws.

Double Mammoth Stand Lamp.

No. 10—Perfection Mammoth Double—66 Candle Power.

Price, without Glass.. $15 00

The value of good light for the preservation of sight is thus set forth by a celebrated expert:

"No superiority in workmanship can be expected unless the vision is preserved, and nothing will do more to preserve it than a sufficient supply of good, steady light.

"When the light is insufficient or of poor quality, or both, the muscles of the eye are strained to their utmost to produce a power of accommodation to enable one to read, write, or even distinguish objects at but a short distance. This strain cannot be kept up for any length of time or frequently incurred without producing grave damage to the vision; the muscles refuse to respond to the nervous influence, and we have a weakness of vision, double vision, short sight, paralysis of the muscles of the eyes, and even total blindness as the resultants."

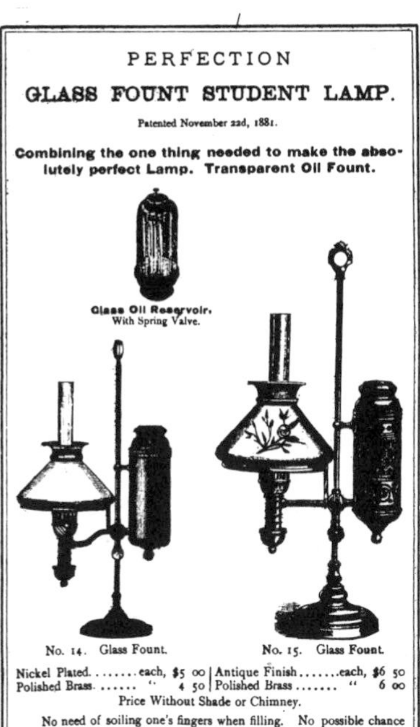
PERFECTION
GLASS FOUNT STUDENT LAMP.
Patented November 22d, 1881.
Combining the one thing needed to make the absolutely perfect Lamp. Transparent Oil Fount.
Glass Oil Reservoir.
With Spring Valve.
No. 14. Glass Fount.
No. 15. Glass Fount.
Nickel Plated........each, $5 00
Polished Brass....... " 4 50
Antique Finish.......each, $6 50
Polished Brass....... " 6 00
Price Without Shade or Chimney.
No need of soiling one's fingers when filling. No possible chance of leaking.

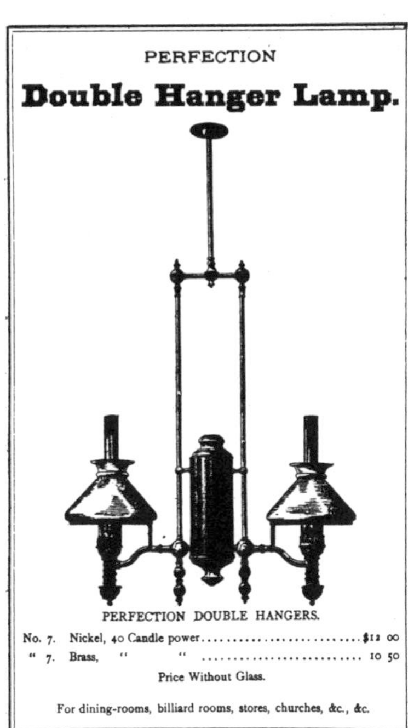
PERFECTION
Double Hanger Lamp.
PERFECTION DOUBLE HANGERS.
No. 7. Nickel, 40 Candle power........................$12 00
" 7. Brass, " " 10 50
Price Without Glass.
For dining-rooms, billiard rooms, stores, churches, &c., &c.

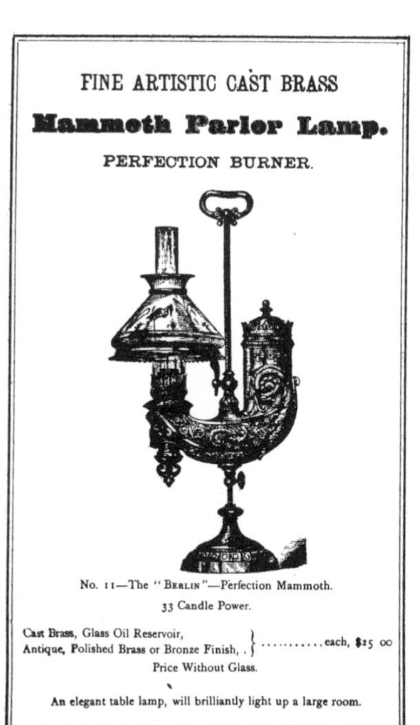
FINE ARTISTIC CAST BRASS
Mammoth Parlor Lamp.
PERFECTION BURNER.
No. 11—The "Berlin"—Perfection Mammoth.
33 Candle Power.
Cast Brass, Glass Oil Reservoir,
Antique, Polished Brass or Bronze Finish, . } ....each, $25 00
Price Without Glass.
An elegant table lamp, will brilliantly light up a large room.

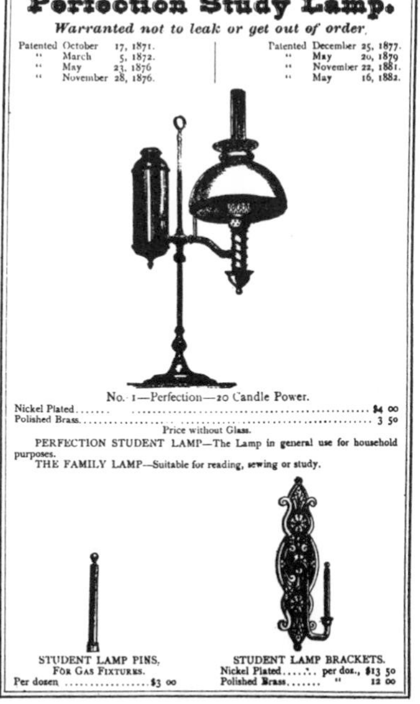
Perfection Study Lamp.
Warranted not to leak or get out of order.
Patented October 17, 1871.
" March 5, 1872.
" May 23, 1876
" November 28, 1876.
Patented December 25, 1877.
" May 20, 1879
" November 22, 1881.
" May 16, 1882.
No. 1—Perfection—20 Candle Power.
Nickel Plated..$4 00
Polished Brass..3 50
Price without Glass.
PERFECTION STUDENT LAMP—The Lamp in general use for household purposes.
THE FAMILY LAMP—Suitable for reading, sewing or study.
STUDENT LAMP PINS,
For Gas Fixtures.
Per dozen $3 00
STUDENT LAMP BRACKETS.
Nickel Plated...... per doz., $13 50
Polished Brass....... " 12 00

2 Sheets—Sheet 1.
F. DEIMEL.
LAMP BURNER.
Patented Jan. 14, 1890.
Fig. 8
Witnesses:
E. R. Brown
E. L. Richards
Inventor.
Fritz Deimel
By
Attorneys.

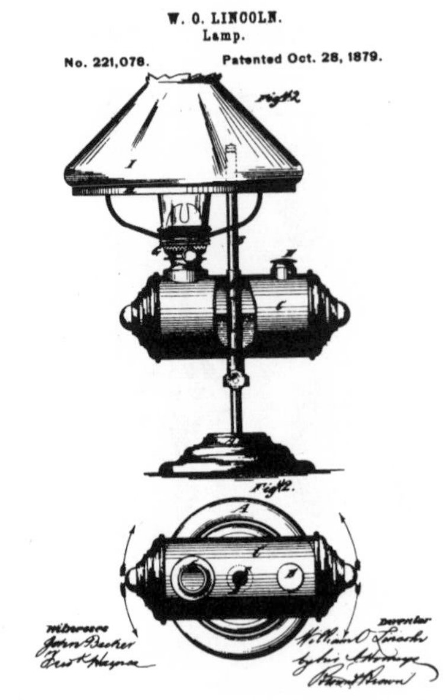
W. O. LINCOLN.
Lamp.
No. 221,078.
Patented Oct. 28, 1879.
Witnesses
John Becker
Inventor
William O. Lincoln
by his Attorneys

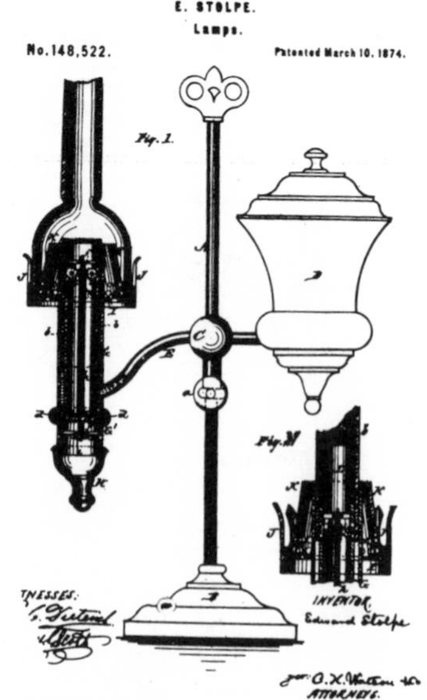
E. STOLPE.
Lamps.
No. 148,522.
Patented March 10, 1874.
Fig. 1.
INVENTOR.
Edward Stolpe
ATTORNEYS.

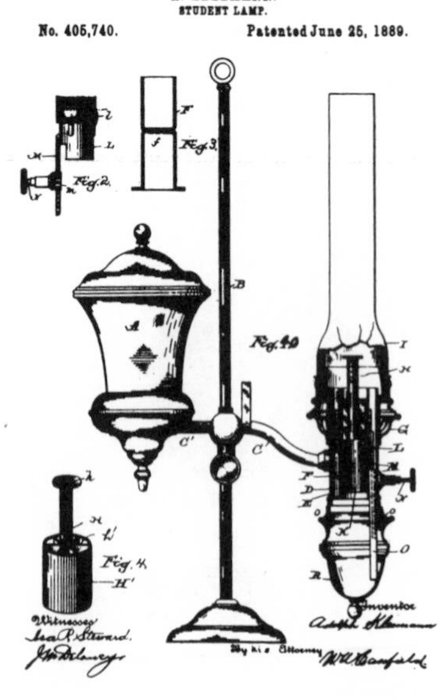
(No Model.)
A. KLEEMANN.
STUDENT LAMP.
No. 405,740.
Patented June 25, 1889.
Fig. 3.
Fig. 2.
Fig. 4.
Witnesses
Inventor
Adolph Kleemann
By his Attorney

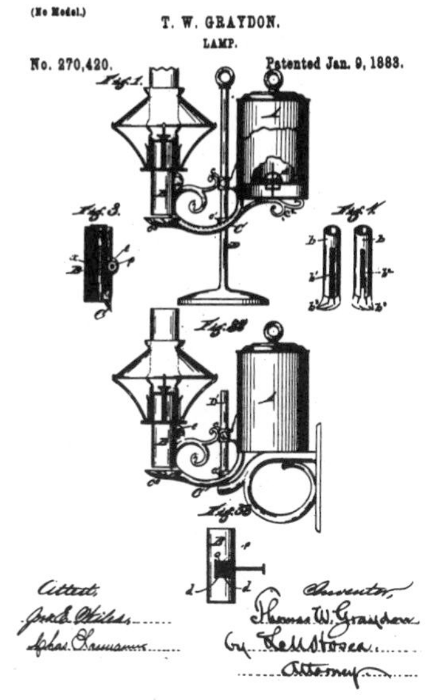

(No Model.)

A. ANGELL.

STUDENT'S LAMP.

No. 270,719. Patented Jan. 16, 1883.

Fig. 37

Fig. 3.

Witnesses

Inventor

Albert Angell

2 Sheets--Sheet 1.

A. M. BLAKE.

Lamp.

No. 159,381 Patented Feb. 2, 1875.

(No Model.)

O. HELLER & W. DONALDSON.

STUDENT'S LAMP.

No. 302,251. Pate July 22, 1884.

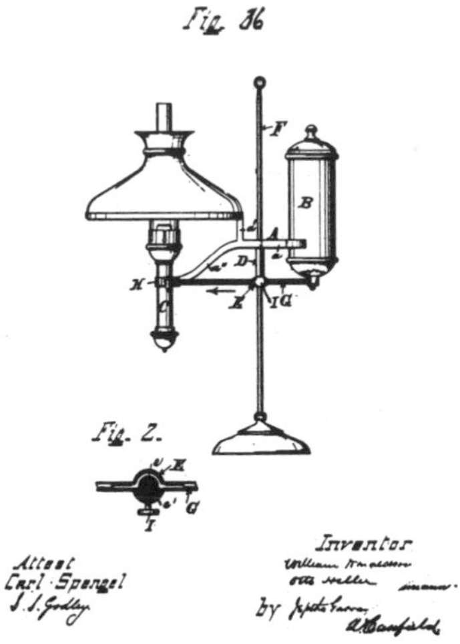

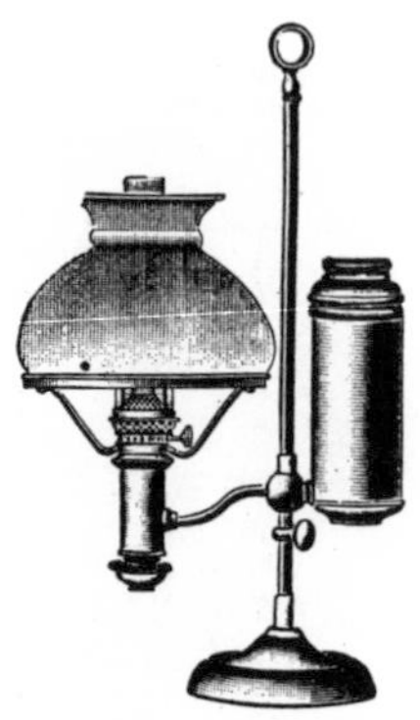

No. 348 Vestal Pendant Lamp.

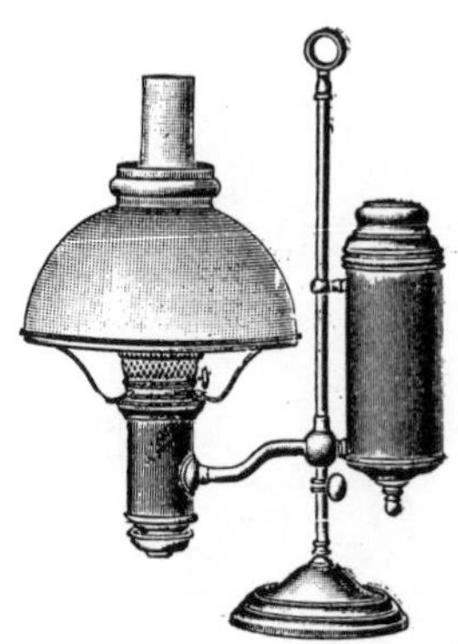

No. 2 Vestal Study Lamp.

Furnished complete with No. 2 Vestal Wick, No. 2 Miller Chimney, 10 inch Shade Ring and Opal Dome Shade.
Height to top of Handle, 20½ in.
Nickel Plated or Old Brass Finish.

No. 1 Vestal Study Lamp
is like above equipped with No. 1 Vestal Burner. Furnished complete with No. 1 Vestal Wick, No. 1 Miller Chimney and 10 inch Shade Ring and Opal Dome Shade.

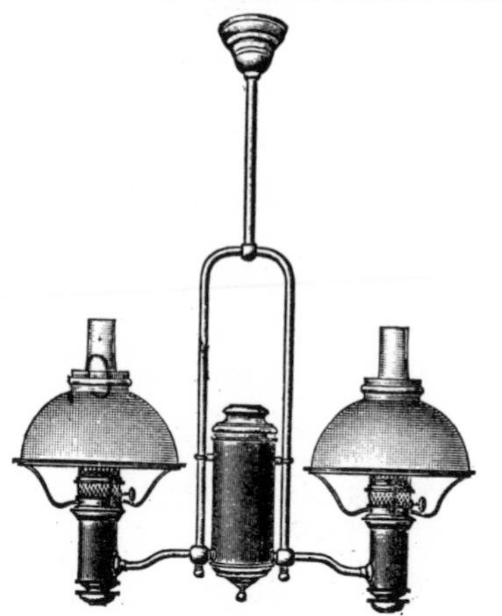

No. 349 Vestal Swing Bracket Lamp.

(No Model.)

J. H. WHITE.

LAMP.

No. 283,177. Patented Aug. 14, 1883.

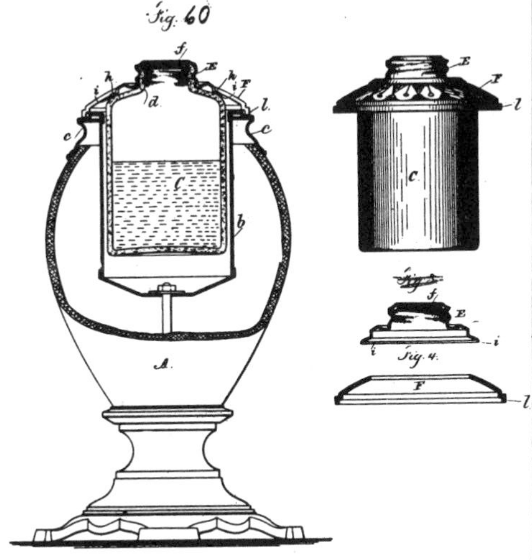

COLONIAL LIBRARY LAMP.

Made in Old English and Japanese Bronze Finishes.
Packed One Dozen in a Case with 10 inch Ring—No Glassware.
Holds 1¼ Quarts of Oil. Burns 6¼ Hours on One Filling.

PRICE ON APPLICATION.

The Plume & Atwood Mfg. Co., Waterbury, Conn.

Chicago. New York. San Francisco.

W. M. & J. J. WALTON.

Lamp.

No. 202,681. Patented April 23, 1878.

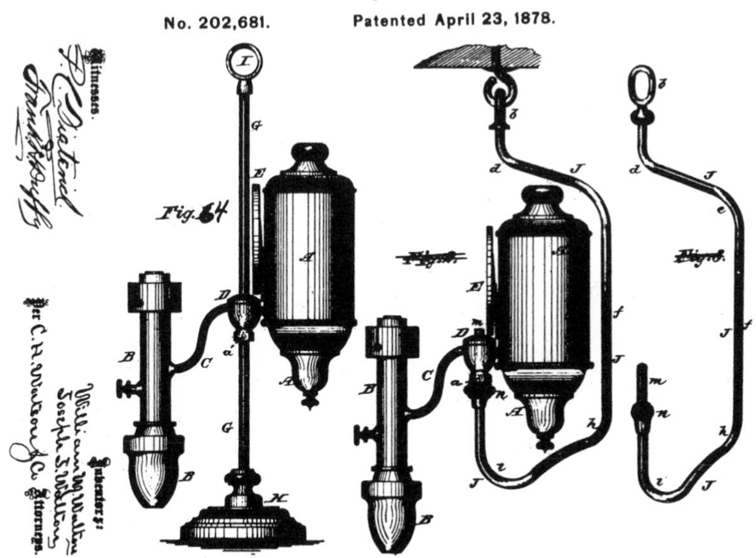

No. 203 in Nickel.
As illustrated, . . .
(Clear globes—opal tops.)

No. 283 Antique Brass,
or Antique Copper.
As illustrated, . . .
(Clear globes—opal tops.)
Capacity 1½ qts.
Burns 12 hours.

Fig. 54 - ANGLE LAMP

The two double-burner lamps shown on this page give the same amount of light. The choice between them is largely personal preference. The 203 pattern is plain in design, and for many purposes this is a desirable feature.

There is one distinct advantage in favor of the 202 pattern: its reservoir is larger and it therefore burns 22 hours on a single filling. This means that it needs filling only once a week or at most three times in two weeks.

Either of these is splendid for lighting dining room, sitting room, library, and for stores, churches, etc. We recommend particularly the Antique Copper finish—a rich glossy black with the raised work struck with copper.

Angle Lamps are the only lamps that can be safely used in low ceiling rooms. The hanging lamps are but 18 inches from top to bottom and the heat passing out the top is comparatively slight. If very close to the ceiling, use Mica Canopies. (See page 16.)

as 1890 this company was listed as agent and assignor of a patent lamp improvement originating by Germany.

American inventors were very active during the 1870's and 1880's. Typical products that saw the market are illustrated from the original patent drawings. It will be noted that the earliest type of shade mount is a metal clamp attached to the standard. Later models have a wire shade holder that fits over the burner. Most of these lamps were made in both the 7-inch and 10-inch sizes. The straight sided cone shade appears to have been used before the domed and mushroom shades. Very few 7-inch shades were made in color, and the majority of those now offered for sale are reproductions. The small or seven-inch single student lamp is most frequently found in nickel. This plating can be stripped off to produce a beautiful lamp of burnished brass.

Double Student Lamps. Practically every variety of single student lamps were also produced as a double one by balancing the oil tank between the two burners. A unique type, especially suited for use as a double lamp, has a horizontal oil barrel with the standard running through its center and with burners mounted on either side. The original patent drawing for this type of lamp is shown. It is found both in brass and nickel plated and is one of the few double student lamps equipped to handle the 7-inch shade. The great majority of double student lamps are large and late varieties with the 10-inch shade.

Student Lamp Types. A system of nomenclature suited to the identification of the various student lamp types would greatly facilitate the exchange of information about them. As an aid in this direction, the author illustrates four typical varieties from old catalogs. He shows the familiar "acorn" type, here called the Colonial Reading Lamp and illustrated from the catalog of an old Connecticut firm, the Bradley and Hubbard Manufacturing Company. He shows a page from the Miller Lamp Company's Catalog of 1900. Their "vestal" type is fairly comon in the 7-inch single variety, but less so in the double, hanging and 10-inh varieties. A Figure gives catalog comments from one of the largest producers of student lamps, the Manhattan Brass Company of New York City. Figures show varieties in the "Perfection" type of lamp, including one that is frequently referred to as the "Horn of Plenty" type. The last decade of the Nineteenth century saw a number of other elaborate cast bronze student lamps. These were expensive and never made in large numbers. A lamp of this late type is known as the "Aladdin."

The Angle Lamp. Here is a lamp destined to almost as great revival possibilities as the student lamp. It was made by the Angle Lamp Manufacturing Company of W. 23rd St., New York City during the late Nineteenth and early Twentieth century. As indicated by illustrations, the lamp exploits a patented principle for getting the flame directly over the place where the most light is desired. These lamps come in brass, nickel and

COLONIAL READING LAMP.

With Duplex Burners, Chimneys and 10-inch Ring Shade Holders.

THE BRADLEY & HUBBARD MFG. CO.

No. 4753.

Wall, Tumbler, Spice & Sport Lamps; Courtesy Antiques.

antiqued copper finish, in the double hanging type and the single wall bracket type. Most of them have clear chimneys and opal white tops. A few of the early ones are found equipped with lovely blue and white swirled glass tops. The lamps convert easily to electrical wiring and many are now being arranged on a standard running through the oil font to serve as table lamps, in substitution for the fast disappearing student type.

Other Patent Lamps. The varieties of patents taken out for grease lamps and the use of other heavy fluids have been already described in Chapter 2. Besides the patent student lamps, other varieties for burning kerosene fuel made their appearance after 1875. The wall lamps fed the fluid downward into burners similar to the student type. They were manufactured by W. Carlton of Boston, Massachusetts.

One of the most interesting late lamps, and a rarity if complete, is the tumbler lamp illustrated and it was patented in 1874. It is an ordinary tumbler filled with a curious boxlike top and handle. Other rarities are **Spice lamps,** and several related types also pictured.

Small dark lanterns, probably intended for bicycles, can be added to the list of those in quest of late Nineteenth century patent lamps. A Figure shows a small kerosene "Sport lamp" with kerosene burner, marked Stevens Patent Sept. 7, 1875. Rare indeed are some of the patent lamps of the late Nineteenth century. When few saw the market, any existent specimen should command the interest of the scores of lamp collectors.

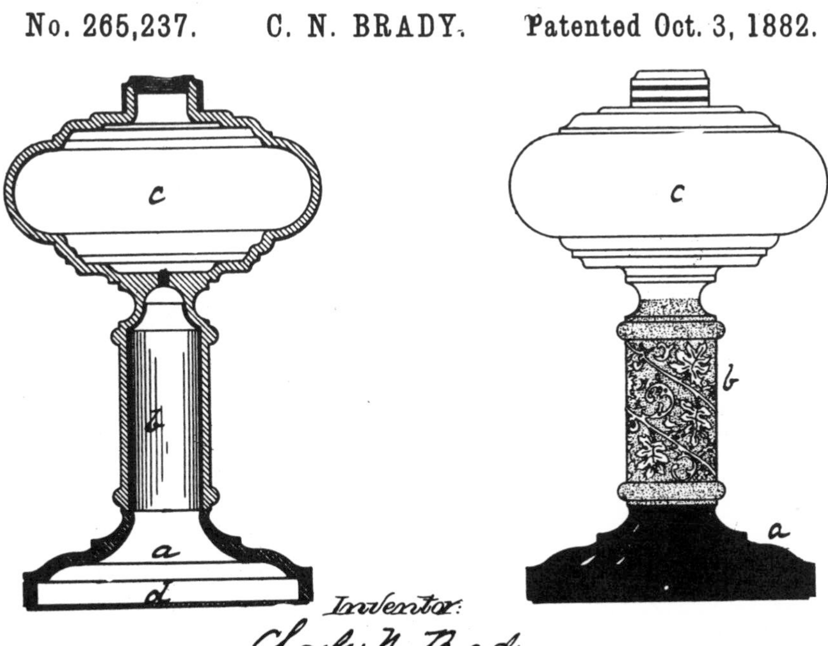

PARIS BRONZES.

THE whole of the beautiful examples on this page are from the establishment of M. Barbédienne, who has contributed to our International Exhibitions perhaps more extensively than any other first-class bronzist, and whose works are consequently better known than those of most of his *confrères*. A considerable number of them will be found engraved in these pages; for, always admirable in design, they are peculiarly well fitted for the eyes of students and young artists. Most of M. Barbédienne's productions are original, but they are also frequently modifications of ancient types, and of those of the classic period of France, the Renaissance, and later periods. That the artists and Art-workmen connected with the establishment are equally at home in all the styles, will be found by a careful study of the various examples given in the course of this work, and the sheet before us itself would go far to prove it. The contrast between the severity of the foot and square pillar of the elegant Candelabrum above to the left, the two graceful Candlesticks, and the daring magnificence of the grand central Lamp, reflected in the Candelabrum above to the right, is very decided, and shows the resources which this establishment has at its command.

ENGLISH AND FRENCH BRONZE AND BRASS WORK.

THE magnificent example of metal work which fills so admirably the central portion of this page is a mixed bronze and brass work by Messrs. Messenger and Sons, of Birmingham. It is one of ten grand gasaliers designed by C. R. Cockerell, R.A., for St. George's Hall, Liverpool, each of which has a hundred and forty lights, is seventeen feet in height, and weighs about one ton. The famous or fabulous bird, the *Liver*, which gave name to the *pool* that now can show the finest docks in the world, is introduced between the stars in the corona above, and in the smaller circle below, while the grand ring is decorated with the armed prows of ancient war galleys and classic masks, and the basket below with Greek foliage, all blended artistically into a most symmetrical whole.

The Lamp and Stand to the left hand is the work of M. Lerolle, of Paris; and that opposite of M. Charpentier. Both are well worthy of those eminent bronzists; the former presents, perhaps, greater novelty in treatment than is usual when classic types are followed in such productions.

MERCURY
With 9 in. Globe

MAGNOLIA
With 10 in. Globe

Chapter VIII
BANQUET AND PARLOR LAMPS

In the last decade of the Nineteenth century, progress in the science of artificial illumination began to bypass the kerosene lamp. Gas lighting, which was known in England as early as 1792, gradually took its place in street lighting in America and was piped into many houses during the latter part of the Nineteenth century. Edison's electric lamp had also made its appearance and bid fair to become the real competitor. And yet, it was during the 1890's that in many respects, the old oil lamp enjoyed its golden age. Development of central burners of the Rochester type had brought a bright, steady and dependable light within the reach of all. Kerosene oil was cheap; gas and electric illumination were expensive, somewhat unpredictable and not always available; and so, while men worked to throw electric power lines all over the country, the oil lamp had its swan song in an era of flamboyance and lavishness. "Beautiful lamps especially designed for each and every room" was the cry of the manufacturers. Gone was the simplicity and functionalism of early lamp design. In their place was overdecoration, ostentation, and in many instances, a sacrifice of illumination in the interest of display.

But there is something fascinating about the late Victorian lamp, in spite of its shortcomings. The charm and whimsicality of these ball globed banquet and parlor lamps has now captured the enthusiasm of home decorators a scarce half century beyond their original period of popularity. Demand is now greater than supply, so that prices have risen very rapidly. A good stock of late Victorian lamps provides the decorator with the proper ingredients for making even the most commonplace of rooms look alert and amusing. Proper identification of the various types is greatly needed.

Banquet Lamps. It is probable that this type of lamp was used as much in the parlor as at the dining table. But the term was used quite generally in catalogues of the period, and there is no doubt that the tall brass pedestal lamps had their illuminated globes high enough from the table to cast the light to advantage. A group of these lamps is illustrated. All have a rather ornate lamp bowl set 15 to 18 inches above an elaborate open work base. The pedestal is formed as a beaming cherib, who holds the lamp bowl precariously above his head. Decorators at first avoided these latter extravagances as too ornate for modern living. Now they have discovered that the statuary base can be painted amusingly to resemble bisque, and as a result there is more interest in figure than in non figure banquet lamps. The proper original shades for these lamps are the ball types. The lamps come in solid brass, antimony and wrought iron.

High China Parlor Lamps. The precursor of what has now become the

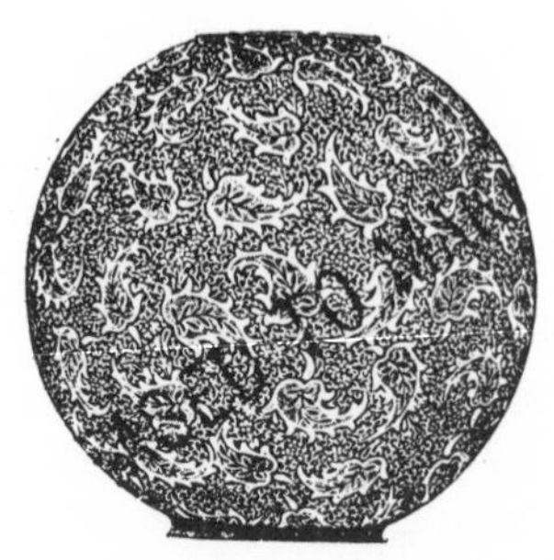

9 and 10 inch Crystal Etched Globes.

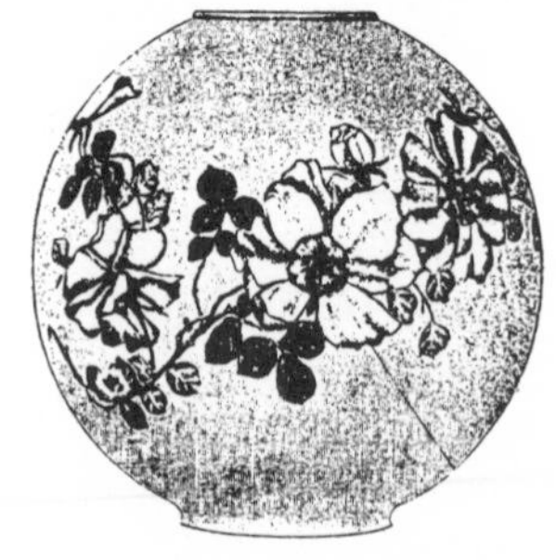

Lumo Parlor Lamp.

9 and 10 inch Decorated Globes.

Vestal Table Lamp.

No. 1166—199 Miller Banquet Lamp.

Furnished with No. 2 Miller Non-Detachable Embossed Metal Fount, Wick and No. 08—4 inch Globe Holder or 10 inch Tripod only.
Has Cast Openwork Base.
Height as shown, 19½ in. Spread of Base, 8¾ in.
Figure Finished in Satin, Silver or Satin Gilt: remainder of Lamp, Polished Gilt Finish.

For Shades to complete these lamps see pages 8 and 9.

No. 1166—199 Miller
Description Above.

No. 1240—222 Miller Banquet Lamp.

Furnished with No. 2 Miller Detachable Fount, Wick and No. 08—4 inch Globe Holder or 10 inch Tripod only.
All Cast Metal.
Openwork Head and Base.
Height as shown, 22¾ in.
Spread of Base, 9¾ in.
Figure, Satin Gilt; remainder of Lamp, Polished Gilt Finish.

No. 1241—231 Miller Banquet

Furnished with No. 2 Miller Detach: Fount, Wick and No. 08—4 inch Globe Holder or 10 inch Tripod only.
All Cast Metal, Openwork Head.
Height as shown, 23 in.
Spread of Base, 10¾ in.
Figure, Satin Gilt; remainder of Lamp, Polished Gilt Finish.

Oil Pots

For use in Lamps with Lift Out Reservoir.

Reservoirs measure 3 ins. in depth, 5 ins. in diameter.

Center Draft.

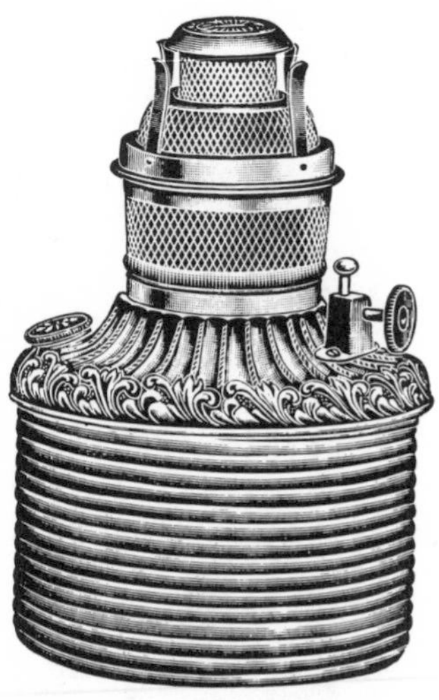

No. 1204. No. 2 Royal.
Embossed.

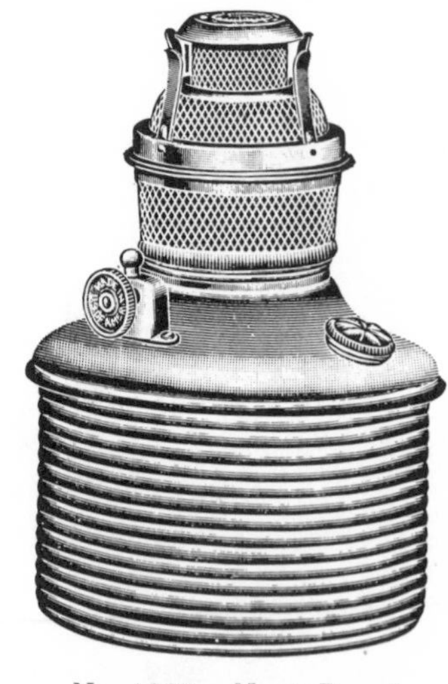

No. 1300. No. 2 Royal.
Plain.

With No. 3 Collar.

No. 1281. No. 3 Collar.

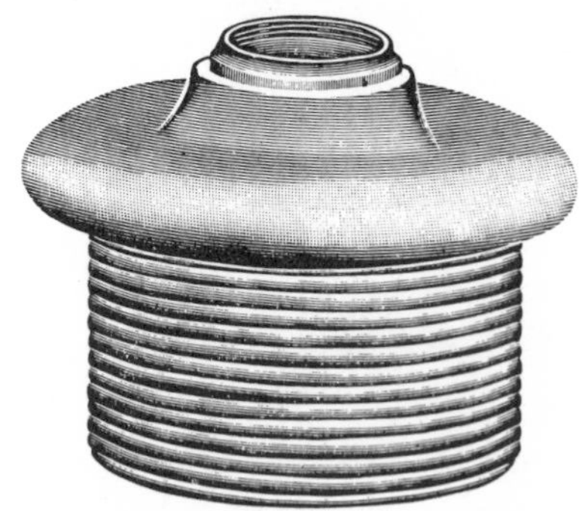

No. 1292. No. 3 Collar.

The above Collar Pots are also made with Center Draft Burner.

No. 1281 with No. 2 Royal Burner is No. 1300.
" 1292 " " 2 " " " " 1420.

Can furnish in any finish to match Lamps, at usual advance over Brass.

Order No.			Per Doz.
No. 1204.	No. 2.	Royal, Embossed, Brass,	$27.90
" 1300.	" 2.	" Plain, "	27.90
" 1281.	" 3.	Collar, " "	13.95
" 1292.	" 3.	" " "	31.00
" 1420.	" 2.	Royal, " "	49.60

fad for late Victorian china and glass parlor lamps begins with the creation of exquisite and rather small high standing oil lamps in the china making centers of Europe, especially of Dresden. The delicate Dresden china lamp with its small ball shade was often to be found in better American homes after 1870. It was never cheap; the hand ornamentation of delicate flowers and figures could not compete with American mass production methods. Yet it set the style for the first American parlor lamps to come from china and glass moulding rooms. The Author gives an example of what is believed to be the oldest type of china parlor lamp, dating probably from the 1880's. Some lamps were decorated with flowers, but the earliest and best are thought to be those in solid color china, such as pale yellow and green. Unlike the later types to be described in subsequent paragraphs, these lamps do not conceal a brass oil font. The china bowl itself is used to contain the oil and has only the small burner opening at the top.

Removable Font Parlor Lamps. In the 1880's J. H. White and other associates perfected a brass oil font which could be inserted into or removed from a surrounding decorative vase of china or opaque glass. Thereby was developed a type of parlor lamp which was to sweep the country twice in popularity, once at its inception and again after the revival of the era in the "Gone With the Wind" motion picture. No lamp type had more imitators nor sold over a wider price range. As evidence of this, the reader can compare the prices quoted on lamps by Mills Bargain House with almost identical forms sold by Macy's of New York. This should give pause to the tendency to buy lamps of this type at very high prices without inspecting the quality of workmanship and decoration. The full range of lamp variants is shown on these catalog pages. Notations can be further supplemented by study of this book's frontespiece. Umbrella and dome shades seem to have appeared first on these lamps at the Chicago World's Fair in 1893. The great claim for such shades was that reading was made more possible by their use. The public, however, liked the ball shade no matter how it dimmed the light and their popularity remained until well into the 20th century. The soft glow of these lamps was just the thing for entertaining beaus in the parlor. This is where the china parlor lamp remained enshrined until its place taken by electricity, it was relegated to the attic to be discovered and wired for lighting "above and below" by the next generation. Most of these lamps were made in Western Pennsylvania and Ohio glass houses. Edward Rorne and Co. of 40 Barclay street, New York and John M. Smyth of Chicago were large distributors.

Brass Parlor Lamps. Metal bowl lamps are late. The early 1900's saw the introduction of brass and copper parlor lamps with bowls shaped very much like the earlier china parlor lamps. Representative samples are shown. Some of the bases have handles. A few will be found with frosted ball shades, but the majority were equipped for mushroom or dome type shades of plain colored glass or of paneled art glass. The brass library

No. 2E96[illegible] Our Princeton Lamp. This is a fine lamp at a very low price. It is decorated with large red poppies and green leaves on a brown and yellow tinted background. It is complete with a 9-inch globe, No. 2 Royal center draft burner, which produces a strong steady light, removable oil fount, No. 2 Rochester wick and chimney, and stands 22½ inches high. This lamp has a massive brass base, finely plated and lacquered. Shipping weight, 20 pounds.
Price **$2.78**

No. 2E971 Art Nouveau Lamp, $2.89. This beautiful lamp is a reproduction of a celebrated piece of French art. It is delicately tinted in purple and embossing is decorated in dark green with beautiful hand painted art figures on both sides of lamp and globe. It has the latest improved Success central draft burner (100-candle power) with large removable brass oil fount. All metal parts are made from satin finished brass. Shipping weight, 30 pounds.
Price **$2.89**

No. 2E973 Cerise Beauty, $2.95. This banquet lamp is made from ruby glass, and when lighted produces a rich ruby light, one of the most cheerful and charming illuminations, which casts a soft ruby glow on all of its surroundings. The handsome embossed satin finished cerise glass and bright gold trimmings go to make up a very striking and artistic lamp. It is fitted with the very best No. 2 Royal center draft burner and a No. 2 Rochester round wick and chimney and has a solid brass removable oil fount. This lamp stands 26 inches high and has a large 10-inch globe. Shipping weight, 25 pounds.
Price......**$2.95**

No. 2E976 The American Beauty Lamp, $2.98. This is one of the prettiest lamps shown this season. The globe measures 10½ inches in diameter; the vase or cylinder to match is of equal size. The lamp measures 26 inches high. The hand painted decorations consist of beautiful American Beauty roses and foliage on a blue tinted background. It has the improved Success central draft burner, and takes No. 1 Belgium chimney and round wick. It produces a strong and steady 80-candle power light. This lamp compares favorably with those sold by crockery dealers at

Victor Lamp, $1.89.

No. 2E965 The embossings of this handsome lamp are dark green, designed to form four rich panels of white, which have beautiful floral centers consisting of wild roses and foliage. It has a removable oil fount made of solid brass and is complete with a large 8-inch globe, No. 3 Climax burner and wick and No. 2 Electric chimney. Height, 21 inches. This is one of the best values we offer. Shipping weight, 20 pounds.
Price.........**$1.89**

No. 2E979 Lucille Lamp, $2.95. Compare this lamp with those offered by your local dealer at $5.00 or $6.00, and you will appreciate this wonderful value. This lamp is strictly the highest grade made. The beautiful pansies and green leaves are very carefully painted by hand by high class artists, every minor detail being brought out true to life. The entire lamp is magnificently tinted in an iridescent luster of light green, forming a deep contrast with the **hand painted flowers.** This lamp is extremely large, measuring 27 inches high and is complete with a 10½-inch globe, No. 2 Rochester chimney and wick. The highest grade center draft burner is used, which produces a strong steady light. Shipping weight, about 25 pounds. Price **$2.95**

No. 2E986 Romeo Lamp, $3.48, is one of the prettiest lamps made in a snow ball design. It is large and shapely throughout. The decoration consists of large hand painted snowballs, highly enameled, with light green leaves. The lamp and globe are richly tinted in a dark green and when lighted, the beautiful snowballs appear true to life. A decoration of this kind appeals to the most critical and is sure to meet with favor everywhere. The burner, which is the highest grade central draft type, produces a 100-candle power light and is complete with No. 2 Rochester chimney and wick. This lamp stands 27½ inches high and has a large 10-inch globe and is adorned with heavy brass crown and base which is finely gold lacquered. Securely packed in a box. Shipping weight, 30 pounds. Price......**$3.48**

No. 2E998 Excel Lamp, $3.89. This is an exceptionally large and handsome lamp at a very low price. It stands 31½ inches high and has an extra large globe 11½ inches in diameter. The decoration consists of large wreaths of delicate pink shaded water lilies and green lily leaves on a light yellow and green tinted background and produces a very pleasing effect when lighted. It is trimmed with a large and massive brass crown and base which greatly adds to the attractiveness of the lamp. It is equipped with the best grade No. 2 Royal center draft burner and removable oil fount made of solid brass, No. 2 Rochester chimney and round wick. This is the largest lamp ever offered at so low a price. Securely packed in a barrel. Shipping weight, 35 pounds.
$3.89

Pansy Lamp, $1.79.

No. 2E958 Our Pansy Lamp is one of the prettiest medium priced lamps made, decorated with hand painted pansies and green leaves on a maroon and yellow tinted background, forming a very rich contrast. Complete with large 9-inch globe, No. 3 Climax burner, shade ring, No. 2 Electric chimney and 1½-inch wick and stands 22 inches high. All metal parts are made of heavy brass, highly polished and lacquered. Shipping weight, 20 pounds.
Price.........**$1.79**

No. 2E[illegible] Kismet Lamp, $4.98. Beautifully decorated by hand. This lamp is the work of high class artists, the decoration consisting of large white and pink chrysanthemums and light green leaves, very cleverly painted by hand and in such a manner that the beautiful flowers are true to life. The entire lamp is most handsomely tinted in pink and light green, forming a fine background for the flowers. No lamp has ever been made that can surpass it in beauty. It is extra large, measuring 26½ inches high and 11½-inch globe and 13-inch base. It has the best central draft burner, which produces candle power light, and removable oil made of solid brass and is complete with 2 Rochester chimney and round wick metal parts, including the fancy cast and large base, are made of brass, gold and lacquered and will not tarnish. No lamp made at any price. Securely pack a barrel. Shipping weight, 40 pounds.
Price..............................**$4.**

No. 2E[illegible] Iris Lily, $5.95. lamp represent largest and best we offer. It me 31½ inches hig has a large 11 globe. The d tion, which co of large purple red iris lilies green leaves beautifully ti pale pink and m background, is tiful to behold. shape is the n offered this se It has a large m brass crown elaborate brass which form a gold plated and protected from and tarnishing heavy coa lacquer. Its bu and illumi powers are passed and equipped with very best grade Central draft b No. 2 Rochester round wick and Rochester chimney. Lamps of this usually sell at from $8.00 to $10.00. securely packed in a barrel. Shipping w 45 pounds. Price..................**$5.**

Decorated Globes.

Decorated Globes for banquet or vase lamps, will fit any 4-inch globe ring.

These globes are beautifully decorated by hand with large pink wild roses and green leaves on a tinted background. Furnished in three tints, pink, yellow or green. Be sure to mention color of tint and size desired.

No
Price

No. 2
of satin
Shipp

Poppy Lamp, $1.98

No. 2E96[illegible] beautiful parlor exceptionally la attractive. It plete with 9-inc and vase, and m 21 inches high decoration con large hand poppies in pink and white. Th and also the v delicately tinted top in light gre the bottom in p has a heavy plated metal scroll design, equipped with Climax burner, wick and No. 2 chimney, and p 60-candle powe Shipping weig pounds.
Price......

Y 8689
Y 8692
Y8696
Y 8687
Y 8695
Y 8690
Y8691
Y 8693
Y8688
Y8694

EXTENSION FLOOR LAMP. With No. 2 B & H Lift Burner.

And No. 198-4 inch Globe Holder or No. 163-10 inch Ring Shade Holder as desired.

When ordering state which Holder is required.

Detachable Fount.

No. 10295.
Wrought Iron. Black.
Height, 51 inches; extended, 68 inches.

Priced **WITHOUT** Chimney or Shade.

lamp as shown has a dark green overlay shade and is very similar to the Rochester burner. Some very large and elaborate parlor lamps were made of copper in low vaselike forms. In reworking such lamps for the modern room it is more effective to make a large shade of fabric than to use a glass or china shade. Brass and copper fonted parlor lamps are due for increased popularity, with schemes developed for the decorative adaptation.

Piano Lamps. In 1893, displays at Chicago's World Fair featured a low decorated type colored glass lamp with an upturned umbrella shade that was referred to as a "piano lamp." Offered in pairs, they enjoyed a limited popularity and are not much in evidence today. This lamp type is mentioned for the sake of completeness and in the hope that variants will subsequently be reported.

Floor Lamps. The creation of an oil floor lamp was something of an accomplishment. There was no precedent for it in earlier lighting devices, unless one drops back to the crude ratchet candle holder stands. Certainly, there is no evidence of whale-oil lamps having been adapted for a floor support. The oil floor lamp was about the last type of kerosene adaptation that made its appearance. Our first instance of the type has been found in a catalogue of 1890. The picture shows a wrought iron oil lamp without its shade. This was at first the typical ball type of the table parlor lamps of the period. Later, in the 1900's, a silk covered wire shade was used with lamps of this type.

The wrought iron floor lamp is not as often encountered as is the brass type whose support for the lamp font is a small attached table with marble or alabaster top. When combined with a large shade of chintz silk or parchment this brass and marble lamp table combination fits very nicely into the modern decorative scheme. Such lamps were never cheap, and the fact they are not available in large quantities is making for a rapid appreciation in value.

Gone With the Wind. The tremendous revival of interest in flower decorated, ball shaded parlor lamps is due in large part to the lavish use of these lamps in the motion picture "Gone With the Wind." Use of such lamps in the Civil War Period is highly questionable historically for they are of much more recent vintage. But the thing that concerns us now is not the historical accuracy of the restoration; rather it is the fact that the revival caught the popular fancy. "GWW lamps," as the type came immediately to be known, developed in interest and prices skyrocketed. Lamps which once retailed for from 95 cents to $3.75 now began to be bought up at prices from $25 to $50 each. Amusing as are these lamps, it was once questioned if collecting interest would uphold such prices. At present moment, demand far exceeds supply. Even when some new lamp type, such as the statuary base banquet lamp of this chapter catches on in popular fancy, the present collecting interest does not wane. People turn to reproductions. Thus we see that the GWW lamp is still not 'gone with the wind.'

EXTENSION HALL LAMP

C3067 — Wt. extension, gold finish frame, smoke bell and open crown, length closed 42 in., extended 56 in., shade ring, 14 in. opal shade with 28 cut glass prisms, allover brown blend, large fruit cluster decoration, No. 2 burners and chimneys. 1 in bbl., 38 lbs.........Each, **$4.95**

C3056—Ht. 27 in.; 10 in. globe, brown & ivory allover blended, large cluster hand painted tulips, openwork base and crown, Success center draft fount. C2521 No. 1 Success chimney. 1 in box, **$5.85**

DECORATED LAMPS

C3051—4 lamps, 2 shapes, ht. 16½ in., 7½ in. globes, ruby, green, pink and buff allover blended tints, apple blossom, lily, poppy and rose decorations, gilt metal bases, regular C2519, No. 2 electric chimney. 4 in bbl., 40 lbs............ ....Each, **95c** (Total $3.80)

C3053—2 lamps, ht. 23 in., 10 in. globes allover storm blue and ruby blended tints, large clusters hand painted roses and peonies, gilt metal bases, No. 3 burners and chimneys. 2 in bbl., 45 lbs.
(Total $3.78) Each, **$1.89**

EXTENSION LAMPS

C3065—Wt. extension, embossed brass frame and bell, length closed 29 in., extended 55 in., white opa cone shade, crystal glass fount, side filler, No. 2 Sun burner and chimney 2 in case, 52 lbs....... .Each, **$2.35**
(Total $4.70)

C3066 — Wt. extension, gilt fram smoke bell, open crown, closed 3 in., extended 55 in., 14 in. shade allover pink, brown & green blended, extra large grape cluster & tulip decorations, side filler, No. 2. burner and chimney. 2 in bbl., 55 lbs
(Total $5.90) Each, **$2.95**

DECORATED GLOBE ASSORTMENT

C3061—5 globes, three 10 in., two 11 in., allover ruby, green, pink, brown and lt. blue tints, American Beauty, tulip, peony and wild rose decorations, 5 in bbl., 47 lbs. .... Each. **95c**

MAGIC
With 8 in. Globe

MINUETTE
With 8 in. Globe

MAGIC
With 7 in. Shade

ROSALIND
With 10 in. Shade

ROSALIND
With 9 in. Globe

GLADSTONE
With 10 in. Globe

OLIVIA
With 9 in. Globe

ALAMO
With 9 in. Globe

ARIEL
With 8 in. Globe

ARIEL
With 7 in. Shade

CLARKE'S Patent "PYRAMID" & "FAIRY" LIGHTS.

Exact size of Clarke's No. 1890 "Pyramid" Lamp and 103 Bracket.

"PYRAMIDS."

To burn 9 hours,
8 in a box,
8½d. per box.

To burn 9 hours,
6 in a box,
6½d. per box.

To burn 6 hours,
12 in a box,
9d. per box.

To burn 6 hours,
6 in a box,
5d. per box.

"FAIRY LIGHTS."

To burn 10 hours,
6 in a box,
1s. per box.

To burn 6 hours,
10 in a box,
1s. per box.

Sold by all Grocers & Dealers.

Artistic Bronze,
No. 103 Bracket,
6d.

No. 1890 Lamp,
4d.

CLARKE'S "PYRAMID" & "FAIRY" LIGHT CO., LTD.

CRICKLEWOOD, LONDON, N.W., *Where all Letters should be addressed.*

Chapter IX

FAIRY, SPARK AND OTHER MINIATURE LAMPS

The history of home table lighting is repeated in all respects by those small miniatures which were mostly used as night lights. Not being a nocturnal animal, man has always felt he could rest more secure if a light was burning in or near his sleeping chamber. The early Colonists were content to sleep near the fireplace in their primitive cabins; but with the development of more elaborate homes and special sleeping quarters, the small glass lamp came into being. As early as 1820 Sandwich made miniature glass lamps for use with whale oil. This was followed in the 1840's by use of other burning fluids such as camphene, which like the whale oil burners, used no chimney. The story of these small glass night lamps was most adequately covered by Dr. Rushford, reproduced on another page. With the coming of kerosene and glass chimneys in the 1870's, we find the Golden Age of such night lamps. Though sometimes thought to have been courting lamps for lovers, it appears they were actually developed as utilitarian bedside lamps to replace candles. Some householders, however, were so intrigued by the soft glow of a candle ensconced in a small art glass shade, that the candle or so-called Fairy lamp presisted in some places well into the present century. The person most responsible for this Fairy-candle light fad, was a Samuel Clarke of London. He patented many varieties and was such a promotion-minded salesman, he could have held his own with any advertiser today. For example, he illuminated a botanical expedition with 1500 Fairy lamps without charge, created models for Queen Victoria's table decorations, promoted a vaporizer for the relief of respiratory ailments, even suggested his Fairy lamp be placed at front and rear doors to keep the burglars from entering. One of his 1880 ads read, "Clark's pyramid lights so shine at night, they keep e'en burglers well in sight." Reproductions of early Clarke ads, along with lists of the highly collectible and expensive originals, appear elsewhere, with the type of special shades that were made. Reproductions, of course, can be purchased for a few dollars but for the average collector, the originals are gone forever.

Clarke's Candles. The original Clarke's Pyramid & Fairy Light Company started at Child's Hill, London. Original patent (10029) was granted to G. M. Clarke in 1844 for an "improved night-light candle." In 1857 a Samuel Clarke took out patent 961 for manufacture of candles made originally under the Pyramid brand name—"Wee Fairy and Cricklite." All registered in the U.S. A feature peculiar to the Clarke candles was the use of Rushwicks using a hard grade of tallow. The following types of glass shades were made for Fairy lamps: Peach blow, Burmese, Nailsea, Satin,

CLARKE'S "FAIRY" LAMPS

IN QUEEN'S BURMESE WARE,

As used by Her Majesty the Queen.

REVERSIBLE.

No. 138. No. 138.

With Decorated Shades, In Queen's Burmese Ware,

"FAIRY" size .. .. ..

"FAIRY-PYRAMID" size

SOCIABLE.

2-LIGHT, No. 177,

In Queen's Burmese Ware.

"FAIRY" size, dec'd

„ plain, .

3-LIGHT, No. 178,

"FAIRY" size, dec'd.

„ „ plain.

"PYRAMID" size, *one-third less.*

No. 249.

In Queen's Burmese Ware.

"FAIRY" size, plain .. .. ..

„ „ decorated .. ..

7-LIGHT CENTRE.

No. 249A —" PYRAMID " size, plain ..

„ „ decorated

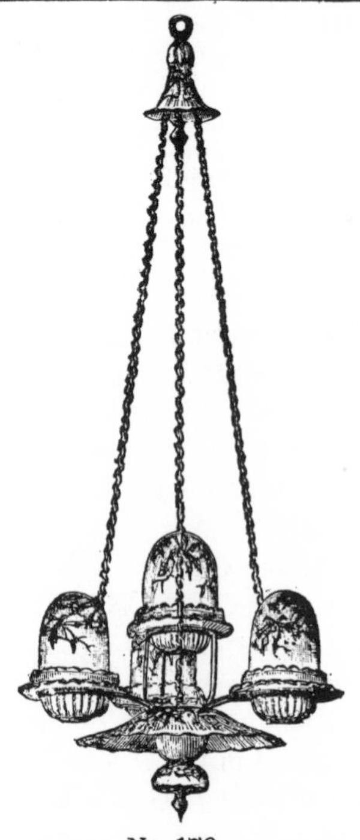

No. 176.

4-LIGHT SUSPENDING,

In Decorated Queen's Burmese.

Overshot, Drag loop, Spangled, Amberina and also Lithophane. Shade stands included nickel, silverplate, brass, glass and porcelain. Some standards were designed to carry as many as seven candle lamps. Names in catalogs show Queen Burmese ware and one Vere Moire (would now be called Nailsea). A fairy size candle burned 10 hours; a Fairy-Pyramid burned 6 hours. Firms supplying lamp parts to Clarke were Royal Worcester, Davanport and Thomas Webb. The business ceased to operate in 1910, when the era of Victorian Art Glass had drawn to its close. In the last days, Clarke's factory tried to supply four-candle light frames to fasten into gasoliers, wall brackets and gas standards. They were for temporary or permanent use but the shade broke whenever the gas was turned on. Late candle lamps which aped Clarke include one by the Diamond Candle Company of Brooklyn and one by the Central Glass Company of Wheeling, West Virginia. The so-called all glass glow lamp is not a Fairy candle but uses alcohol.

Miniatures. The world in miniature has long held fascination for the collector. Not all these objects belong to the Fairy (candle) class. Some are toy replicas of household equipment, made for the play of children; others were executed by the artisan as a **tour de force** and intended for the curio cabinet; still others are cut down versions of larger implements which served well-defined needs in the daily life of the past. Most miniature lamps belong to this last and practical class. Made throughout the Nineteenth century, these served illuminative functions in the era between the candle and the electric bulb.

One who studies a collection of miniature lamps may be skeptical that their feeble beams were of much lighting value. Most lamps, when lighted, are dimmer than a regular candle. In fact, their presence seems to enhance rather than dispel the surrounding gloom. Why then were so many of these small 'spark' lamps used? The answer seems to be supplied by words impressed on a lamp of 1870 vintage, "Patent Safety Night Lamp." Our ancestors just emerging from the age of the tallow candle apparently saw in the new oil lamps a safe means of keeping alive a faint spark of light through the hours of darkness. Certainly this was the chief reason for the popularity of the small night lamp during the last half of the century.

Early Spark Lamps. The fact that so many small lamps have handles shows that they were meant to light the way to bed, as well as to burn beside the sleeper. Earlier, perhaps, the high price of oil fluids made the miniature burner an economic necessity. We know, for instance, that the first glass lamps made at Sandwich in the 1820's were of the small or miniature variety. They had blown fonts and pressed glass bases and stood from four to five inches in height. Even earlier, probably, are the all-blown glass 'spark' lamps, some of which were so small as to be formed in the three-part mold of a decanter stopper.

Whale Oil Ship Lamp

Drop-burner lamps.

GLASS NIGHT LAMPS

by

Edward A. Rushford, M. D.

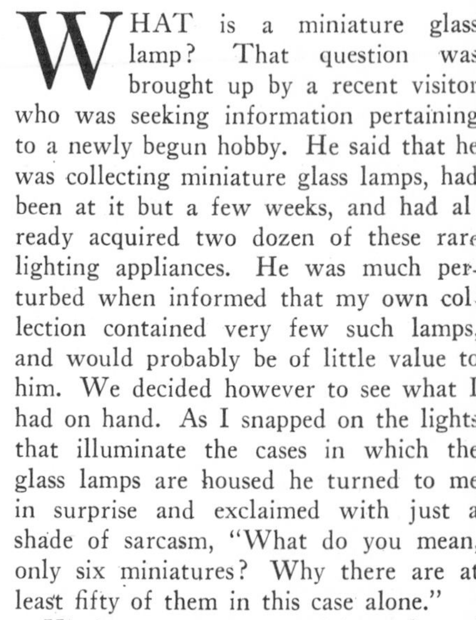

WHAT is a miniature glass lamp? That question was brought up by a recent visitor who was seeking information pertaining to a newly begun hobby. He said that he was collecting miniature glass lamps, had been at it but a few weeks, and had already acquired two dozen of these rare lighting appliances. He was much perturbed when informed that my own collection contained very few such lamps, and would probably be of little value to him. We decided however to see what I had on hand. As I snapped on the lights that illuminate the cases in which the glass lamps are housed he turned to me in surprise and exclaimed with just a shade of sarcasm, "What do you mean, only six miniatures? Why there are at least fifty of them in this case alone."

His interest was centered in a class of small glass lamps that has been variously termed night, chamber, bed, courting and sparking lamps, and by some collectors and writers, miniature lamps. But there

Variations of early blown glass night lamps of the cork-disk burner type.

are very few of them that are true miniatures. To prove this contention Mr. Webster's dictionary was brought into action, and it says that a miniature is "a representation on a much reduced scale." A lamp deserving of the title of "miniature" should therefore be a reduction to scale of some other lamp.

THE lamps in question are small of stature, most of them around three or four inches in height, and none of them over six inches. But they possess certain characteristics of form that are not to be found in lamps of larger size, and during their period of use they served a very definite purpose in household illumination. Experience has shown that the greater part of miniature lamps were either models or toys, or were a part of the equipment of doll houses. And in spite of the fact that the majority of them will function just as well as their larger brothers, they served no definite purpose in lighting the home.

To illustrate these points I conducted my visitor to my daughter's collection of small and miniature lighting appliances, which contains some fifty lamps. Here we found examples of many of the main lamp types from an ancient stone saucer lamp to the first electric light bulbs used on Christmas trees. And I was able to find in my own collection the big brother of every one of those lamps that were made of stone, pottery or of any of the metals. But it was a very different story with the glass lamps, because very few of them had big brothers. The ultimate result of the discussion was the conclusion that miniature glass lamps are rare items.

There are many reasons why the collecting of these small lamps will prove to be a most satisfactory hobby. They require little space, a fair sized cabinet will house a goodly number of them. There are still enough of them obtainable to form a comprehensive collection without

More variations of Blown glass night lamps. All made for the cork-disk burner except one with threaded burner (center 6). Bottom 9—Blown reservoirs on pressed bases.

exhaustive effort. The prices are still reasonable. The percentage of reproductions is so small, and the fakes so apparent, that even the beginner if careful, is in little danger. There is a delicacy of line and texture to be found in the lamps of the whale oil period, rarely found elsewhere, and an infinite variety of symmetrical forms, finding relief from time to time in those charmingly lopsided little fellows that are really the gems of any collection. All in all there are few collectables that present greater charm than a group of these lamps properly housed and arranged. But if one has ideas along these lines delay is inadvisable for there is a growing scarcity of some of the earlier types.

A DEFINITE name should be found for these lamps, and glass night lamps seems to be the most appropriate. This was the name most commonly used in the days of their active service, and the one most frequently found in the old catalogs. They came in handy for many purposes, but their principal service was connected with the act of retiring for the night. Their burners were made with but a single wick tube, and this was smaller than were the tubes of the lamps used in routine household duties and for reading. Consequently their flames were small, but hardly small enough to account for the term "spark" lamp. They produced sufficient light to permit a person in a normally steady state, to negotiate a darkened hall, or a dimly lighted stairway leading to the bedroom. There were probably larger lamps in the room that could be lighted if one was fastidious in his preparations for the night, though a sleepy person can turn in without brilliant illumination. In many homes, and especially if the family was sizeable, a number of these night lamps were to be found on a convenient table in the lower hall. Close by there was a larger lamp, and a holder of spills or, in later days, matches. When the time came to retire each member of the family found a freshly cleaned and filled lamp waiting in the hall, ready to be lighted.

It is reasonably certain that the period of greatest popularity of the glass night lamp was the half-century between 1820 and 1870. It is probable that they were in use before 1820, and it is known that they were being illustrated in catalogs as late as 1875. The examination of a great many of these lamps has brought out certain facts that should be of interest to the collector, whether beginner or veteran. But may I first suggest that every lamp collector acquire the habit of picking up every loose burner, no matter what the type, that he may see lying around. Old lamps without burners are painfully common, and many a fine lamp has been made complete through this habit of picking up strays.

10

Lamps with blown reservoirs and pressed bases.

During the period in which these lamps were used, four main types of burners were employed, drop burners, whale oil and fluid burners, and those developed for kerosene. The average lamp collector finds that the lamps of the first three types are the most interesting and attractive. One should know the difference between burners and the proper lamps in which to place them, there is nothing more ridiculous than to find a whale oil burner reposing in the reservoir of a typical kerosene lamp. Substitutions were made as new burners were invented, but the new burner would be of an advanced type rather than an earlier one. The drop burner is the simplest of all, a small, circular tin plate with a tube of tin piercing its center, and generally provided with a slender tail-like handle curled up at the end. These burners were dropped into the opening in the lamps' reservoirs, and as a rule fitted quite loosely.

Miniature glass lamps.

THERE are two types of whale oil burners, termed cork-disk and threaded, and the former is the earlier type. The lamps made for the cork-disk burner are by far the most desirable of all the night lamps. The burner is made of two circular tin plates holding a disk of cork between them. They were pushed into the reservoir of the lamp, as one pushes a cork stopper into a bottle. They are smaller in every way than are the burners used in glass lamps of ordinary size, and support but a single wick tube. The larger burners generally have two wick tubes, but never more. The majority of cork-disk burners, large and small, have the word PATENT stamped on the upper plate. This is one of the many lamp mysteries of the past yet to be solved. By some it is thought to indicate the early work of some American inventor, whose records were destroyed in the burning of the United States Patent Office. Others believe that this burner was invented by John Miles, the Englishman, who patented what we now know as the whale oil burner, in 1787. He called it the solid burner, and in his specifications told how he constructed his metal lamps and burners so that they would "screw or squeeze into each other, air-tight." He did not mention cork-disks however, and these burners have not been found in metal lamps. We are told that in the early days blown reservoirs were

Center—The Handy night lamp. Left and Right—Bulbous lamps with "Fluid" burners.

"Fluid" lamps, Salt shaker type.

the collars were held fast. To determine whether a rough necked lamp was of the whale oil, burning fluid or kerosene period requires a knowledge of the style changes in glass night lamps.

Whether or not the drop burner lamps were ever made in this country has been a much discussed question. The majority of those found here today certainly had their origin on the continent of Europe, where their use continued to a much later date than the simplicity of their burner would lead one to believe. This is especially true of the small lamps of this type, they are much heavier and strikingly different in form than are those lamps that are American to a reasonably degree of certainty. The claim of American origin is generally made for larger lamps of the drop burner type, lamps proportionately lighter and of more pleasing form. Their defenders possess at least one strong argument, the fact that the early glass blowers came from Europe, and unquestionably made their products in the manner and forms that they were accustomed to.

The average sizeable collection of glass

imported from England, and pressed bases were applied to some of them in our own glassworks. If this is true they probably arrived here, burner equipped, and the word may indicate an English patent, possibly by Miles.

THREADED burners were first made of pewter and later of brass, and screwed into a collar of the same metal cemented to the neck of the lamp. These burners were used on whale oil lamps of the late period and those intended for burning fluid and kerosene. Burners were easily lost and some times the collars as well, and the collector may find himself at a loss in determining the type of a lamp without a collar. But there is a very simple rule with few exceptions that is a big help. The drop burner lamp has no neck about the opening in the reservoir. Both the cork disk and the threaded burner lamps have short necks encircling the opening, this neck was left smooth for the cork-disk burner, but was roughened, either by chipping or by gouging if a threaded burner was to be used. The roughening furnished a better hold for the cement or plaster-of-Paris with which

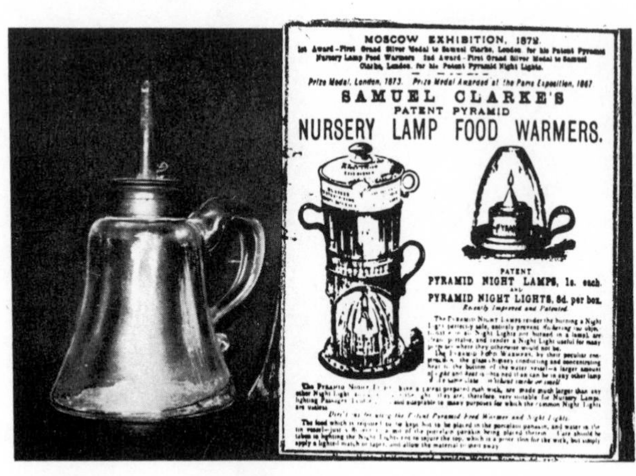

Miniature hand lamps.

night lamps will contain a few drop burners, many whale oils of the cork-disk type, very few with threaded whale oil burners, probably not as many as there are drop burners, and a goodly showing of fluid lamps. The tastes and the luck of the collector may produce some variance to this rule. But one is sure to be struck by the great variety of forms to be found among those little lamps made for the earlier form of whale oil burner. So great a variety that it almost seems that no two were made alike. Two other features are noticeable in lamps of this type, their light weight, and the extreme rarity of one whose form is not pleasing.

A DETAILED classification of these lamps according to form would be extremely complicated, and would serve no real purpose. Lamps with cork-disk burners may be roughly divided into two main groups, those with and those without handles. As a rule handled lamps had no stems, the bottom of the reservoir forming the base of the lamp. And the reverse is also true, handles are rarely found on stemmed lamps. Exceptions to these rules are rarities to be sought for. The comparatively small number of drop burner night lamps, and whale oils with threaded burners gives little chance to establish rules, but it can be said stemmed burning fluid lamps are very uncommon.

In figure 1 there are shown three drop-burner lamps, the one in the center of very small size and deep ambre in color. Colored night lamps of all the main types were made, and some combinations of color have been found. They are very desirable but of such rarity as to command astounding prices. The curled handles of two of the drop burners are quite noticeable.

Figure 2 shows three of the form of night lamps most frequently termed sparking or courting. The romantic stories connected with these terms are decidedly illogical, and should be forgotten. The first lamp is still filled with the whale oil that served its last burning, and the lack of symmetry displayed by the lamp in the center only adds to its charm. The Christmas candy effect so often employed in applying handles is here quite apparent. Figures 3, 4 and 5 present examples of lamps with spreading thickened bases, showing variations of three of the common types.

The tapering reservoirs of the first two lamps in figure 6, suggest a transition between the two main divisions. In the center is one of those rare glass night lamps with a threaded whale oil burner. The lamp at the right, those shown in fig. 7, and the first two lamps of fig. 8, are some of the forms to which the term wineglass has been given. The use of this term is not objectionable because it does give one a mental picture. But the theory that these lamps were made in the same moulds that produced wineglasses seems doubtful because of the small capacity of their reservoirs. Lamps that fit this theory are quite rare, the one in fig. 7 is the only lamp of the six that is large enough to qualify.

Five of the lamps shown in figs. 7 and 8 have the

Small kerosene lamps.

button stem, a feature of much of the stemware of their period. The first lamp of each of these groups is a marked example of that charming lopsidedness that is not infrequently encountered in these little light producers. The lamp in the center of fig. 7, a bit off center in form, is an example of the much sought for clam water glass. The lamps in fig. 9 have stepped bases, with the inside pressed in a manner giving the effect of a waterfall. Such lamps are said to be a combination of foreign and domestic workmanship, the reservoirs imported from England and the bases applied here. A lamp with a circular stepped base is shown at the left of fig. 10, and at the right is an example of another type whose base resembles an inverted cup plate.

THE lamp in the center of fig. 10 has a bit of a story connected with it. Calling on one of my dealer friends in Boston's famous Charles St., I was greeted with "I've been hoping you would be in, I've a little glass lamp I want you to see." And he dug out this lamp from the lower drawer of a remote bureau. As I took it I was struck first by its extreme light weight, then by the comparatively small size of its base, and finally by the appearance of the brass collar, from which unfortunately, the burner is missing. "There's something wrong with this lamp Fred," said I. "You're darn right there is," said he. "Turn it over." And he added mournfully. "And I paid six dollars for a pair of them." On the under surface of the base I found a curious raised mark, apparently Japanese, resembling the letter F pointed in the wrong direction, and placed between the outstretched arms of a V. Fred refused to sell it to me at any price, but finally gave it to me after exacting a solemn promise that I would use it as a horrible example of the pitfalls that lie in the way of the careless.

In fig. 11 are shown three true miniature glass lamps from my daughter's collection. The first two, a threaded whale oil and a drop burner are marked reductions to scale of lamps in my own collection. The lamp on the right is a half size reduction of a lamp-type common in late whale oil and early burning fluid periods; it carries a whale oil burner for two wicks.

In the center of plate 12 may be seen an example of a rather curious type of small lamp that is not uncommon. This one is marked "The Handy Night Lamp" but others have been found bearing the title of "The London Lamp," a name which has given rise to the theory that they are of English origin. The tin burner slips over the neck of the reservoir and when complete should have the small, circular tin reflector attached. As there are pick slots in the burner tubes, and frequently ventilation openings in the top, they must have been intended for oil burning.

The small glass lamps intended for the use of burning fluids are very easy to distinguish when the burners are present. Burning fluid was a very dangerous combination of alcohol and turpentine, and because of its explosive tendencies caused much property damage, and many accidents and deaths. To lessen the danger, by keeping the fluid as far from the flame as possible, long, slender and generally tapering tubes were employed to hold the wicks and the burners were made without pick slots or ventilation openings.

The majority of fluid night lamps will be found to belong to one of three principal types, depending on their form. For this reason most fluid lamps may be readily recognized even though the burner is missing. Another help is the fact that while pewter was used almost exclusively for the collars and burners of whale oil lamps, brass and pewter seem to have been equally popular for the making of these parts of fluid lamps. As for the three principal forms of these lamps the first may be called bulbous, a term well fitted as may be judged by numbers one and three of plate 12. The second type has been dubbed the salt shaker lamp and a glance at plate 13 will indicate the suitability of this term.

Miniature Lamps in Dr. Freeman's collection.

Opaque Glass Lamps, Plain and Decorated *(1835–1885)*

Most of the early Nineteenth century lamps burned camphene and are equipped with a characteristic circular wick-holder of pewter. Lamp chimneys do not appear until the 1850's, and some of these miniature lamps have a patent brass burner with a flat wick for kerosene. Lamps of the mid-century are also somewhat larger than at the beginning, in fact you can tell something of the age of a lamp by its smallness of size.

At mid-century, colored and opaque glass began to take their place along with clear glass lamps. An especially rare type of this era is the Aladdin All Night Lamp which burns camphene and has a tin sconce at its back.

Kerosene Night Lamps. The golden age of the miniature lamp was in the 1870's. The collections illustrated show six different patents granted in this decade alone. Among lamps of the period of the 'Little Nutmeg' patent and the brass-base 'Patent-lite' of 1871. The 'Little Buttercup' is a handled patent light that comes in amber, amethyst, blue green and clear glass. The 'Banner Improved' has an opaque white font and chimney, and there is a glass lamp mounted on a special brass base which resembles a candlestick. The illustrations include also the 'Little Jewel,' which comes in several colors, a rare miniature overlay, and the 'Little Harry,' patented Oct. 28, 1873 .

The Time Light. The most interesting and probably the rarest of the 1870 group of patent lamps is the 'Time Indicating Lamp' as shown. On the base is also impressed the words "Grand Vals Pride of America. Time and Light.' It has been suggested frequently that this lamp was used as a 'courting' light. The lamp, when filled, indicates a level marked 8 p.m. (the proper hours for calling). Then as the oil is burned, the levels 9, 10, 11, etc. are indicated. Six a.m. will find the oil in the bottom of the font, but of course no self-respecting swain would have stayed to this late hour. This mention of courting lamps recalls that some collectors regard all types of spark lamps as intended for entertaining the beau in the parlor. Certainly their feeble glow would have been welcome to a generation whose lovemaking was altogether too highly supervised. But at the expense of dissipating a pleasantly romantic notion we must doubt if any miniature lamps were ever used for sparking. Their more usual place would have been in the bedroom or beside the sick-bed. In days before it was considered fit for one to read in bed, the Time-Light would have served only to remind the wakeful of the passing of the hours. So faint was its glimmer that we may even question if the oil level could be read properly. Perhaps the light was just sufficient to guide the hand to the font, where familiar fingers could assist by "feeling" the hours indicated by the oil level.

Miniature GWW Lamps. In the 1880's and 1890's miniature lamps became larger and more elaborate. The low handled types disappeared, and taller lamps of opaque white and colored glass took their place. Some colored globe shades appear along with the inner clear glass chimney and bird and animal figures were occasionally molded into the bases. The

rarest of these is the swan base lamp. Miniature GWW lamps, such as are shown are now much sought after.

The Fairy Lamp. Special mention should be made of the so-called "Fairy Lamp," a two piece dish and globe type usually made for burning a candle. Most of these Fairy Lamps are beautiful examples of the glass-makers art. They come in Satin Glass, Nailsea, Peachblow, Burmese and other types of late Victorian art glass. As mentioned earlier the best known is Clarke's Fairy Lamp and introduced to this country at the World's Fair in 1893. Hobbs, Bocunier and Company also made Fairy Lamps, in fact most of the glass manufacturers of this era carried some such decorative lamps in their line.

Miniature Metal Lamps. It must not be thought that all miniature lamps are made of glass. The Author shows an all-pewter lamp of typical early vintage. There are also a number of brass lamps that burn camphene and one looks like a dish-type candlestick and has impressed upon its base the following notation, "Good-Night, BB Co., Pat. June 1869." There is also a Britania metal lamp whose handle suggests the overly ornate 1880's, a tin 'Sterling' lamp of 1875, and the 'Home' lamp with tin reflector. Even a miniature bracket lamp is represented in this collection. Then there are the various Rochester Burners which bring the miniature lamp into the Twentieth century. A Figure reproduces a catalog page that shows the all-brass night lamps in use around 1900.

Toy Lanterns and Christmas Tree Lights. Two other types of miniature lamps are the tiny lanterns carried outdoors and the early Christmas Tree lights. Small brass lanterns with clear or colored shades are fairly common and date from the 1870's. The first type was carried by a ring on a chain. The latest type of lantern illustrated is the 'Diamond' pattern. Cautionwise, it carried a tin guard around the chimney.

Most intriguing of all miniature lights are those intended for the holiday season; so varied are their shapes and placement that some would not have their original purpose easily recognized. The first glass Christmas Tree light that the author found was offered to him as a **bucket** by the dealer who owned it. Subsequently, many different types of glass 'buckets' have been found for holding the Christmas Tree candle away from the highly inflammable branches. The blue Thousand Eye light appears to be the most sought of the pattern glass Christmas lights. As an indication of the odd shapes and uses of holiday lighting, one illustration pictures a **'Glory Light.'** The pair of glass fonts that hang from the iron center support can be filled with oil and lighted for a festive occasion. Perhaps this identification of what has sometimes been called a 'flower holder' will encourage a further study of the lighting possibilities of certain other miniature gadgets of the Victorian era.

Bedroom Night Lamps

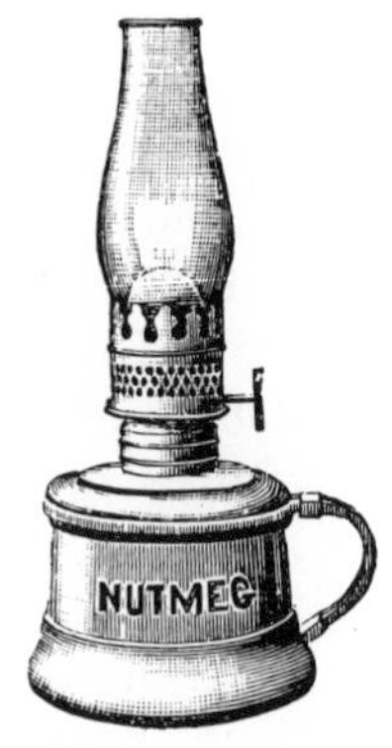

No. 181. Nutmeg.
7 ins. high.
Glass Bowl, Wire Handle.

No. 1516 Nutmeg Burner.

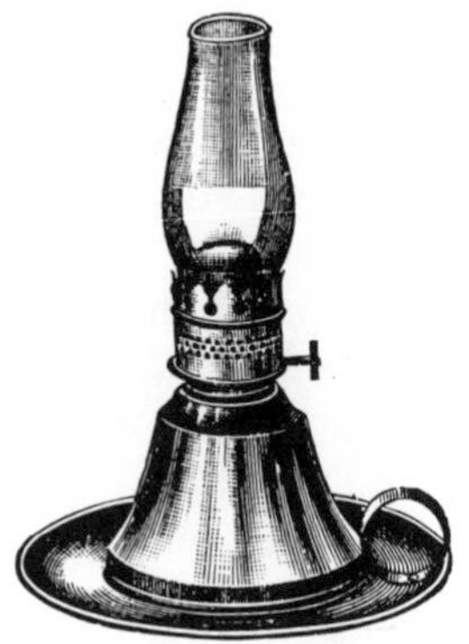

No. 182. Cottage.
6¾ ins. high.
All Metal.

No. 1516 Nutmeg Burner.

No. 2127. Acorn.
5¼ ins. high.
All Metal.

No. 733 Acorn Burner.

All above take Nutmeg Chimney and Wick.

No. 181 Lamp is packed regular in assorted colors, Flint. Opal and Blue.

No. 1290. Little Brownie.
7½ ins. high.
All Metal.

No. 739. Hornet.
7¾ ins. high.
All Metal.

No. 2130. Fireside.
6½ ins. high.
All Metal.

Burns 40 hours.

ACME

Nobby Brass Night Lamp. **Stellar**  **Pearl Brass Night Lamp.**  **Acme Night La**

Float lamps (Carleton Brown Collection)

ELABORATE CRYSTAL STANDS WHICH CAN BE USED AS WELL WITH ELECTRICITY

R. H. SPALDING,

Successor to H. Porter, and sole Manufacturer of

PORTER'S PATENT COMPOSITION BURNING FLUID,

ALSO,

SUPERIOR CAMPHENE AND ALCOHOL.

Manufacturer of and Dealer in

FLUID AND OIL CHANDELIERS,

Astral, Solar, Hanging and Side Lamps, Portable and Study Lamps of every description, Girandoles, Candelabras, Hall Lanterns,

China and Terra Cotta Ware, Globes, Shades, Glass Prisms, &c.

WHOLESALE AND RETAIL,

NOS. 8 & 9 TREMONT ROW, BOSTON,

Opposite the Head of Hanover Street.

Chapter X
HANGING LAMPS

Of the several varieties of oil lamps not previously mentioned, especial interest will be found in those which were made for hanging from the ceiling, or for other semi-permanent attachments, such as in street lighting. Hanging lamps appeared in the hallway of the home as early as 1800. They seldom arrived in other rooms of the house until the latter part of the same century. By this time, of course, the burners had been much improved and means for holding the lamps safely aloft had been developed. These are one type of lamp for which no great demand yet exists among decorators and collectors. Modern decorators have tended to eliminate the hanging lamp, except for the hallway. When favor changes to the ceiling fixture, there will still be a few left of the items described in this chapter as having originally illuminated the rooms of our Victorian grandparents.

Hall Lamps. Hall lamps of the early 1800's were usually a heavy clear etched glass globe or cylinder with a minimum of brass fitments. An oil lamp, not unlike those made for table use would be placed inside the cylinder for light. The insertion of the lighted lamp must have been quite an effort, for no way was provided for lowering the fixture to within easy reaching distance. The lighted lamp had to be carried up to the fixture, by stepladder or some related contrivance. As time went on, however, a chain and counterpoise weight were developed for extension of the fixture, and thus the lighting process was greatly facilitated. In the later improvements, as the globe fixture was pulled down the lamp font on the other end of the chains would rise to a position where it could be easily lighted. Old catalog pages from different companies are reproduced to show the typical hall lamps of the late Victorian era. These globes came in such sought after colors as cranberry, blue and candy stripe pink. A few satin glass hall lamp globes may be found; also some late etched cylinders, not especially differing in form from the early type shown in this chapter.

Library Hanging Lamps. Next in popularity to the hall lamp, both today and in a bygone era, was the hanging lamp for use in the library or dining room. These fixtures, with their gorgeous domes of colored and flower decorated opaque glass enjoyed a well deserved popularity from the 1880's until the First World War. As shown in five different Figures at least, three types of shades were used. The earliest and most desirable type is of cranberry or some related variety of colored glass. Next comes the flower decorated and plain opaque glass shade, and finally, in the 1910 period, the art glass shade. As shown in catalogs by Frostoria, some of these hanging lamps have a decorated glass oil font to match the shade,

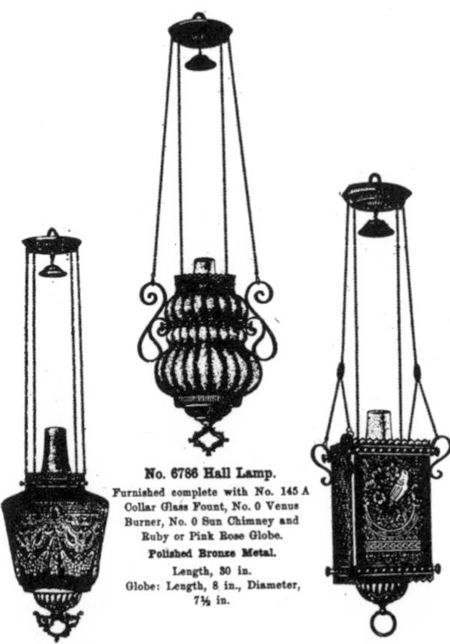

No. 6786 Hall Lamp.
Furnished complete with No. 145 A Collar Glass Fount, No. 0 Venus Burner, No. 0 Sun Chimney and Ruby or Pink Rose Globe.
Polished Bronze Metal.
Length, 30 in.
Globe: Length, 8 in., Diameter, 7½ in.

No. 6847 Hall Lamp.
Furnished complete with No. 131 B Collar Glass Fount, No. 2 Favorite Burner, No. 2 Sun Hinge Chimney and Crystal Etched Globe.
Polished Bronze Metal.
Length, 30 in.
Globe: Length, 8 in., Diameter, 7½ in.

No. 6767 Hall Lamp.
Furnished complete with No. 131 B Collar Glass Fount, No. 2 Favorite Burner, No. 2 Sun Hinge Chimney and 4¾ x 8 inch Ruby Etched or Enameled Glass.
Polished Bronze Metal.
Length, 34 in.

Library Lamps.

No. 08579
Furnished with No. 21½ Vestal Fount, No. 2 Vestal Burner and Wick, No. 2 Miller Chimney and No. 08579-15 inch Hexagon Shade of Cast Metal Openwork, over Panels of Green and Amber, Light Amber or Olive Green Art Glass.
Old Brass and Black Finish.
Length closed, 28 in., extended, 64 in.

No. 08580
Furnished with No. 21½ Vestal Fount, No. 2 Vestal Burner and Wick, No. 2 Miller Chimney and No. 08580-16 inch Hexagon Shade of Cast Metal Openwork, over Panels of Green and Amber, Light Amber or Olive Green Art Glass.
Old Brass and Black Finish.
Length closed, 28 in., extended, 64 in.

Library Lamps.

No. 08349
Furnished with No. 2 Miller Detachable Fount, Wick and Chimney; 14 inch Decorated Dome Shade and Vase to match.
Bronze Metal or Antique Copper Finish.
Length closed, 35 in., extended, 71 in.

No. 08300
Furnished with No. 2 Miller Detachable Fount, Wick and Chimney; 14 inch Decorated Dome Shade and Vase to match.
Bronze Metal.
Length closed, 36 in., extended, 72 in.

Library Lamps.

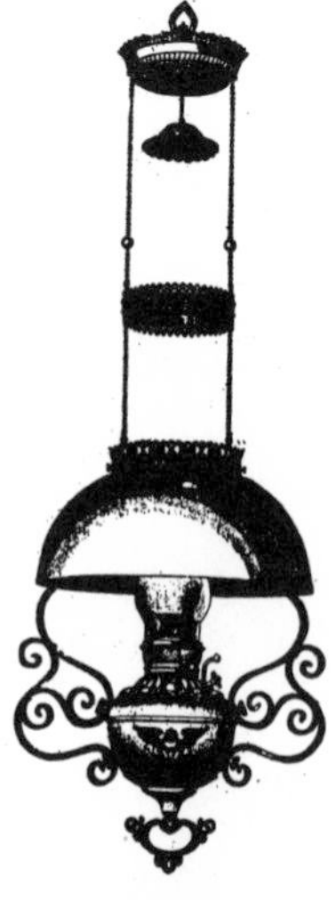

No. 08501
Furnished with No. 2 Miller Detachable Fount, Wick and Chimney; 14 inch Opal Dome Shade.
Vase, Shaded Brass; remainder, Polished Gilt Finish.
Length closed, 35 in., extended, 71 in.

No. 08438
Furnished with No. 2 Miller Detachable Fount, Wick and Chimney; 30 Prisms and 14 inch Opal Dome Shade.
Polished Brass or Antique Copper Finish.
Length closed, 37 in., extended, 73 in.
Embossed Metal Vase.

No. 41. ASSORTMENT. Six Library Lamps Complete. Polished Bronze Metal.

Trimmed with 14 inch Shades of Attractive Designs, in Assorted Decorations with Tinted Grounds and B Collar Founts to match, No. 2 Solar Burners, No. 3 Wicks, No. 2 Sun Chimneys and Band Lamps with 30 Prisms each. Patented Automatic Spring Extensions.

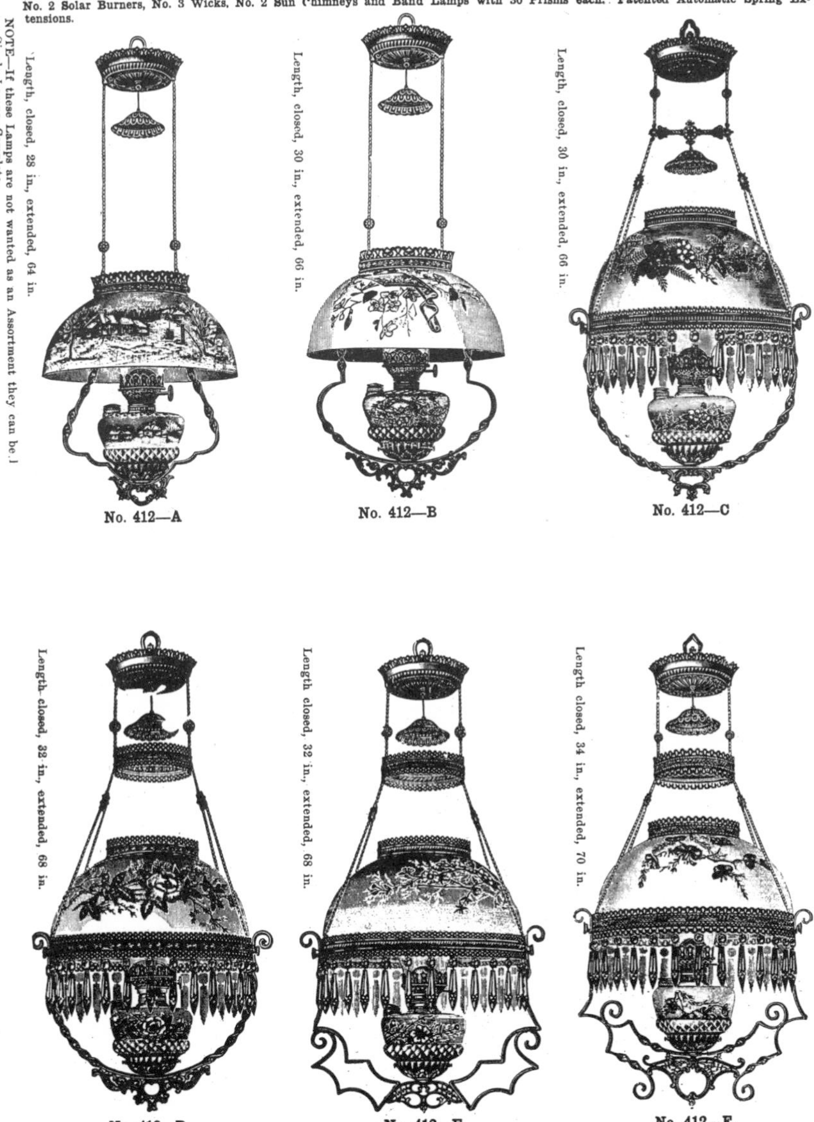

No. 412—A | No. 412—B | No. 412—C

No. 412—D. | No. 412—E. | No. 412—F.

No. 412 ASSORTMENT. Six Lamps Complete.

Packed in 2 Bbls. { Approximately, Gross, 70 lbs.; Net, 33 lbs. Cubic Measurements, 9 ft., 2 in.
" " 50 " " 28 " " " 7 " 8 "

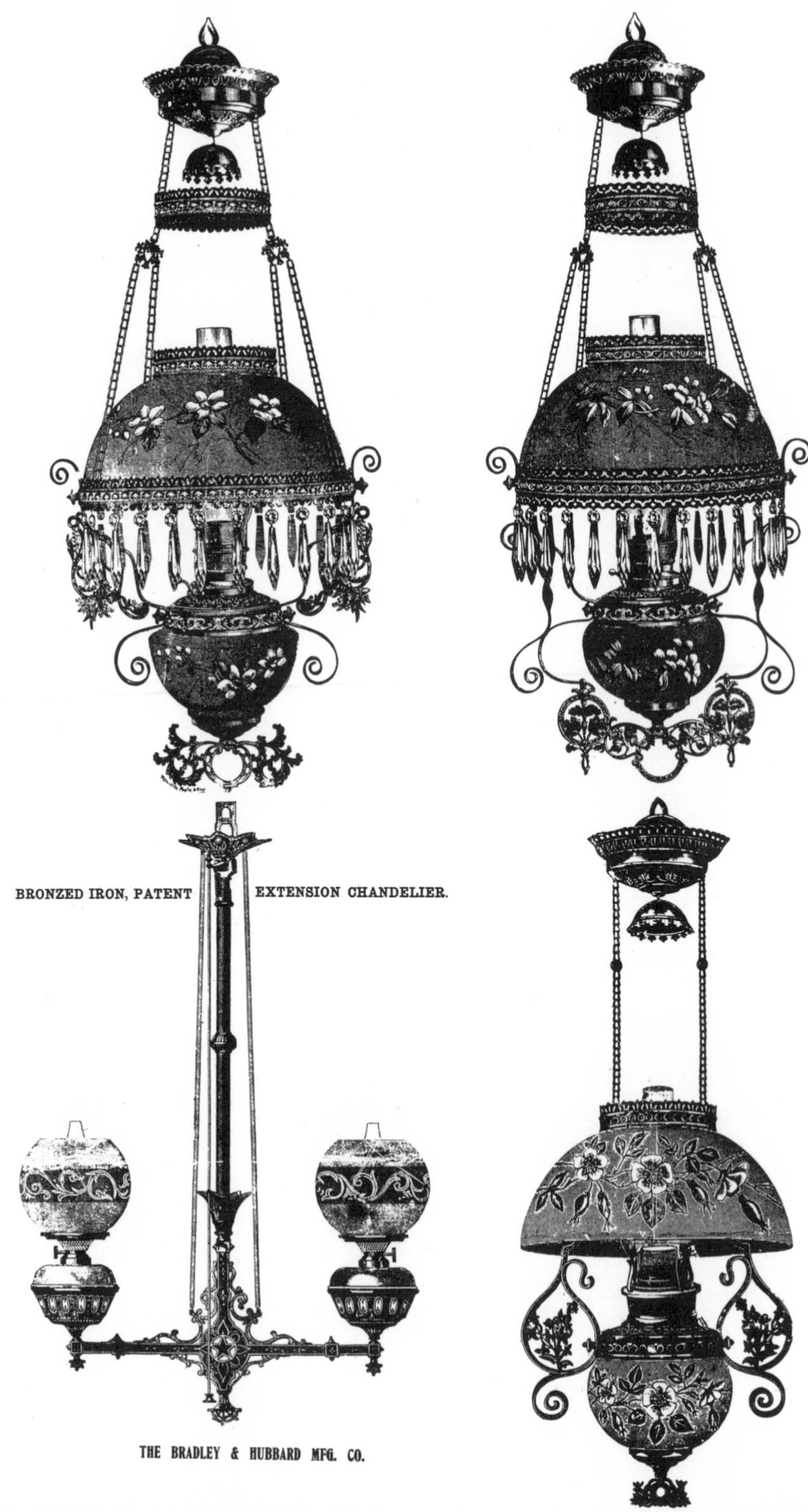

THE BRADLEY & HUBBARD MFG. CO.

No. 428—D.
Length closed, 33 inches; extended, 69 inches.

No. 428—E.
Length closed, 35 inches; extended, 71 inches.

No. 428—F.
Length closed, 34 inches; extended, 70 inches.

No. 428 ASSORTMENT. Six Lamps Complete.

Packed in 2 Bbls. { Approximately, Gross, 63 lbs.; Net, 32 lbs. Cubic Measurements, 9 ft., 2 in.
" " 49 " " 21 " " " 6 " 6 "

No. 428 ASSORTMENT. Six Library Lamps Complete. Polished Bronze Metal.

With Patent Automatic Spring Extensions. Trimmed with 14 inch Opal Dome Shades, B Collar Glass Founts, No. 2 Solar Burners, No. 3 Wicks, No. 2 Sun Chimneys, and Band Lamps with 30 Prisms each.

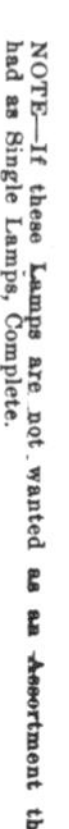

NOTE—If these Lamps are not wanted as an Assortment they can be had as Single Lamps, Complete.

No. 428—A
Length closed, 27 inches; extended, 63 inches.

No. 428—B
Length closed, 30 inches; extended, 66 inches.

No. 428—C.
Length closed, 32 inches; extended, 68 inches.

others have a metal or plain glass oil font, and some have a brass oil font. Pendants were optional on this type of lamp, but most purchasers took them. These must have added greatly to the brilliance of the lamp, as the family, held together within the radius of its rapture, spent the long winter evenings reading about the table. In the modern interior, such lamps are still useful to help create the cheery and homey atmosphere of the mid-Victorian sitting room at its best.

Parlor Chandeliers. A few hanging lamps were made along very elaborate lines for use in the parlor and drawing room of the wealthy. None of these are illustrated since they are no longer found in any great abundance. Instead, there are illustrated besides the all-glass pendants some representative samples of parlor hanging lamps of more modest proportions. Such fixtures are the original source of the many "hand lamps" which now lie on the back shelves in antique shops. They feature an extension chandelier which holds detachable lamps in an ornate iron bracket.

Store Lamps. What sort of lamps lighted the old country store and added a bit of illumination to the philosophers seated around the cracker barrel? The answer is found in the hanging lamps reproduced in Harp-type. The distinguishing feature of most lamps of this type is the large 15-inch tin reflector shade. The part away from the light is painted a dark green, that on the lower side is left bright. The lamp font is usually of brass, though late ones often had a nickel finish. Occasionally a white opal glass shade is found on such lamps. All are distinguished for their prim severity and were used in kitchens as well as in public halls and in stores.

Car Lamps. A very interesting variety of hanging lamp can be collected occasionally from old railway and street cars. Figures of patents show the types most likely to be encountered. In some ways a cross between student and hanging lamps, these old illumination devices for moving vehicles were supposedly characterzied by their "safety." Certainly, if wired for use in the home with electricity, their safety and usefulness would increase. No one has yet done much in the way of such adaptations of car lights, hence this area may be watched with interest.

Coach Lights. No survey of oil lamps would be complete without at least a brief mention of the coach light. Lamps of considerable antiquity belong to this group, but our attention will be confined to the late varieties such as were used on carriages during the latter part of the Ninteenth century. The characterstic type has a square boxlike reflector lamp chamber sometimes silver plate and with plate glass windows on two sides. Below the reflector chamber is an elongated hollow tube which serves to attach the lamp to the carriage and to hold the oil reservoir. An opening above the reflector chamber carries off the heated air and provides occasion for a proper "topping" to the entire structure. These coach lamps are now greatly in demand for use beside doorways. Value is mainly dependent upon size. Small late coach lanterns for carrying are not in demand.

No. 236 Harp Lamp.

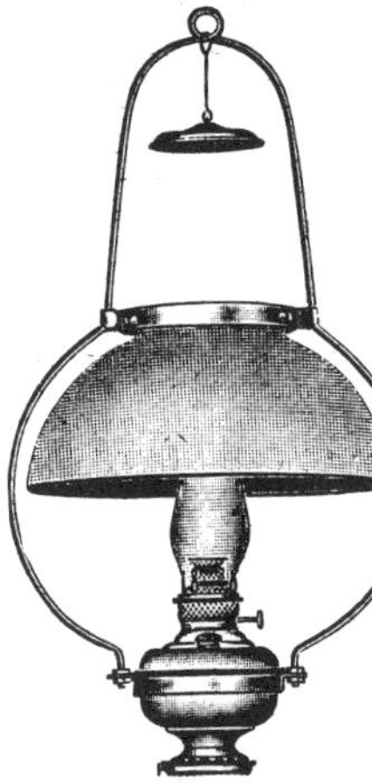

No. 237 Harp Lamp.

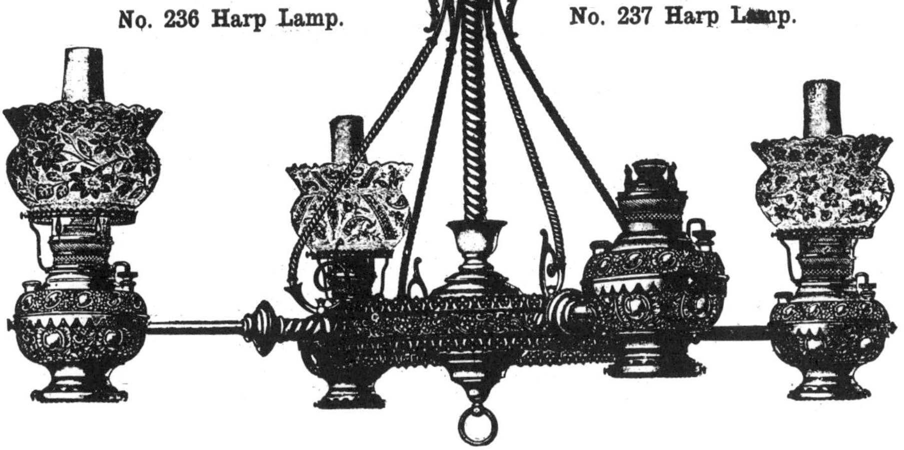

No. 0900 Miller Non-Extension Chandelier.

Suitable for Halls and Public Buildings.

No. 228 Harp Lamp.

Furnished complete with No. 30 Vestal Fount, Wick, No. 2 Miller Chimney and No. 169—15 inch Tin Reflector.
Polished Brass Finish or Nickel Plated.
Reflector with Green Top.

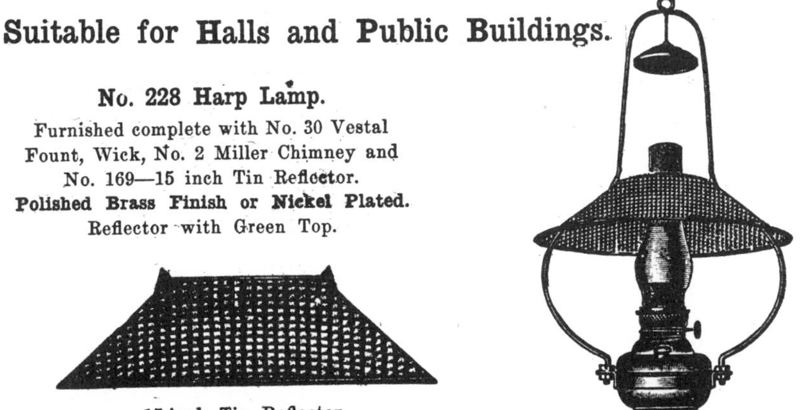

15-inch Tin Reflector.

American Exhibitors at the Paris Exposition whom First Prizes were Awarded.

Street Lights. There was a time when practically every village boasted a few oil street lamps, but that day is now gone. Only occasionally can discarded remnants now be picked up, restored and used outside the old house to give authenticity and color. For gas lights see later pages. Baltimore in 1817 became the first American city to be lighted wholly by gas. Boston got its system working in 1822, and New York in 1827. Gas fixtures for street lighting still abound in some cities. As they disappear from the streets, we may be assured they will find a place in the garden of those who are trying to recapture the spirit of a by gone day.

Two types of street oil lamps should be recognized. One has an early patented square type of reflector unit or often no more than a four sided glass-box which sat on the post with a oil-lamp set in its bottom. The other is the Dietz type of post lantern also shown on an accompanying page. Besides the street light, collectors will also look for examples of the early oil lamps which swung from Pullmans and Railway coaches, those which were used to illuminate stores, offices and lecture halls. The carriage lamps on horse drawn vehicles provide another category, to say nothing of these oil-lit vehicle lamps found on early Twentieth century autos and bicycles, the valuable **Sheffield-plated-hearse lamps,** the many boat and steamship lamps and even those used in **torchlight** processions and as signals to fire fighters or strung up for band concert lighting in pre-electric torch days. All have received some pictured mention here for specialized collectors trying to recapture the street lighting splendors of a bygone day.

The Social History of Lighting by W. T. O'Dea (Routledge, London, 1958) talks about "bad light" as something that preceded "the good glow of the kerosene lamp which lights the home." One can agree that light for travel, light for work, light for worship, the theater, sports and fun, all required different equipment. We show pictures of such travel lights as those for boats and carriages; **mine lights** and lighthouses all had special devices. Especially condemned by all users of such equipment was feeble oil flames, the guttering of candles outdoors, the failure of snuffers, dousers, and extinguishers to quell flames that got out of control. Primitive survival of man's oil attempt to light the night outside a home was "The Stormy Petrel" (an oily fish which was tacked on a pole and set afire to guide the weary wayfarer to safety. Fireflies have also been tried to aid in street lighting along with more conventional lamps. But not until 200,000 electric lamps (using a 5,000 kilowat supply from Niagara Falls) were operated for 1900 Pan-American Exposition, did man really began to see in the dark.

We call attention especially to our old catalogs showing oil lamp parts put out in the late Nineteenth century by the Miller Co. and by Plumb & Atwood. The latter still makes many old lamp parts and its modern successor (Dorset Division of the J. B. Williams Co., Thomaston, Conn.) sells three fine brass reproductions using original Rochester burner forms easily converted from kerosene to electricity if so desired.

Royal Fount with Harp

And 10-inch Opal Dome Shade.

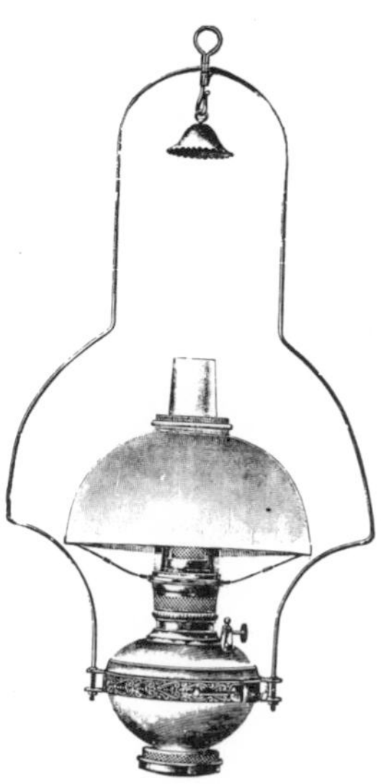

Order				Per Dozen. Brass.	Nickel.
No. 1197.	No. 1.	Royal Fount Plain,	complete as shown in cut,	$40.15	$42.65
" 1191.	" 1.	" " Embossed,	" " "	40.15	42.65
" 867.	" 2.	" " Plain,	" " "	41.75	44.25
" 1007.	" 2.	" " Embossed,	" " "	41.75	44.25

Founts listed separately on page 52, Harps on page 66.

No. 3 Mammoth Banner Fount and Harp

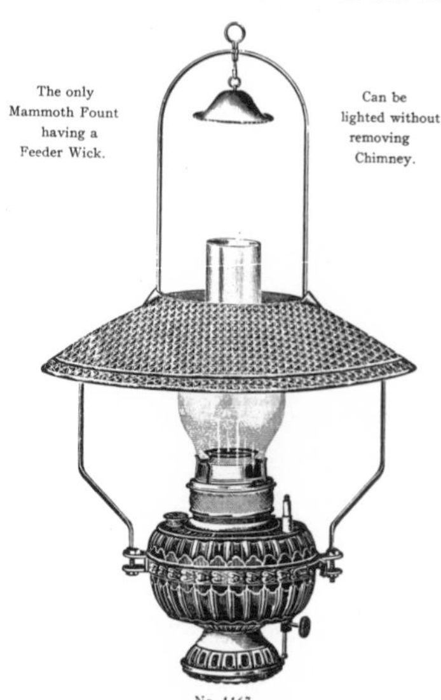

The only Mammoth Fount having a Feeder Wick.
Can be lighted without removing Chimney.

No. 1167.

With 20-inch Tin Reflector.

Order			Per Doze Brass.	N
No. 1167.	No. 3.	Founts and Harps only,	$62.00	$
" 1167.	" 3.	" Complete as shown in cut,	72.85	

Packed 1 doz. Founts and Harps only in a case—9½ cubic feet.

Weight 96 lbs. Gross, 46 lbs. Net.

Chimneys and Reflectors packed separately.

No. 3 Mammoth Banner Fount and Harp

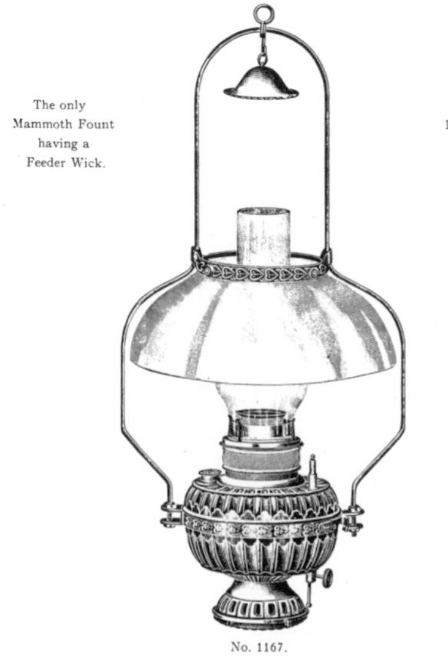

The only Mammoth Fount having a Feeder Wick.
Can be lighted without removing Chimney.

No. 1167.

With 14-inch Porcelain Dome Shade.

Order			Per Dozen. Brass.	Nickel.
No. 1167.	No. 3.	Founts and Harps only,	$62.00	$68.20
" 1167.	" 3.	" Harps and Crowns only,	65.10	72.10
" 1167.	" 3.	" Complete as shown in cut,	82.15	89.15

Packed 1 dozen Founts and Harps only in a case—9½ cubic feet.

Weight 96 lbs. Gross, 46 lbs. Net.

Glassware packed separately.

No. 3 Plumwood Mammoth Fount and Har

Takes No. 3 Plumwood Chimney and Wick.

No. 1267.

With 20-inch Tin Reflector.

Order			Per Doz Brass.	N
No. 1267.	No. 3.	Founts and Harps only,	$68.20	$
" 1267.	" 3.	" Complete as shown in cut,	79.85	

Packed 1 dozen Founts and Harps only in a case—9½ cubic feet.
Weight 99 lbs. Gross, 48½ lbs. Net.
Chimneys and Reflectors packed separately.

No. 3 Plumwood Mammoth Fount and Harp

Takes No. 3 Plumwood Chimney and Wick.

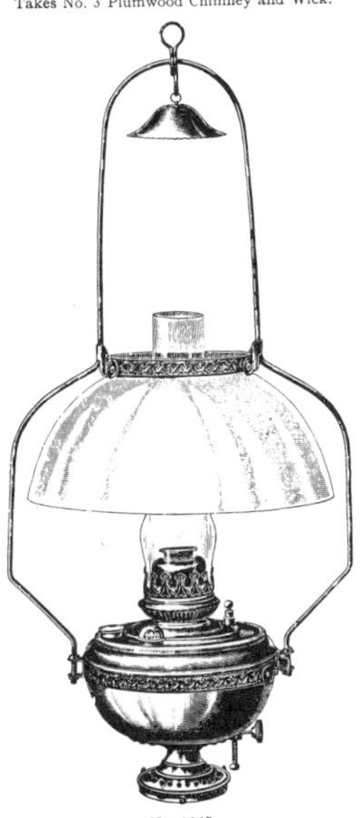

No. 1267.
With 14-inch Porcelain Shade.

Order			Per Dozen. Brass.	Nickel.
267.	No. 3.	Founts and Harps only,	$68.20	$74.40
267.	" 3.	" Harps and Crowns only,	71.30	78.30
267.	" 3.	" Complete as shown in cut,	89.15	96.10

Packed 1 dozen Founts and Harps only in a case—9½ cubic feet.

Weight 99 lbs. Gross, 48½ lbs. Net.

Glassware packed separately.

No. 2 Plumwood Fount with Harp

Takes No. 2 Plumwood Chimney and Wick.

Fount No. 1416.
Harp No. 1504.
With 15-inch Tin Reflector.

Order			Per Dozen. Brass.	Nickel
No. 1416.	No. 2.	Plumwood Founts only,	$32.55	$34.10
" 1416.	" 2.	" " Complete as shown in cut,	45.75	48.10

For price of Harp only and Side Wall Bracket for this Fount see pages 66 and 67.

Harps

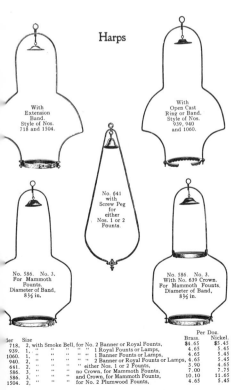

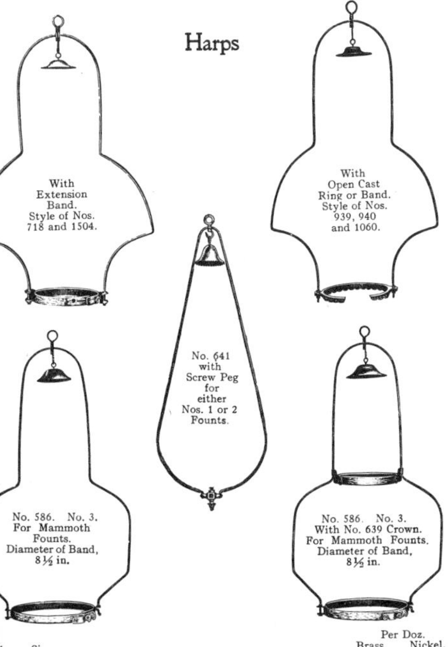

Order	Size		Per Doz. Brass.	Nickel.
718.	2,	with Smoke Bell, for No. 2 Banner or Royal Founts,	$4.65	$5.45
939.	1,	" " " " " 1 Royal Founts or Lamps,	4.65	5.45
1060.	1,	" " " " " 1 Banner Founts or Lamps,	4.65	5.45
940.	2,	" " " " " 2 Banner or Royal Founts or Lamps,	4.65	5.45
641.	2,	" " " " either Nos. 1 or 2 Founts,	3.90	4.65
586.	3,	" " " no Crown, for Mammoth Founts,	7.00	7.75
586.	3,	" " " and Crown, for Mammoth Founts,	10.10	11.65
1504.	2,	" " " for No. 2 Plumwood Founts,	4.65	5.45

Harp with Extension Fixture and Crown

Fits the Banner, Plumwood or any Mammoth Fount.
8½ inches in Diam.

Illustration shows cut with our No. 1267 Plumwood Fount and 14-inch Dome Shade.

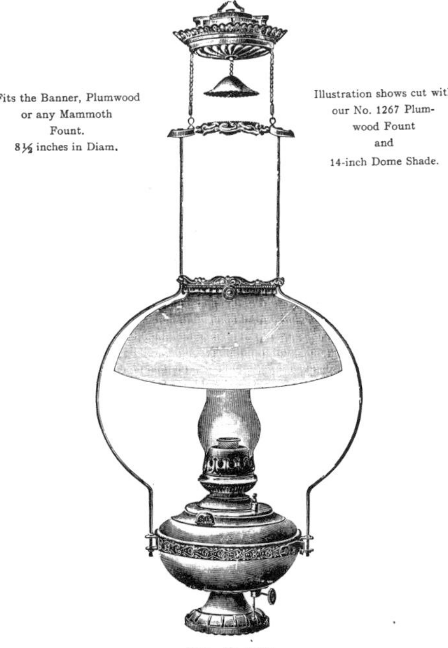

Harp No. 1330.
Fount " 1267.

Order			Per Dozen. Brass.	Nickel.
No 1330.	No. 3.	Harp with Crown and Extension,	$ 46.50	$ 48.05
" 1330.	" 3.	" Complete as shown in cut,	126.35	134.10

S. W. SQUIRES.

STREET-LAMP.

.182,865. Patented Oct. 3, 1876.

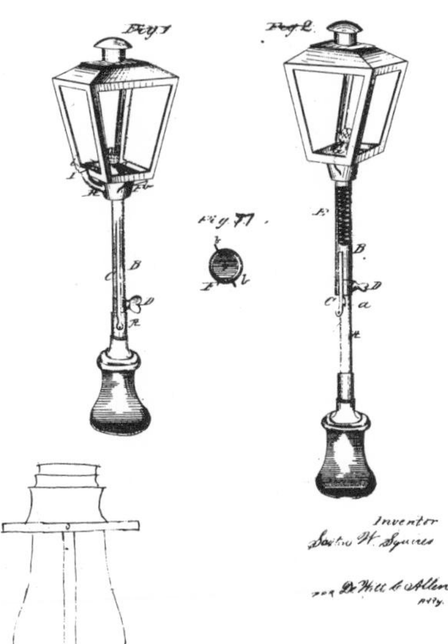

(No Model.) 3 Sheets—Sheet 1.

J. KIRBY, Jr.

CAR LAMP.

No. 367,109. Patented July 26, 1887.

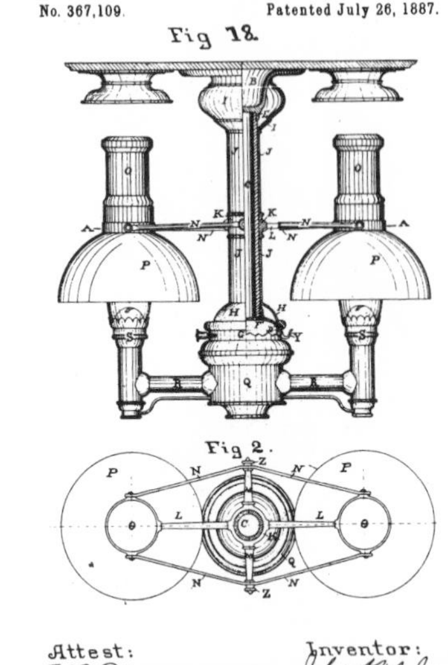

Dietz.

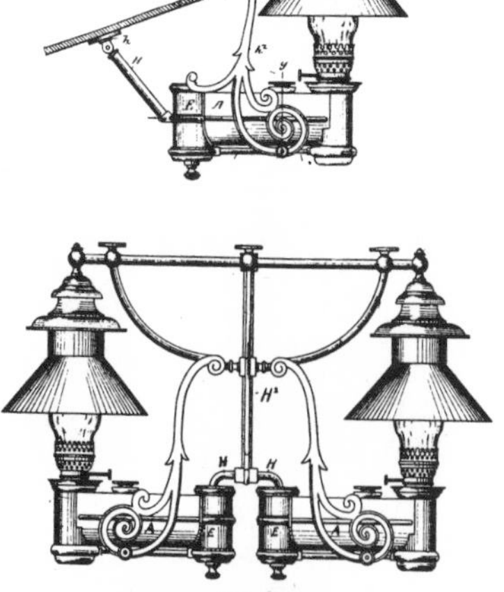

(No Model.) 3 Sheets—Sheet 2.

F. A. TABER.

LAMP HOLDER FOR CAR AND OTHER LAMPS.

No. 349,186. Patented Sept. 14, 1886.

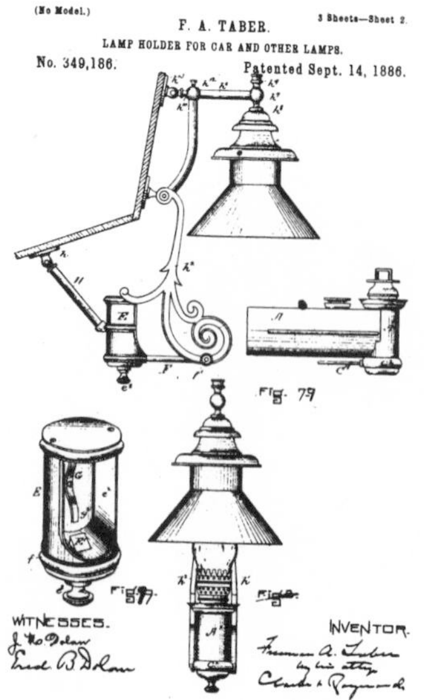

Modern Adaptations of Oil Lamps. It seems fitting to close our survey of oil lamps with a few comments on their adaptation for modern use. This is the day of electric power and one of the virtues of the old oil lamp is its easy conversion into a new form of illumination. It is like having all the old beauty with none of the attendant bother.

Various devices are on the market that help in the conversion of oil lamps. One is a screw-in plug that replaces the old burner and is threaded at one end for taking an ordinary electric lamp socket. There are also complete units, such as shown in this chapter, which simulate the old type burners. The proper wiring for many old lamps, and astrals especially, is to let the wire enter only above the bowl or oil font. GWW lamps are usually wired "above and below," so that light will show in both the ball shade and in the base. In all things, care should be taken not to damage the old lamp in the adaptation process. Wanton punching of holes or tearing away of certain parts can only decrease authenticity and value.

The old lamp catalogs, which supply so much of interest in this book, have come from various sources. The concern of Edward Miller and Company of Meriden, Connecticut, founded in 1844 and incorporated in 1866 was one of the largest devoted to lamp manufacture. A representation of their plant on another page gives some idea of the magnitude of the venture. Their catalogue included student lamps, parlor, banquet and portable lamps of every type. Some whose taste runs to sperm-oil lamps of early Sandwich vintage may feel that the lamps described in these last pages are unbearably ugly; but an impartial judge would probably admit them a considerable merit. Combined with late Victorian furniture in the proper setting, lamps of these types supply an amusing whimsy and air of rightness to the decorative scheme. They are far more mellow than the garish modern reproductions of old lighting fixtures. Time will undoubtedly show an ever increasing use of old oil lamps in modern settings.

DIETZ" PIONEER STREET LAMP

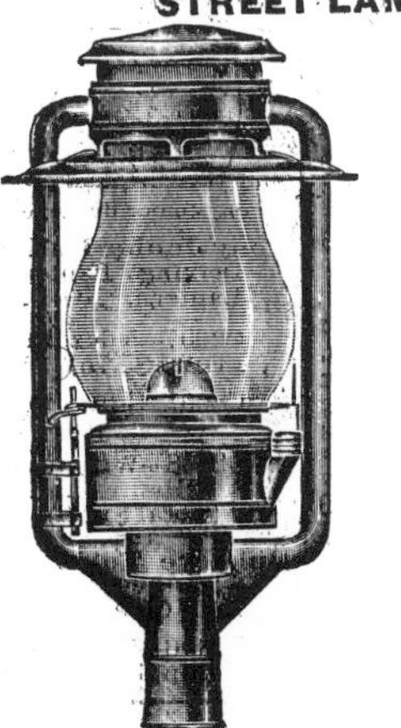

reet Lamp—Cold blast principle.

EUREKA" DRIVING LAMP

Smallest lamp of its kind. Ideal for use on all light driving vehicles.

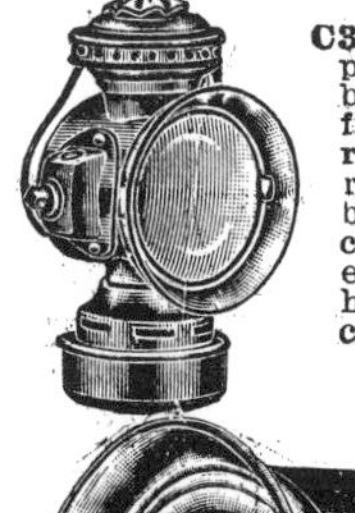

C3751—Ht. 7½ in., patent wing lock burner, 3 in. plain front lens, 2 in. ruby rear lens, removable parts, burns 10 hours, clamp holder with each. For left hand side. 1 in carton.
Each, $1.05

SMALL LANTERNS

Complete with burner, wick and globe.

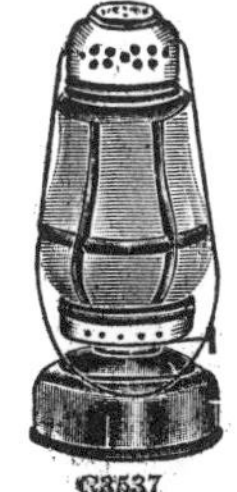

C3537

C3538-40

"DIETZ" DRIVING LAMP
For Left-Hand Side

For horse drawn vehicles. Strongly made, easy to operate. Complies with all night driving laws.

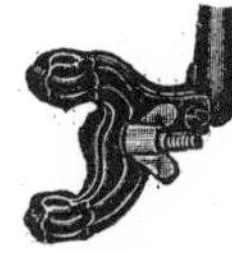

Dashboard Clamp—Used with C3750, C3751 and C3752 lanterns on buggies.

C3754—1 in pkg.
Each, 20c

Chapter XI
VICTORIAN LIGHTING ARRANGEMENTS

Lighting arrangements of mid and late Victorian homes tended to become increasingly ornate and ostentatious. The oil lamp had found its best and safest illuminant with the coming of kerosene. The homes which could afford it developed a lamp for every room in the house and kept them all ablaze as a status symbol. Glass and china manufacturers, metal workers and artsy craftsmen vied with each other in turning out a plethora of lamp fonts, globes and statuesque bases with special decorative effects. Seldom was any thought given to either the economic need, or the efficiency of home illuminating. Rockefeller and his petroleum millionaires were interested in just one thing: use of more and more oil. He encouraged people to buy many manufactured lamps, even promoted a cheap Rochester burner for the poor, not so much because it gave a brighter light than a small kitchen handlamp, but because it burned more kerosene. From having groped around in the semi-darkness during their early years, Queen Victoria's Godchildren went on a lighting binge that has yet to run its full course! Part II of this book picks up that thread and takes us through the many later concomitants of our "Gone with the Wind" Era, from vapors and gaslights to the early electric lighting devices that are today's collector items.

"Let there be light," was certainly the motto of Victorian high society. Of all the activities in a big house, arranging the lamps in preparation for an evening party, was not only a great lady's pleasure but also a major cleaning-chore for her maid-servants. Man, never a nocturnal animal, emerged during this period as the reigning father of a large brood. In his big home he was desirious of showing it off after the sun went down. Party going, home entertainment and even the family dining table became highly ritualistic and status-oriented. Not only were there innumerable tomes on how to comport oneself as hostess or guest; the proper lighting of each room to achieve "maximum effect' was loudly tooted in ladies magazines. Oil paintings and 'chromos' were to have special lighting thrown upon them. Mantle-lights, library table lamps, foyer and entrance lights (to say nothing of ceiling chandeliers) formed such an array that there was little of further interest to be seen in a room. Not only were oil lamps being placed everywhere, those who could afford the new-fangled gas lighting were having it piped into every room, each with an especially designed fixture. On the stairway newel posts were ripped open so as to hold a light. Outside the house was also 'lit up'—porches, garden gazebos, the porte-co-chere and horse-block had for the first time gas (and later electric) wiring to dispel the gloom. If not the most tasteful period of Victorian

High Society, candles

Gin Palace, gas

Cadgers Club, oil

Life in London, 1821 by I. R. and G. Cruickshank

New York salon lit by Edison lamps, 1881

Picture gallery, New York City, lit by Edison lamps, 1881

ENGLISH, AUSTRIAN, AND FRENCH LAMPS, Etc.

THE Lamp-stand, or Lampadaire, on the left of the sheet is the production of a well-known English maker, Mr. Charles J. Phillp, of Birmingham, and a most graceful work it is.

The Pendant, which occupies the upper place in the centre, is by one of the most famous Art-workmen in Austria, Herr D. Hollinbach, of Vienna, and is a perfect gem, an exquisite design exquisitely worked out.

Beneath is a Gasalier, one of the most beautiful productions of Mr. Matifat, of Paris, a rich and original composition —probably for an Oriental destination, by the introduction of the palm trees—a beautiful example of Parisian work.

The last figure, the graceful Lamp-pillar to the right hand, is one of the beautiful artistic castings in iron of the Coalbrookdale Company, and is worthy of the reputation of that famous establishment; the general outline of the work is most agreeable to the eye, and the details are charming throughout.

homelife, certainly these last phases manifest an impulsive upward thrusting of life in which mechanical inventiveness and the daring of domestic architectural delights were matched by an awakened humaness and love for very ornate things. From the limitations of hand-craftsmanship (whose accomplishments of fine living had once served only the Lords), the Industrial Revolution had given the successful factory owner an urge to build his own castle while his wife displayed conspicuous consumption in lavish home fetes.

While social history is not a prime purpose of this book, today's collector will find the whole gamut of cultural taste, popular fashion and love of home refinements, easily traced by the study of Victorian lighting arrangements. Pictures which follow give insight into the intentions of lamp makers as well as into the needs and ideals of the lamp users. Indeed, the development of such exuberant visual expressions brings before us, even today, a nostalgic gleam for that ornately elegant society preceding World War I. These decades scholars have called, "Western civilization's most common and prosperous years." Most late Victorian lamps were primarily decorative. Lighting to read or to work by was of secondary consideration. That is perhaps a part of their present day charm, when indirect lighting takes care of the utilitarian feature of sight and lets the old types serve only as decorative accessories. Before rushing after out-moded oil and gas lamps, Art Nouveau and Tiffany shades that drive antiquers wild, let us consider the developments which brought on such changes.

From earliest time, man has endeavored to produce artificial light so as to utilize more thoroughly the hours of darkness for purposes of work or of pleasure. As no human can see in the dark, Victorians were exceptional only in having at their command better illuminants than their forefathers and more time for after dark play. Until the first application of electricity in the late Nineteenth century all artificial light was produced by fire. Recall the first problem: getting the oil light source into the right place (either from floor or table) and having got it there, so placed, it would not easily be knocked over and so set the place afire. The solid-based table lamps with marble and iron bases were a distinct aid; but as Victorian lights went ever nearer the ceiling (recall the chandeliers and metal fixtures holding lamps aloft), the next problem was to get the light down more to eye level with suitable shades and globes. At first art for arts sake was not good enough for people playing with oil fires; but with the advent of gas lighting and electricity, the originators of Art Nouveau and The Arts & Crafts Movement were free to construct gay lighting devices very often of inefficient lighting facility. This brings us to the third Victorian problem, too much lighting in the home and one that still plagues us even today. The phenomenally rapid developments of lighting methods in the late Nineteenth century are usually held responsible for such over-illumination. First with cheap and relatively safe kerosene, then with cheaper central gas piping and on to the carbon arc, vapour and incandescent lamp, more and more artificial illumination beat upon the human eye. For a comparatively small amount of candle power enough light was often thrown out to be even dangerous to the eyesight of the home's occupant.

In order to acquire an understanding of bad Victorian lighting practice, consider such factors as eyestrain, having a flame glare, the direction from which lamp light enters the eye, the indiscriminate use of highlights and shadows and the relation of color to one's mood: Glare (direct or reflected) was sometimes alleviated by diffusion of the concentrated light source through a shade. More frequently it was left bare to be diffused improperly upon any surrounding surfaces. In civilized man, the axis of the eye is tipped downward with its nerves equipped (as in reading, in writing and in handwork) to receive a strong stimulus from below. Straining results when a strong light stimulus is given the eye from above. The eyelids serve as protective function and so does the broad-brimmed hat of the cowboy. Since it is likewise desirable to avoid strong illumination (no matter how well diffused in the upper part of the room), one can see that the Victorian's predilection for chandeliers and gasoliers probably did their eyes considerable harm. One good thing that did result from a multitude of table lamps at below eye-level was the fact that the lack of constancy in the height of such flames resulted in changing light and shadow effect which might help to prevent fatigue. As for the effect of the colors of lights on human moods, this probably was one of the best, if least understood aspects of Victorian lighting. The influence of color upon mood was felt very strongly by our sentimental grandparents. Lamp shades in greens and violets were thought to have a quieting narcotic-like effect, while those of the red and yellow ends of the spectrum were thought to be lustful and stimulating. The warm yellow glow of the oil-lamp flame would be turned up or down with various shades used to help give a party, ballroom or courtship corner "the proper atmosphere." On the other hand, gas light with its cooling green and blue tones could be used to "soothe and rest the tired spirit." Given to over sentimentality, Victorian society dames did seem to know something about changing lighting color effects to suit the temperaments and emotional purposes of their guests. A bright warm gay light which was felt pleasant in the dining room was sometimes kept even more brilliantly lighted in the drawing room to tire out and to fatigue "bores invited" just to kill off one's social debts. But let an acceptable young man come just to pay his respects to the family who has a daughter of marriageable age, then "quietly the lights were dimmed" (to the cooler shades of rosebud pink and blue) in hopes he would linger a bit longer.

Most Victorian interiors had their lighting effects arranged, however, with disregard for the particular requirements of the room for family living.

The drawing room or back parlor may have incorporated a beautiful marble fireplace, but its over mantel ornamental picture often could not be seen at all due to inadequate artificial lighting. Only in recent years have interior decorators and optical specialists developed proper compositions of bright and of dark areas in lighting a room. What we do have are the discards from our bygone days; gas reflectors, table and dome lights, chandeliers and sidewall brackets; one can mount a breath-taking but eye-saving lamp and visually recapture the late Victorian lighting adapted for modern living.

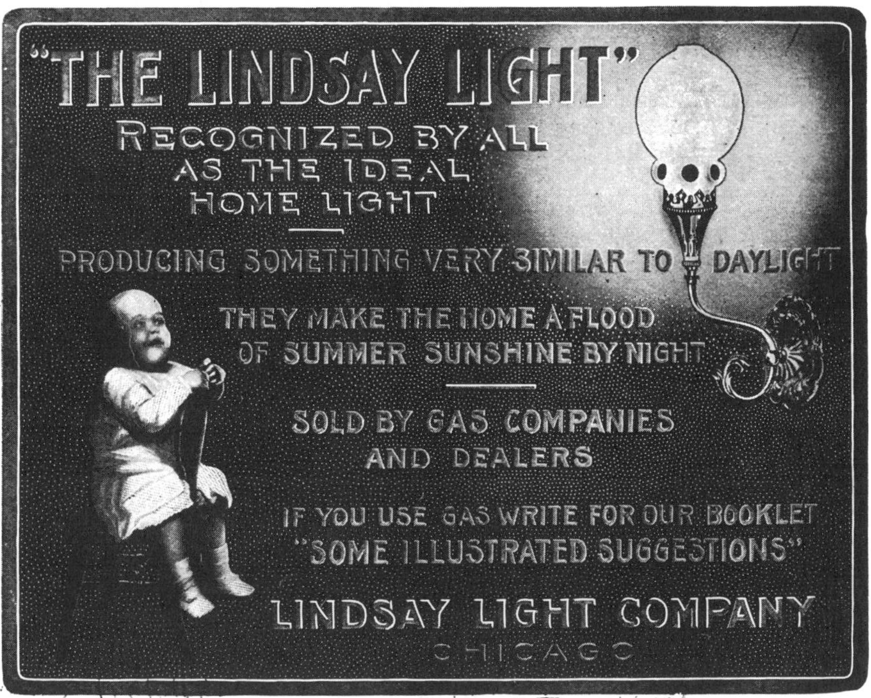

GAS! GAS! GAS!

Medals of the highest merit have been given to the undersigned by the American Institute of the State of New York, as well as several other States, for our superior Workmanship and Design of beautiful

Gas Fixtures, Chandeliers, Lamps, &c. &c.

These compliments, however, bear no comparison to the daily awards made by the elite, who visit our great Manufacturing Depot at

No. 376 Broadway,

Where an Assortment of

GASALIERS, CHANDELIERS, BRACKETS,

LAMPS, GIRANDOLES, &C.

ARE CONSTANTLY SUPPLIED.

OUR STOCK IS PROBABLY THE LARGEST IN AMERICA.

Designers and Modelers are almost daily producing New Patterns.

☞ WHOLESALE DEALERS ARE PARTICULARLY INVITED TO GIVE US A CALL. ☜

SPLENDID CHANDELIERS, WITH LARD OR FLUID HEADS,

Made for Mansions or Churches, where Gas is not introduced.

ARCHER, WARNER & CO.

376 BROADWAY, NEW YORK.

ARCHER & WARNER,

119 CHESTNUT STREET, PHILADELPHIA.

Chapter XII
DEVELOPMENT OF GAS LIGHTING

So intent has been the acquisition of Victorian oil lamps that only now are collectors turning to those almost forgotten but equally fine examples that remain from the Gas-light era. The 1880 gas street lamps in iron or in copper with their blown glass globes have all but disappeared from antique sales rooms. Next comes the craze for brass, crystal and polychrome gasoliers which once adorned the houses of the well-to-do. Here is the genesis of that development. Though quite ancient, substituting gas flame for oil lights was quite late in reaching America.

The history of artficial lighting is full of unanswered questions, and one that concerns us here is **why** when ancient's, like the Chinese knew the illuminating properties of natural gas, would western scientists take so long in discovering how to develop the idea commercially. One of the problems was how to control gas flow. The earliest form of true burner was the 'rat-tail' consisting of a metal tube enclosed at one end and perforated by a single hole. By 1808 the **Cockspur Burner** in which the tube end was pierced by three small holes to give a triple flame and the **Cockscomb Burner** in which the holes were even more numerous gave a light of about one candle power for every cubic foot of gas burned per hour. The **Batswing Burner** of 1816 (a small pear-shaped steel burner) gave a little more light and so did the **Fishtail Burner** of 1820, followed by the **Bunsen Burner our first true gas burner** and still used today. The development of the gas burner, shown on a separate page indicates how painfully we progressed to the efficient and incandescent light of **Welsbach Burner** of 1885-1895.

The Chinese probably first used "gas" for lighting by piping natural gas found in their salt mines. Around 1664 a natural gas well in Lancashire, England (found very close to a coal mine) suggested to Dr. John Clayton that artficial gas could also be made thereby. He distilled coal in a retort and succeeded in collecting some of the coal-gas in bladders which when touched by a match, burst into flame. No practical application was made of this finding until over a century later when Professor J. P. Minclelers at Louvain University distilled coal and other substances to light his lecture room with gas. 1802 saw the tentative introduction of **"Bengal Lights"** (flaming open burners from an apparatus which distilled its own gas from wood and coal solids). Early burners (Cockspur and the Cockscomb) were an adaptation of the 1790 argand round wick burner to gas lamps. The fish-tail burner was an improvement because its two impinging flames spread into a flat fan-shaped shield.

As yet there was no attempt to substitute gas for oil burning lamps in

THE DEVELOPMENT OF THE GAS BURNER

the home; but the possibilities of street lighting (once gas mains could be laid down) were considered in many cities. F. A. Wintzler, called the father of the central station idea, started in London (1810) the first company attempting to supply gas lighting service to the public. But it was not until 1838 when W. H. Fox Talbot discovered that finely divided lime could raise a gas flame to white incandescence and in 1855 when R. W. von Bunsen invented the even better burner (which bears his name) that anyone thought very seriously of using artificial or natural gas to replace kerosene and other oil illuminants in the home.

Probably the greatest new development that spurred the wealthy to have their rooms piped with gas was not the fact that there could be instant light in every room, but was the invention of brighter gas mantels about 1885. We shall pass quickly over the early difficulties of maintaining standard pressure even from controlled expansion tanks holding artificial gas. Natural gas was even more unpredictable; pressure often dropped to nothing in cold weather and gave off pungent evil smelling odors when fully operating. The principle methods for making artificial gas was coal. When heated out of air it produces a solid residue known as coke, and some volatile matter known as coal gas; douse the coke with hot steam and it gasifies to make water gas; this mixed with coal gas is what was distributed in pipes to city families to light their streets and their homes. Flames even with covered glass chimneys burned rather feebly, until along came the Welsback gas mantel to raise an incandescent glow.

Following the discovery of how to make gas from coal and the unparalled success of lighting London streets and homes, many American concerns took up the challenge. Baltimore was the first city to use gas commercially in 1820, with a contract for street lighting. Sparked by Rembrandt Peale's sensational use of it to light his museum, other cities quickly followed suit but it was not until 1875 that the use of gas for home lighting began to make any great progress. The Philadelphia Centennial Exposition used gas, of course; but even the wealthy were convinced that gas was smelly and also not very brilliant; this last objection was met for all time by the gas mantels of Dr. Carl Auer von Welsbach in 1885 and used in nearly its original forms down to today. Welsbach's inverted saturated cotton fabrics in a solution of salts, burned out its organic matter and attached the resulting mantel to the burner tip of the gas fixture. His first mantel gave a marked green light, his next development patented the use of thoria which added strength to the mantel; finally in the 1890's he produced an incandescent mantel composed of thoria and cerea, and this when given a final collodion coating allowed the mantel to stand up under trying commercial abuse and gave us the incandescent bright lights that made the gas chandeliers shown in these pages sparkle with real brilliance. Small wonder then that until the coming of more practical and cheaper power from electricity, the gas light era enjoyed a grand holiday.

THE SIEMENS REGENERATIVE GAS LAMP.

BRILLIANT LIGHT! GREAT ECONOMY!!

WATKINS'

PATENT PORTABLE

Makes its own GAS at a cost of LESS THAN 1-2 A CENT AN HOUR!

The Cheapest and Best Method for LIGHTING STREETS, PARKS, and PRIVATE GROUNDS.

GAS ATTACHMENTS.

These Attachments can be placed in any Stree Lanterns now in use, doing away with all stree mains and service pipe; and the duration of ligh can be *graduated to any desired number of hour* from the time of lighting.

A. H. WATKINS,

294 Harrison Avenue, BOSTON, MASS

Chapter XIII
GAS LIGHT FIXTURES

The long-time collector of old lamps has a few thrills coming when he finally turns attention away from the whale oils, Betty's and Student types of earlier days and to those of gas lighting. Iron, brass and copper were the hallmarks of fixtures in this era, with just a few plated in gold or silver. Goods came packaged in the following finishes: polished brass and black polished brass, polished old iron, old brass, copper, gold bronze, Roman gold, Sali-gold, Rich gilt, steel and black wrought iron. Extra charges were made for such finishes as Dark Oxidized Copper, Mottled Oxidized Copper, Oxidized Silver, Silver and Black, Polished Silver, Butler's Silver, Nickel and Ormolu.

We divide gas lighting fixtures into five distinct types.

A—**Table lamp** in which a heavy base and columar pipe was attached to a portable gas hose and the whole job topped off with a special burner and reflecting globe.

B—**Combination Newels** were those which could be mounted on a newel post or attached to a table or ledge. Since there was no necessity any longer for an elaborate oil font, the base of these lamps resembled candles or open work vases. Many of them featured a cluster of several imitation candles complete with bobeches and finished off with an opalescent globe which could be used for a flambeau or even used for electricity. Styles included the Colonial, the Louis XV, the Empire, the French Stalactite, the Gibson and the Rococo with many size variations offered in each.

C—**Lanterns Outdoor** (porch) and the indoor (hall) were offered in numerous French styles with lovely cut glass or engraved etched glass globes. Hall lights attached to the ceiling were offered both as artificial candles, as globes with Welsbach burners, and as combination effects, uniting gas and electric wiring in the same fixture.

W—**Wall Brackets** included the special toilet lights using gas alone, with some as combinations. Bedroom, living and dining room side brackets are among the most sought after examples of this bygone era, partly because of their own convoluted **Art Nouveau Turning** or straight **Boxy Types** of Mission Arts & Crafts lineage. That many are being adapted into decorative table lights today is shown in our final chapter.

E—**Gas Chandeliers** complete our 5-point study of gas-light fixtures. By all odds, the most desirable for the going neo-Victorian mode, these **Gaseliers** are everything one could want in a piece de resistance for the room. Pictures show the special features of billiard room chandeliers, those designed for the dining room, the nursery and those loaded with crystal and gilt intended only for ballrooms.

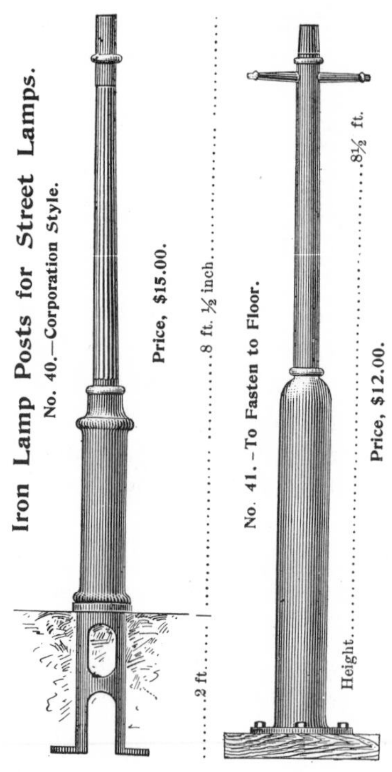

Iron Lamp Posts for Street Lamps.
No. 40.—Corporation Style.
Price, $15.00.
8 ft. ½ inch.
2 ft.
No. 41.–To Fasten to Floor.
Height 8½ ft.
Price, $12.00.

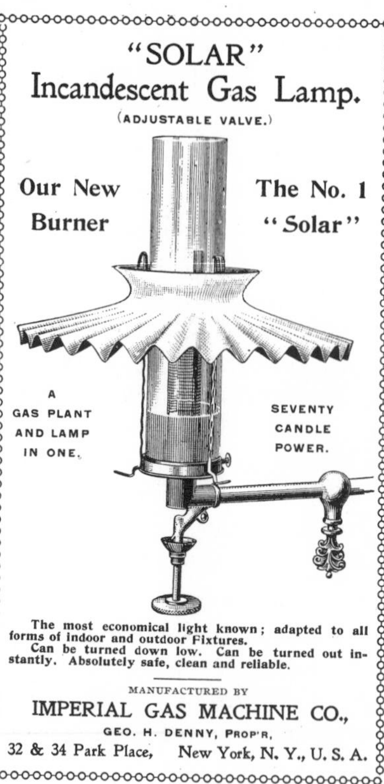

Two-Light Pendant, No. 13.

To Hang or Fasten to Celling.

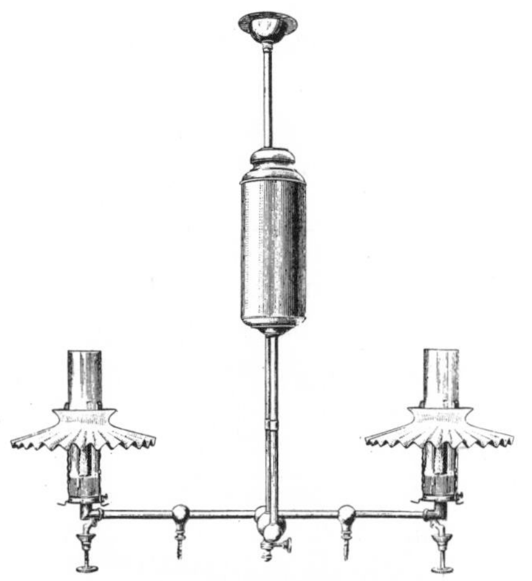

Price, complete, $11.00.

Length, 37 inches. Spread, 22 inches.

Detachable Fount. Made of Brass throughout, Nickel Plated and highly polished.

This Pendant is adjustable—may be raised or lowered by Set-Screw.

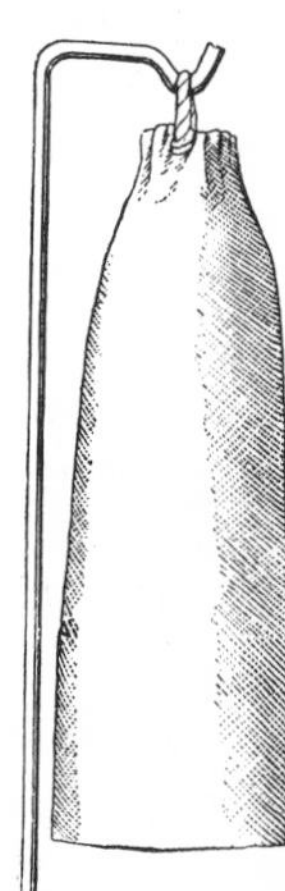

"Solar" Gasolene Mantles.

$3.00 per Dozen.

Especially designed for **Gasolene Gas.**

☞ **Use Only the Best Mantles—they are Cheapest in the end.**

For Incandescent Goods in the Shape of Globes, Shades, Chimneys, etc., designed for use on "Solar" Fixtures, *write us for Catalogue.*

☞ NOTE: We have a large variety of Globes, Shades, etc., other than those shown in accompanying illustrations, in plain, etched, and colors, designed for our Solar Fixtures.

Two-Light Pendant, No. 23.

To Hang or Fasten to Ceiling.

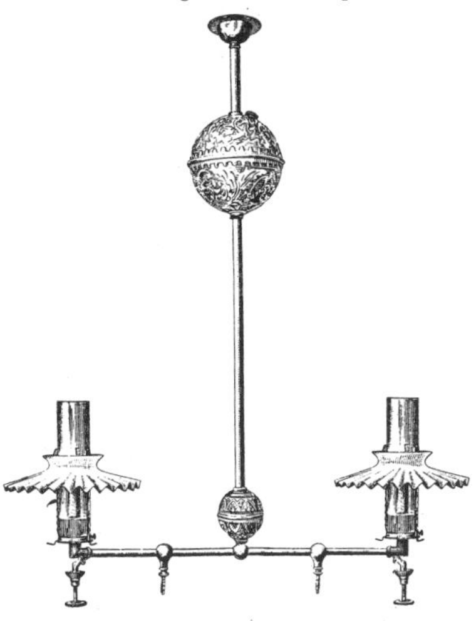

Length, 36 inches. Spread, 33 inches.
Reservoir, 3 Pints.
Of Heavy Solid Brass, polished.

Price, complete, $12.00.

Same Fixture also in 4 Lights.

Price, $15.00.

Above Fixtures furnished any desired length specified.

Arc Lamp and Reflector, No. 32.

For Porch and Out-of-Door Lighting.

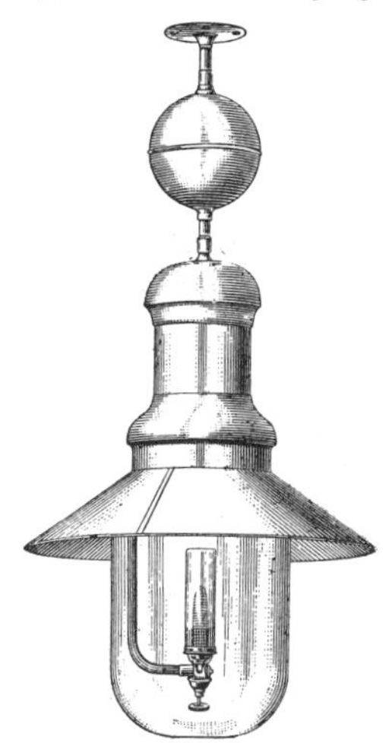

Heavy and finished in Dark Green or Maroon.

Length, 38 inches.

The most perfect and convenient lamp of the kind ever brought out.

Casts no shadow. All the light utilized.

Price, complete, $11.00.

Vestibule Lamp, No. 31.

(To Suspend.)

Wind-tight. Insect-tight.
Size, 8 x 12 inches. Length of Stem, 22 inches.
Reservoir holds 3 Pints.

Designed for open halls, piazzas, and all exposed places where Fixture can be suspended from ceiling.

Heavy, finished in Maroon, Green or Black.

Absolutely **proof** against **wind** and **insects.**

Price, complete, $11.00.

Square Side Lamp, No. 30.

For Side of Wall, Building or Fence.

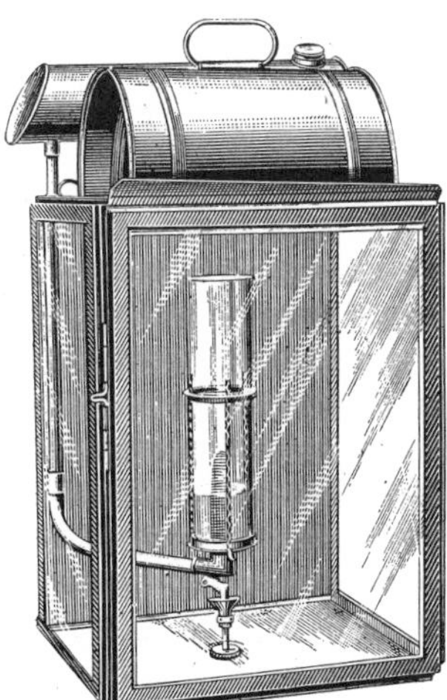

Size, 9 x 13 inches. Wind and Insect Proof.

Reservoir holds 3 pints.

Designed for out-of-door use and exposed places. Finished in Maroon, Green, or Black.

Price, complete, $5.50.

Note: This Lamp also made with 3 sides, or triangle shape at same price.

Harp Pendant, No. 21.

To Hang or Fasten to Ceiling.

One-Light Pendant, No. 22.

To Hang or Fasten to Ceiling.

Iron Bracket for Dome Street Lamps, No. 45.

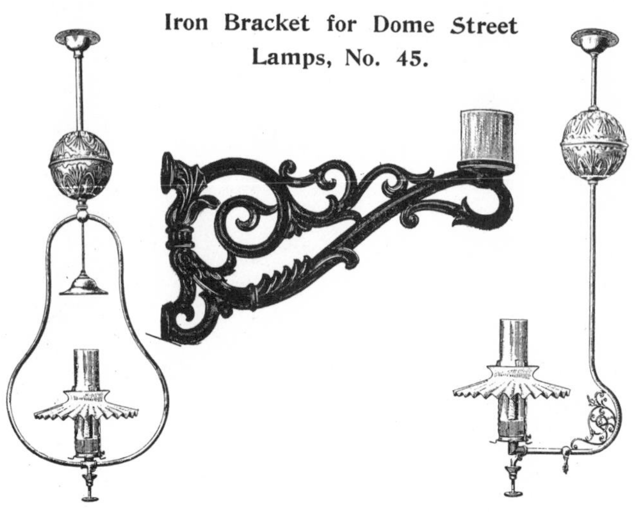

Length, 33 inches. Reservoir, 1 Quart.

Made of Brass throughout. Polished and highly finished.

Price, complete, $7.50.

Length, 33 inches. Reservoir, 1 Quart.

Made of Brass throughout. Polished and highly finished.

Price, complete, $7.00.

Wall Lamp, No. 20.

Japanned Fount. Brass Tubing.

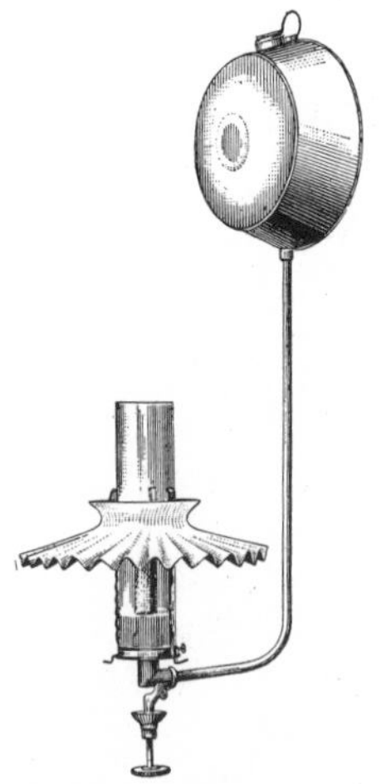

Length, 22 inches. Reservoir, 3 Pints.

Price, complete, $4.00.

The same Burner and just as fine a light as furnished with our best finished Fixtures.

☞ **Fourteen (14) different styles of Fixtures adapted to all outdoor and indoor lighting.**

Dome Street Lamp, No. 33.

With Socket for Post or Bracket.

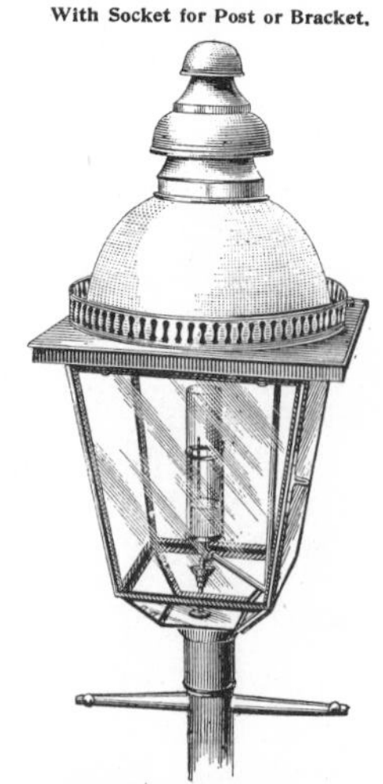

Height, 29 inches. Width, 16 inches.
Reservoir holds 2 Quarts.

Price, complete, $12.00.

An exceptionally neat design of Lamp for Street, Park and Public Square lighting, with Opal Dome Top and Copper Canopy. Not affected by wind or temperature. Insect-tight.

Plain "Corporation" Style Street Lamps.

Price, complete, $10.00.

Student Lamp, No. 10.

Detachable Fount.

This Lamp may be raised or lowered, it being fixed to Standard by Set-Screw.

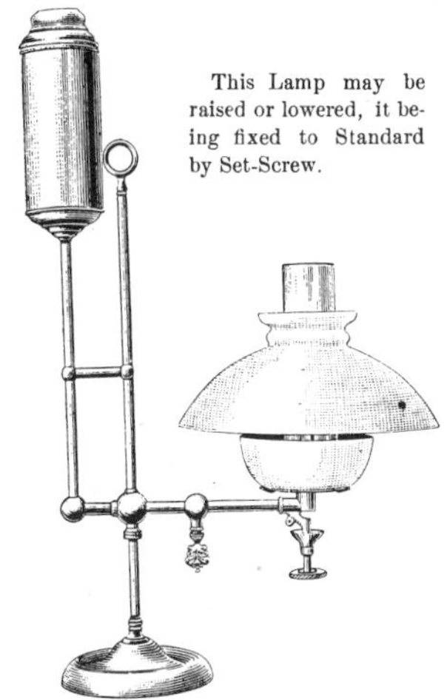

Price, complete, $8.00.

Fount holds one pint.

This style is one of the most desirable and attractive forms for table or portable use. Made of Brass, Nickel-plated and highly polished.

Any style of Shades, Globes or other appurtenances for Incandescent Gas Burners may be used with this and all other Lamps and Fixtures manufactured by us.

OUR NEW BURNER, The No. 2 "Solar."

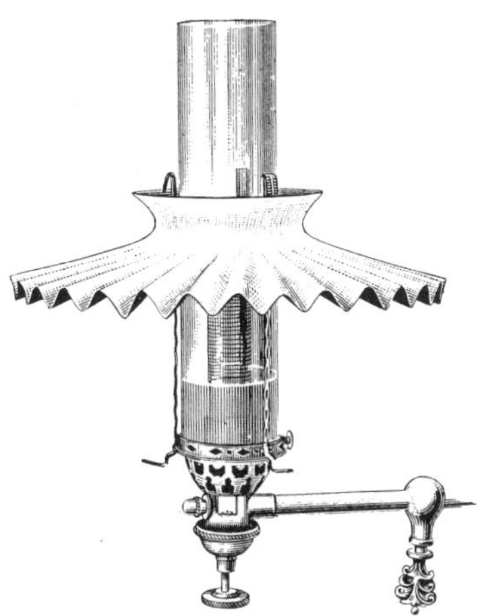

The "Solar" Burners are Self-Cleaning—clean themselves every time the light is turned out.

Prices are f.o.b. New York.

If you have no account with us, send us with your order P. O. or Express Money Order to cover same. Send us at same time references to insure further shipments on open account, payable in 30 days.

Bracket Swing Lamp, No. 11.

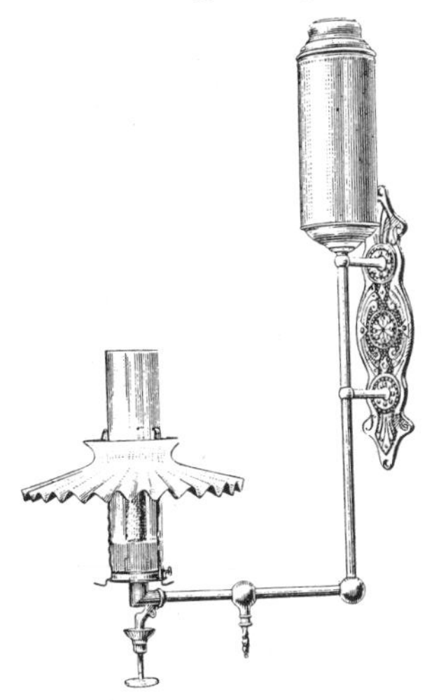

Price, complete, $7.00.

Fount holds 1 Pint.

Detachable Fount, made of Brass throughout, Nickel Plated and highly polished.

The finest line of Nickeled Brass Fixtures with Detachable Founts in the United States.

One-Light Pendant Fixture, No. 12.

To Hang or Fasten to Ceiling.

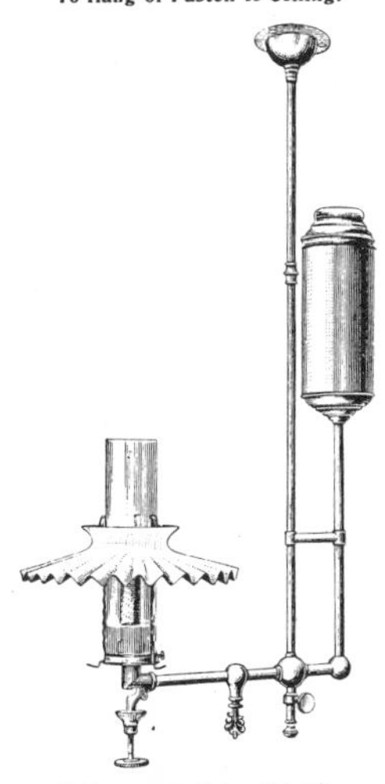

Price, complete, $7.00.

Length, 37 inches.

Detachable Fount. Made of Brass throughout. Nickel Plated and highly polished.

This Pendant is adjustable—may be raised or lowered by Set-Screw.

AN IMPROVED INCANDESCENT GAS LAMP.

W. C. VOSBURGH M'F'G CO

(LIMITED)

MANUFACTURERS OF

Gas and Electric Fixtures

269 to 281 State Street

BROOKLYN, N. Y.

Telephone, "62 Brooklyn."

WESTERN BRANCH:

114 and 116 WABASH AVE., CHICAGO, ILL

It is a pity that more of these fine fixtures were not preserved as decorative adjuncts to the mixed modes of current interior decoration. To get the right parts together and mounted with the proper globes or shades, is what actually makes these various types such a delight for the new as well as for the older type of lamp collector.

ORNAMENTAL METAL WORK

The Statuette of imitation bronze or iron was put to work to support gas jets.

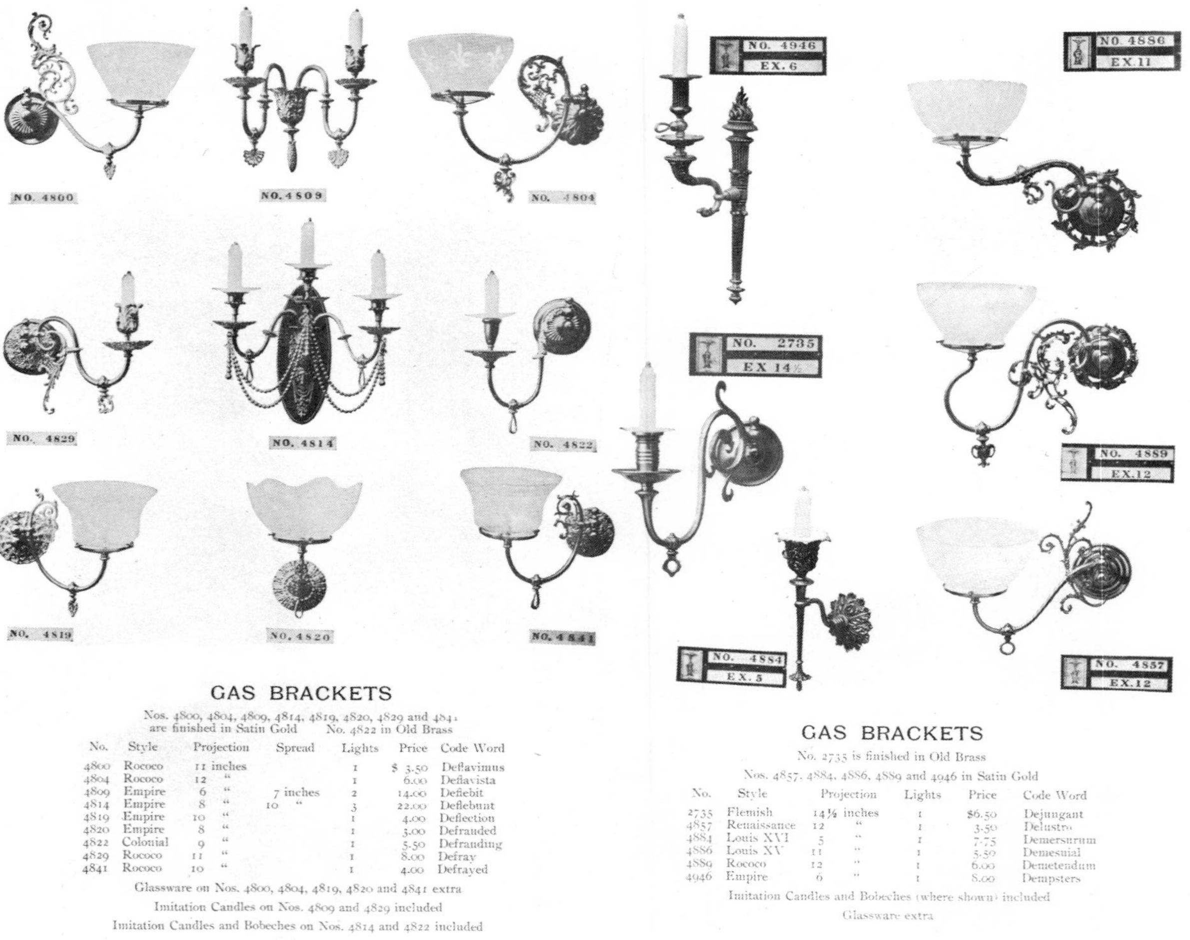

GAS BRACKETS

Nos. 4800, 4804, 4809, 4814, 4819, 4820, 4829 and 4841 are finished in Satin Gold No. 4822 in Old Brass

No.	Style	Projection	Spread	Lights	Price	Code Word
4800	Rococo	11 inches		1	$ 3.50	Deflavimus
4804	Rococo	12 "		1	6.00	Deflavista
4809	Empire	6 "	7 inches	2	14.00	Deflebit
4814	Empire	8 "	10 "	3	22.00	Deflebunt
4819	Empire	10 "		1	4.00	Deflection
4820	Empire	8 "		1	3.00	Defrauded
4822	Colonial	9 "		1	5.50	Defrauding
4829	Rococo	11 "		1	8.00	Defray
4841	Rococo	10 "		1	4.00	Defrayed

Glassware on Nos. 4800, 4804, 4819, 4820 and 4841 extra

Imitation Candles on Nos. 4809 and 4829 included

Imitation Candles and Bobeches on Nos. 4814 and 4822 included

GAS BRACKETS

No. 2735 is finished in Old Brass

Nos. 4857, 4884, 4886, 4889 and 4946 in Satin Gold

No.	Style	Projection	Lights	Price	Code Word
2735	Flemish	14¼ inches	1	$6.50	Dejungant
4857	Renaissance	12 "	1	3.50	Delustro
4884	Louis XVI	5 "	1	7.75	Demersurum
4886	Louis XV	11 "	1	5.50	Demesuial
4889	Rococo	12 "	1	6.00	Demetendum
4946	Empire	6 "	1	8.00	Dempsters

Imitation Candles and Bobeches (where shown) included

Glassware extra

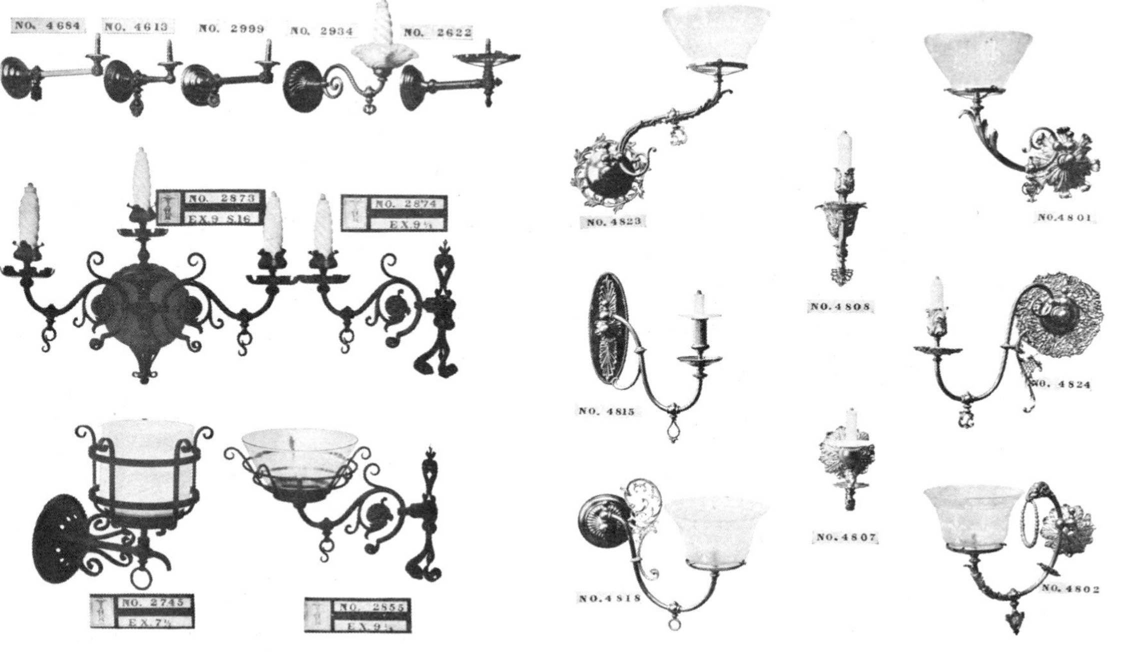

GAS BRACKETS

Nos. 2622, 2934, 2999, 4613 and 4684 are finished in Rich Gilt or Polished Brass
Nos. 2745, 2855, 2873 and 2874 in Wrought Iron

No.	Projection	Spread	Lights	Price	Code Word
2622	5¾ inches		1	$ 1.60	Decourt
2745	7½ "		1	9.50	Decrowned
2855	9¼ "		1	10.00	Decrowning
2873	9 "	16 inches	3	18.50	Decrusant
2874	9¼ "		1	9.25	Decubabunt
2934	7 "		1	3.50	Decubito
2999	6¾ "		1	.72	Dedalera
4613	4½ "		1	.60	Dedalian
4684	6½ "		1	.68	Dedalico

Opalescent Twist Cylinder for No. 2745, Clear Glass Globe for No. 2855.
Imitation Candles and Bobeches (where shown) for
Nos. 2873, 2874 and 2934 included

GAS BRACKETS

Nos. 4801, 4802, 4807, 4808, 4818, 4823 and 4824 are finished in Satin Gold
No. 4815 in Old Brass

No.	Style	Projection	Lights	Price	Code Word
4801	Louis XV	11 inches	1	$ 7.50	Deistical
4802	Louis XVI	12 "	1	8.00	Deitadinho
4807	Louis XVI	6 "	1	7.00	Deitatem
4808	Empire	7 "	1	9.00	Deitatis
4815	Colonial	10 "	1	9.00	Dejabais
4818	Rococo	12 "	1	4.50	Dejacion
4823	Louis XV	11 "	1	5.50	Dejariamos
4824	Rococo	12 "	1	10.00	Dejasteis

Glassware on Nos. 4801, 4802, 4818 and 4823 extra
Imitation Candles on Nos. 4808 and 4824 included
Imitation Candles and Bobeches on Nos. 4807 and 4815 included

NO. 4862 EX 10

NO. 4854 EX 12

NO. 4853 EX 15 S.15

NO. 4874 EX 10

NO. 4872 EX 11

GAS BRACKETS

Nos. 4853 and 4872 are finished in Old Brass

Nos. 4854, 4862 and 4874 in Satin Gold

No.	Style	Projection	Spread	Lights	Price	Code Word
4853	Colonial	15 inches	15 inches	2	$21.00	Dejurabor
				3	26.00	Delenirent
4854	Empire	12 "		1	3.25	Dejauger
4862	Renaissance	10 "		1	6.00	Dejectamus
4872	Colonial	11¾ "		1	4.50	Dejuncto
4874	Rococo	10 "		1	9.00	Dejuncturo

Glassware extra except Imitation Candles and Bobeches for No. 4853 included

GAS BRACKETS

Finished in Rich Gilt or Old Brass

No.	Style	Projection	Spread	Lights	Price	Code Word
4948	Gothic	12 inches	15 inches	3	$20.00	Demeterent
4951	Gothic	11 "	17 "	2	14.50	Demoticus
				3	15.00	Demotique

Glassware extra

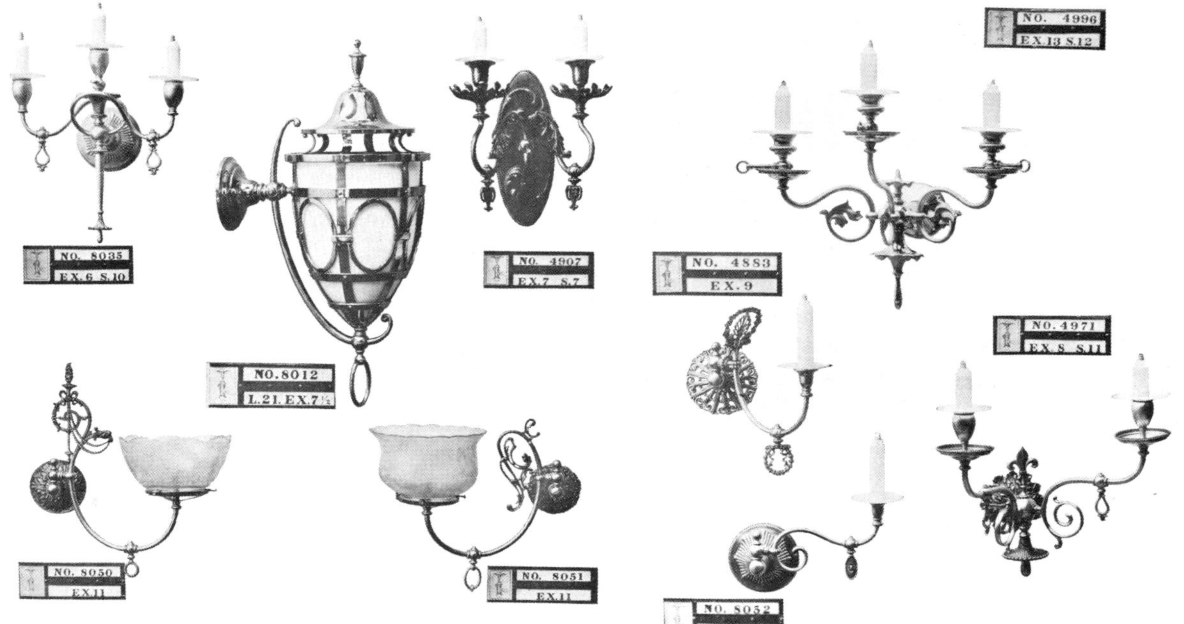

GAS BRACKETS

Nos. 4907, 8050 and 8051 are finished in Satin Gold
Nos. 8012 and 8035 in Old Brass

No.	Style	Projection	Length	Dia. of Globe	Spread	Lights	Price	Code Word
4907	Louis XV	7 inches			7 inches	2	$16.00	Demurring
8012	Colonial	7½ "	21 inches	7 inches		1	20.00	Denuberent
8035	Colonial	6 "			10 "	3	15.00	Dentones
8050	Empire	11 "				1	5.00	Denuam
8051	Rococo	11 "				1	3.75	Denubendo

Imitation Candles and Bobeches for Nos. 4907 and 8035 and
Straw Opalescent Globe for No. 8012 included
Glassware for Nos. 8050 and 8051 extra

GAS BRACKETS

No. 4883 is finished in Satin Gold
Nos. 4971, 4996 and 8052 in Old Brass

No.	Style	Projection	Spread	Lights	Price	Code Word
4883	Empire	9 inches		1	$ 4.50	Delenitrix
4971	Colonial	8 "	11 inches	2	15.00	Demptos
4996	Gothic	13 "	12 "	2	16.00	Demurmuro
				3	21.00	Demurrable
8052	Colonial	10 "		1	4.00	Deportaret

Imitation Candles and Bobeches included

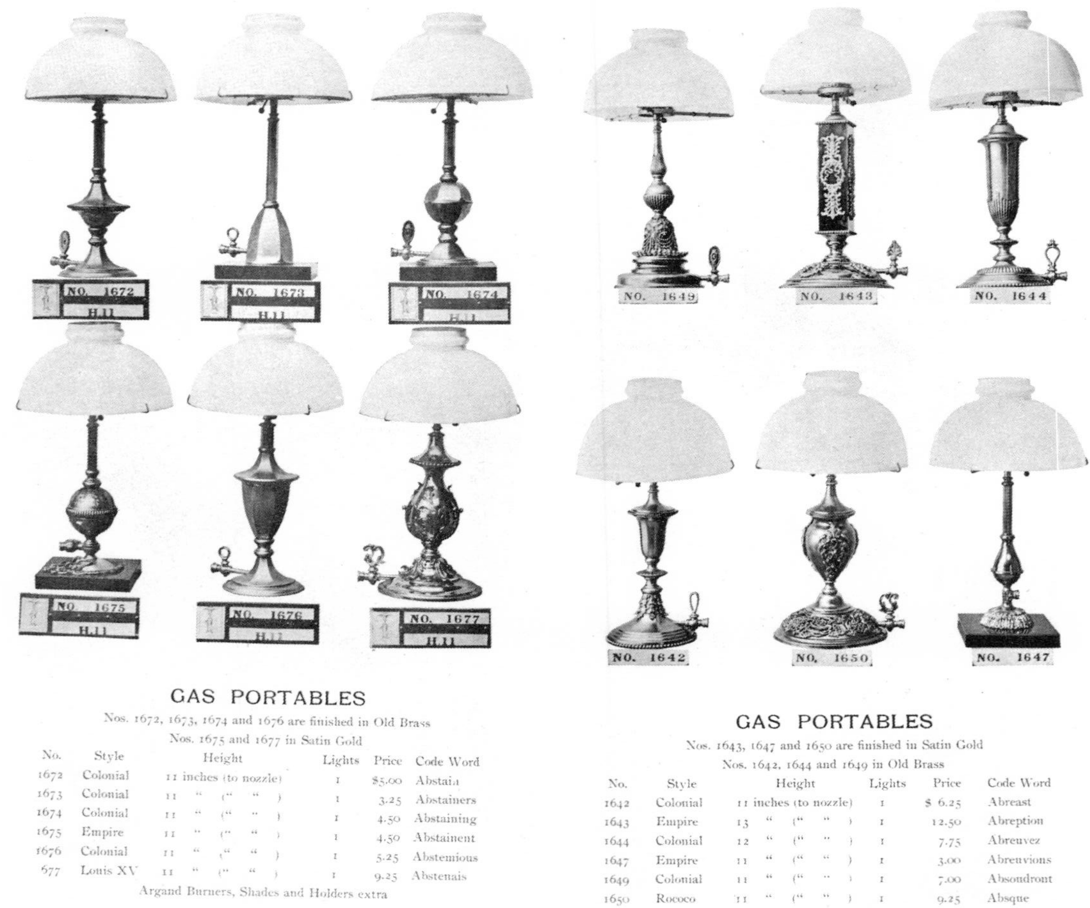

GAS PORTABLES

Nos. 1672, 1673, 1674 and 1676 are finished in Old Brass
Nos. 1675 and 1677 in Satin Gold

No.	Style	Height	Lights	Price	Code Word
1672	Colonial	11 inches (to nozzle)	1	$5.00	Abstain
1673	Colonial	11 " (" ")	1	3.25	Abstainers
1674	Colonial	11 " (" ")	1	4.50	Abstaining
1675	Empire	11 " (" ")	1	4.50	Abstainent
1676	Colonial	11 " (" ")	1	5.25	Abstemious
677	Louis XV	11 " (" ")	1	9.25	Abstenais

Argand Burners, Shades and Holders extra

GAS PORTABLES

Nos. 1643, 1647 and 1650 are finished in Satin Gold
Nos. 1642, 1644 and 1649 in Old Brass

No.	Style	Height	Lights	Price	Code Word
1642	Colonial	11 inches (to nozzle)	1	$ 6.25	Abreast
1643	Empire	13 " (" ")	1	12.50	Abreption
1644	Colonial	12 " (" ")	1	7.75	Abreuvez
1647	Empire	11 " (" ")	1	3.00	Abreuvions
1649	Colonial	11 " (" ")	1	7.00	Absoudront
1650	Rococo	11 " (" ")	1	9.25	Absque

Argand Burners, Shades and Holders extra

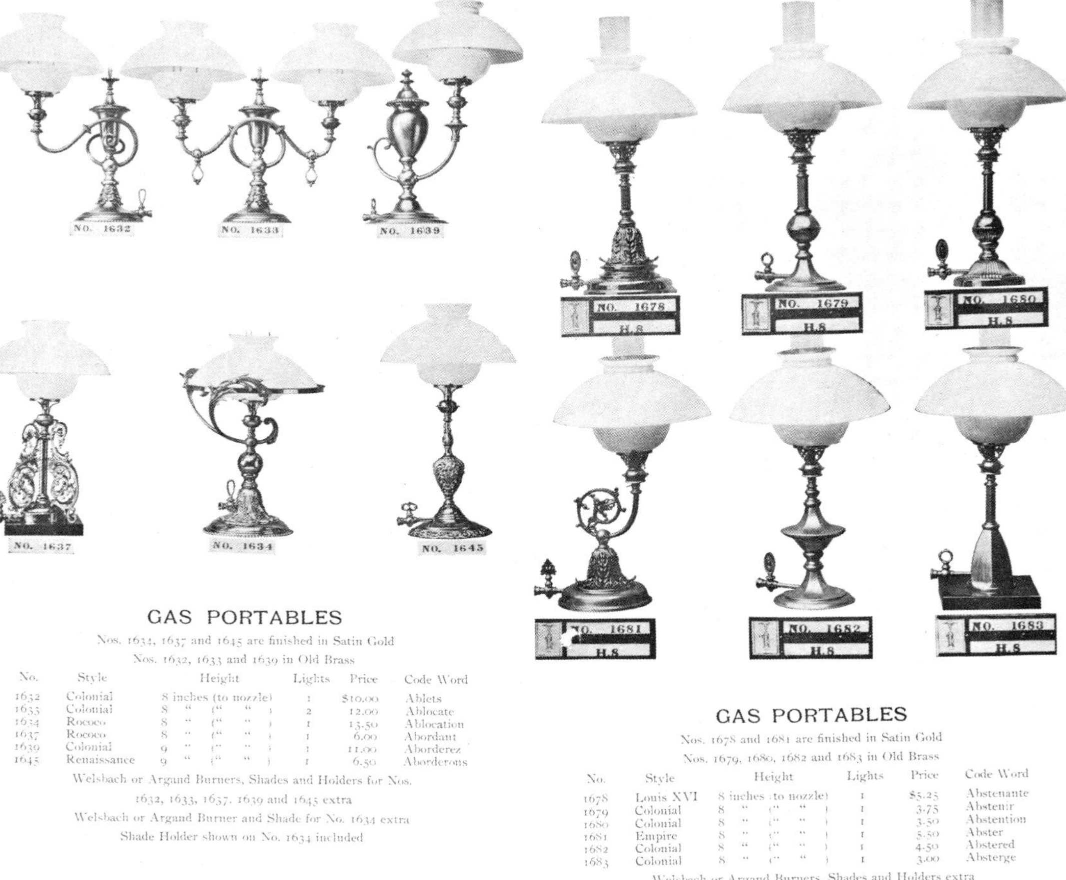

GAS PORTABLES

Nos. 1634, 1637 and 1645 are finished in Satin Gold

Nos. 1632, 1633 and 1639 in Old Brass

No.	Style	Height	Lights	Price	Code Word
1632	Colonial	8 inches (to nozzle)	1	$10.00	Ablets
1633	Colonial	8 " (" ")	2	12.00	Ablocate
1634	Rococo	8 " (" ")	1	13.50	Ablocation
1637	Rococo	8 " (" ")	1	6.00	Abordant
1639	Colonial	9 " (" ")	1	11.00	Aborderez
1645	Renaissance	9 " (" ")	1	6.50	Aborderons

Welsbach or Argand Burners, Shades and Holders for Nos. 1632, 1633, 1637, 1639 and 1645 extra

Welsbach or Argand Burner and Shade for No. 1634 extra

Shade Holder shown on No. 1634 included

GAS PORTABLES

Nos. 1678 and 1681 are finished in Satin Gold

Nos. 1679, 1680, 1682 and 1683 in Old Brass

No.	Style	Height	Lights	Price	Code Word
1678	Louis XVI	8 inches (to nozzle)	1	$5.25	Abstenante
1679	Colonial	8 " (" ")	1	3.75	Abstenir
1680	Colonial	8 " (" ")	1	3.50	Abstention
1681	Empire	8 " (" ")	1	5.50	Abster
1682	Colonial	8 " (" ")	1	4.50	Abstered
1683	Colonial	8 " (" ")	1	3.00	Absterge

Welsbach or Argand Burners, Shades and Holders extra

GAS PORTABLES

Finished in Old Brass

No.	Style	Height	Lights	Price	Code Word
15031	Colonial	19 inches (to top of shade)	1	$13.00	Acrotomous
15040	L'Art Nouveau	20 " (" " " ")	1	26.00	Acteth
15041	Mission	18 " (" " " ")	1	22.50	Acteurs
15042	Mission	19 " (" " " ")	1	12.00	Actifs
15043	Mission	20 " (" " " ")	1	15.00	Acting
15044	Moorish	22 " (" " " ")	1	15.00	Actiniform

Welsbach Burners and Shades extra except Art Glass Shade for No. 15041 included

10 inch Mosaic Art Glass Dome for No. 15043 $17.50 extra

GAS PORTABLES

Finished in Old Brass

No.	Style	Height	Lights	Price	Code Word
1777	Gothic	11 inches (to nozzle)	1	$11.25	Acronycal
1781	Colonial	12 " (" ")	1	9.00	Acropolis
1793	Flemish	12 " (" ")	1	15.00	Acrostic
1794	Renaissance	12 " (" ")	1	12.00	Acrosti[illegible]
1798	Renaissance	13 " (" ")	1	10.00	Acroterial
1799	Renaissance	13 " (" ")	1	18.00	A[illegible]rium

Welsbach Burners and Shades extra

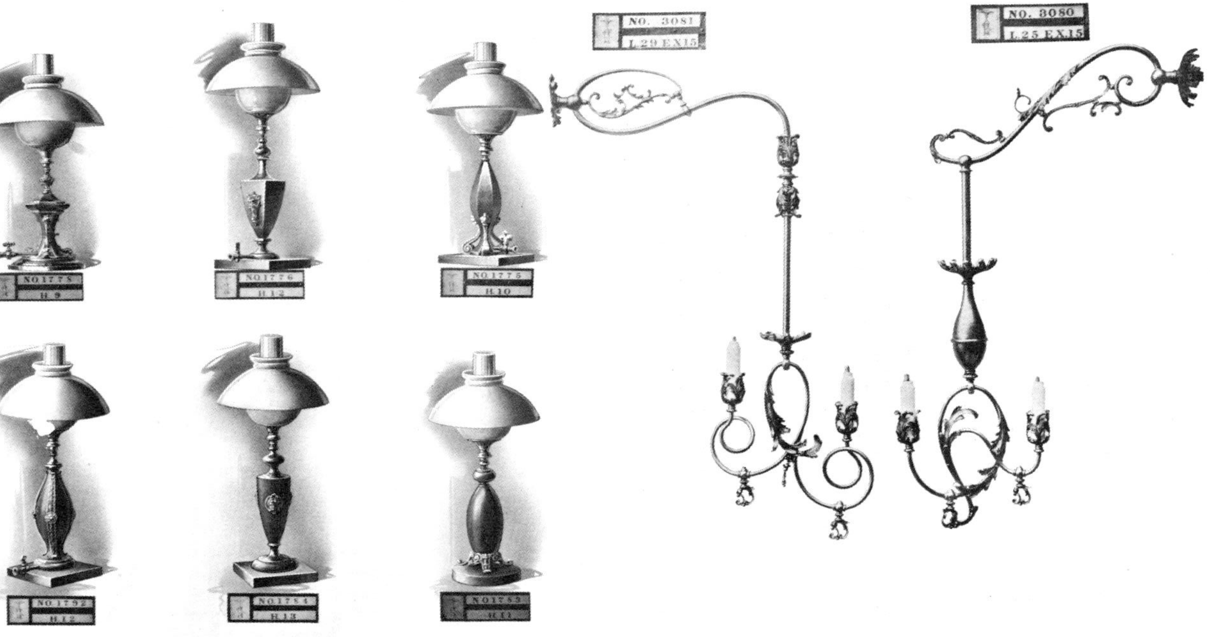

GAS PORTABLES

Finished in Old Brass

No.	Style	Height	Lights	Price	Code Word
1775	Gothic	10 inches (to nozzle)	1	$ 9.00	Acrobatic
1776	Renaissance	12 " (" ")	1	7.75	Acrochord
1778	Renaissance	9 " (" ")	1	10.00	Acrogen
1783	Renaissance	11 " (" ")	1	9.00	Acrogenous
1784	Colonial	13 " (" ")	1	7.75	Acrolith
1792	Colonial	12 " (" ")	1	9.00	Acromion

Welsbach Burners and Shades extra

GAS TOILETS

Finished in Satin Gold

No.	Style	Length	Projection	Spread	Lights	Price	Code Word
3080	Louis XV	25 inches	15 inches	7½ inches	2	$18.00	Earnest
3081	Louis XV	29 "	15 "	7½ "	2	17.00	Eavesboard

Imitation Candles included

NO. 6144

GAS CHANDELIER

LOUIS XIV

Finished in Satin Gold

Length 72 inches Spread 30 inches

6 Lights $200.00 Retnaret

Glass Shades extra

NO. 6185

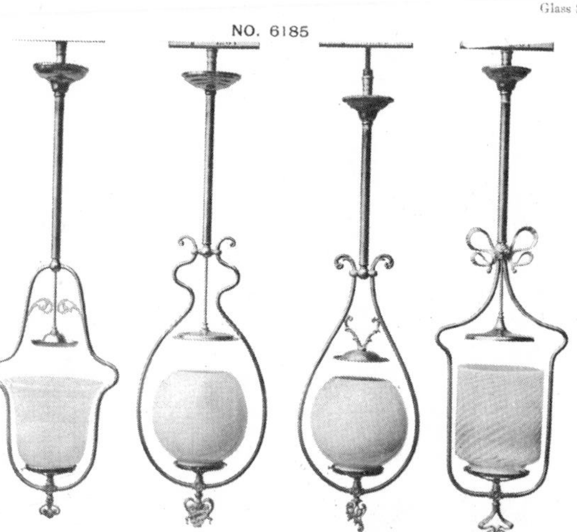

GAS HALL LIGHTS

Finished in Old Brass or Polished Brass

No.	Length	Lights	Price	Code Word
2431	37 inches	1	$7.25	Carina
2432	37 "	1	7.25	Carinarian
2433	35 "	1	7.00	Carinated
2434	37 "	1	6.75	Carinatin

Straw Opalescent Globe for No. 2431 included

Glassware for Nos. 2432, 2433 and 2434 extra

GAS LANTERNS

No. 2402 is finished in Satin Gold

No. 2411 is Wrought Iron but can be made in Old Brass at the same pric

No.	Style	Length	Lights	Price	Code Word
2402	Rococo	38 inches	1	$18.00	Caridean
2411	Colonial	38 "	1	33.50	Carides

Opalescent Globe for No. 2402 and Roughed Inside Globe for No. 2411 in

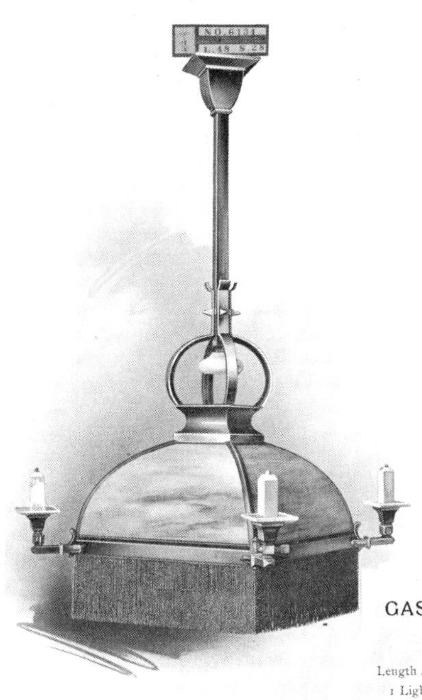

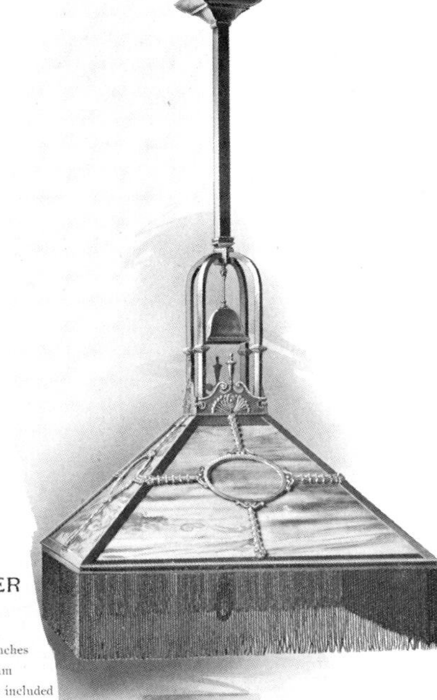

NO. 6186
GAS CHANDELIER

COLONIAL

Finished in Old Brass

Length 42 inches Spread 22 inches

1 Light $42.00 Retusarum

Art Glass Dome and Seed Bead Fringe included

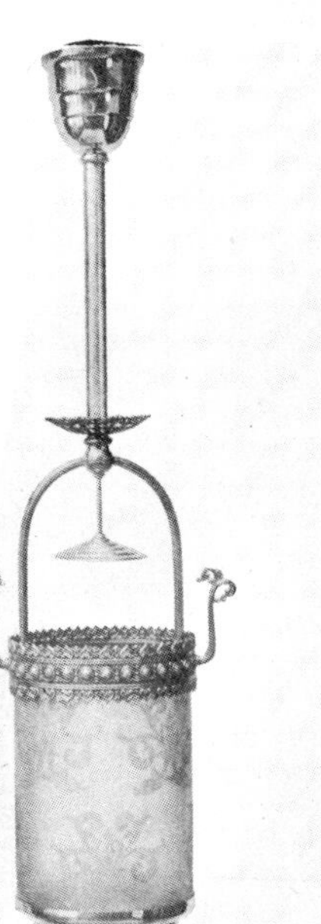

GAS LANTERNS

No. 2333 is finished in Satin Gold

No. 2350 in Old Brass

No.	Style	Length	Lights	Price	Code Word
2333	Empire	39 inches	1	$13.50	Caribon
2350	Colonial	38 "	1	28.00	Careworn

Silver Etched Globe for No. 2333 and 6½ x 8¼ Beveled Glass (Roughed Inside) for No. 2350 included

GAS LANTERNS

Finished in Old Brass or Wrought Iron

No.	Style	Length	Spread	Lights	Price	Code Word
2403	Mediaeval	42 inches	9½ inches	1	$24.00	Caries
2407	Colonial	36 "	15 "	1	38.00	Carillon

Roughed Inside Cylinder for No. 2403 and 7 x 9 Glass (also Imitation Candle) for No. 2407 included

GAS NEWELS

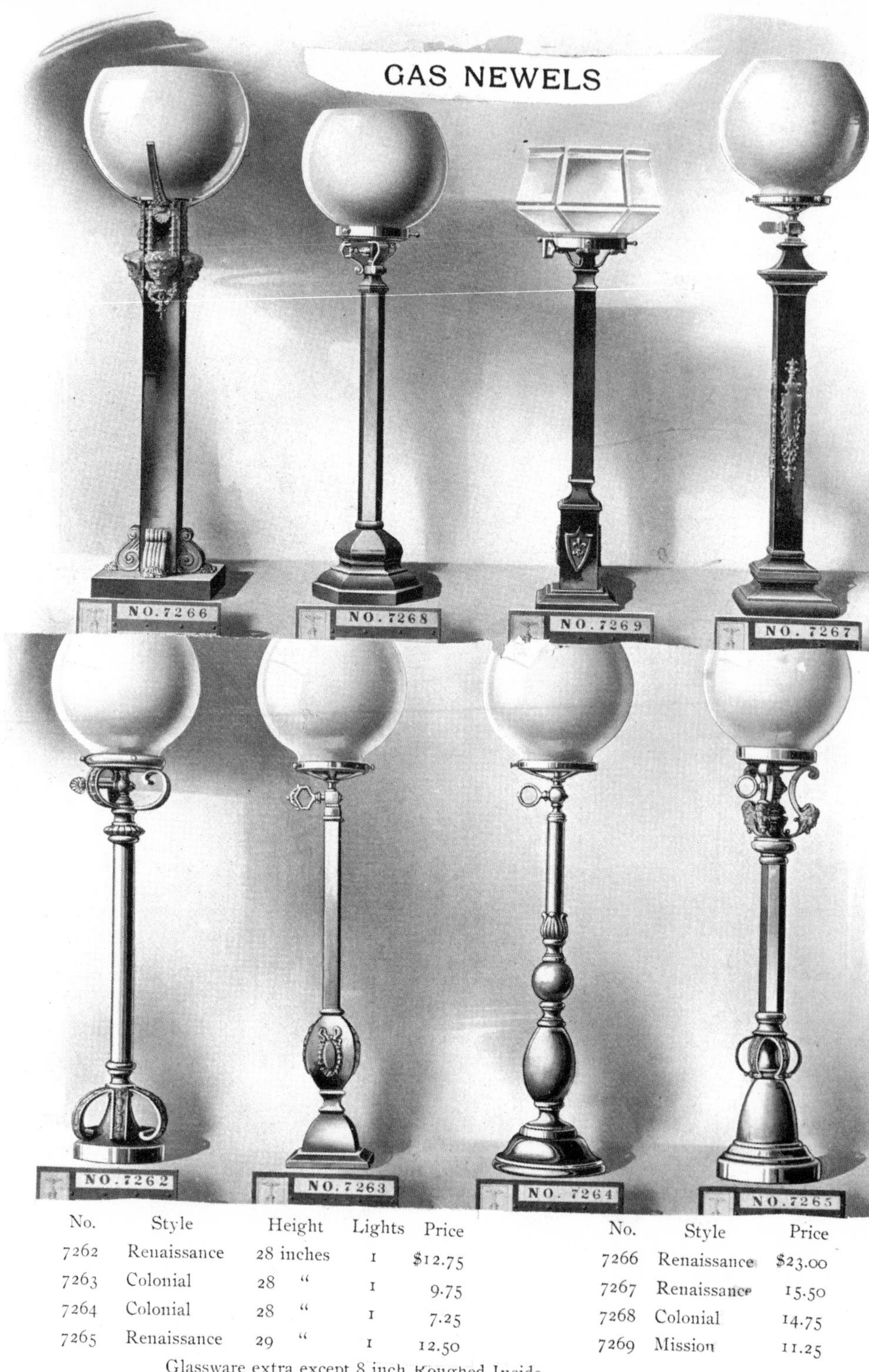

No.	Style	Height	Lights	Price
7262	Renaissance	28 inches	1	$12.75
7263	Colonial	28 "	1	9.75
7264	Colonial	28 "	1	7.25
7265	Renaissance	29 "	1	12.50

No.	Style	Price
7266	Renaissance	$23.00
7267	Renaissance	15.50
7268	Colonial	14.75
7269	Mission	11.25

Glassware extra except 8 inch Roughed Inside

VE present a design for a gas-chandelier selected from the ibition-rooms of Messrs. Archer, coast & Co., of New York. It n the style of the time of Louis V., and is intended for the draw-room or library. With the ex-sion centre-light attachment, which known as the "Excelsior," and ented under that name in May, 4, it is also especially adapted for in the dining-room. The attach-nt admits of the lowering of the tre-light, an argand burner, from main body of the chandelier to desirable distance. The mech-sm of the attachment is plain and ple in construction, and its ope-on is free from many of the in-ate contrivances peculiar to slide-ndeliers as heretofore made. The in body of the chandelier has six ners springing from the same nber of upright bars grouped und the central standard. The ns are ornamented with enfoliated igns under each globe, which are ported by gracefully-curved rods, minating in sharp points, and serv- as a relief to the more positive s of the former. The general ect of the chandelier is light and ceful, and yet the central stand-

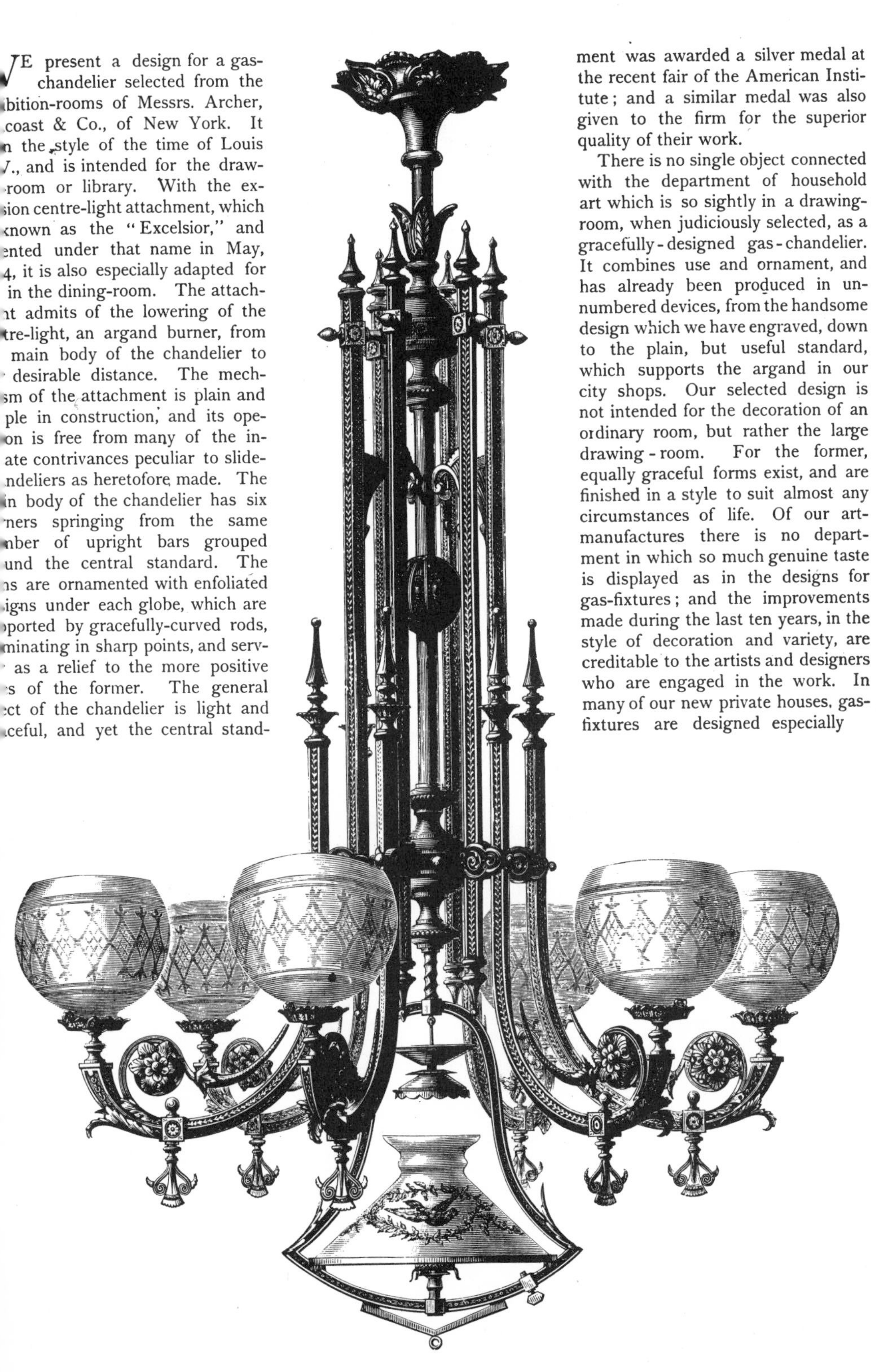

ment was awarded a silver medal at the recent fair of the American Institute; and a similar medal was also given to the firm for the superior quality of their work.

There is no single object connected with the department of household art which is so sightly in a drawing-room, when judiciously selected, as a gracefully-designed gas-chandelier. It combines use and ornament, and has already been produced in unnumbered devices, from the handsome design which we have engraved, down to the plain, but useful standard, which supports the argand in our city shops. Our selected design is not intended for the decoration of an ordinary room, but rather the large drawing-room. For the former, equally graceful forms exist, and are finished in a style to suit almost any circumstances of life. Of our art-manufactures there is no department in which so much genuine taste is displayed as in the designs for gas-fixtures; and the improvements made during the last ten years, in the style of decoration and variety, are creditable to the artists and designers who are engaged in the work. In many of our new private houses, gas-fixtures are designed especially

5991½ 5984½ 5993½ 5994½

5991 5984 5993 5994

Plate A.

Phoenix Glass Company

4204½ 5724½ 5559½ 4847½

4204 5724 5559 4847

5705 4422 5721 5115

Plate B.

4962½ 5751½ 5216½ 5589½

4962 5751 5216 5589

5635 5656 5585 5703

Plate C.

5110½ 5649½ 5458½ 5874½

5110 5649 5458 5874

Chapter XIV
GAS LIGHT SHADES AND GLOBES

Functionally, gaslight shades were at first close approximates to those used on oil lamps. Both illuminants needed something to assure a steady flame and to keep out drafts. But whereas the kerosene lamp might use a glass chimney so as not to dim or diffuse its feeble light, the higher candle power of the gaslight (especially with a Welsbach mantle) made for glare. As a result we find relatively few gas shades, globes or domes in clear glass. Acid dipping could turn a clear lamp chimney or globe into a soft translucent shade. And, as time went on, more and more glass suppliers turned to colored, frosted, milkwhite and egg-shell effects, finally burst into an all-out blaze of color.

In making a study of all such shales, one should recall the period of their use. Mid-Victorians, like today, were gadget conscious—keen to adopt each new modernity; they also loved the gay use of color in the home. Furniture, utensils and even table glass bedecked in a riot of different hues. This is the period of **Victorian Art Glass** for the parlor what-not and whole sets of dishes in some colored glass pattern. By the 1880's, when gas lighting had really taken hold, it is not surprising that the open gas globes began to appear in Daisy and Button blue, Amerbina swirl and even as etched Cameo in color. We shall not here attempt to show all varieties of these glass shades that emerged in this era. Best that can be done in space at our disposal is to give a nomenclature to different types that are today collectable; if not now used on gas or converted electric fixtures, many serve as displays in the collector's 'display window.' Here are the styles:

A—**Globes for inverted burners,** or **Globes for upright incandescent burners**

B—**Decorated ball and bowl shades for table lamps** (similar to G.W.T.W.)

C—**Imitation candles & bobeches for gas burners**

D—**Etched white-glass globes**

E—**Rich cut-glass globes with bobeches for chandeliers**

F—**Smoke-shades and smoke-bells**

G—**Hall globes and chandelier domes**

H—**All others.**

A really undiscovered area in old lamp collecting is the shades and bottoms which went together to make a home table lamp in our gaslight era. A few would pass for kerosene lamps whose shades they imitated. Others struck out boldly for new decorative effects and these (see pages which follows) are among the most desirable to find. We have actually seen a

No. 6568
Etched, $8.40 per dozen
Entreaty { Telegraphic Code

No. 6483
Etched, $10.20 per dozen
Entreat { Telegraphic Code

No. 6220
Etched, $7.20 per dozen
Entrance { Telegraphic Code

No. 6964
Etched, $24.00 per dozen
Entomb { Telegraphic Code

No. 6043
Etched, $7.20 per dozen
Enthusiast { Telegraphic Code

No. 6475
Etched, $7.20 per dozen
Empiricism { Telegraphic Code

No. 8061
Etched, $12.00 per dozen
Entangle { Telegraphic Code

No. 6620
Roughed Inside, $4.80 per dozen
Entail { Telegraphic Code

No. 6410
Etched, $7.80 per dozen
Ensnare { Telegraphic Code

No. 8054
Etched, $7.20 per dozen
Enslave { Telegraphic Code

No. 6517
Roughed Inside, $9.00 per dozen
Ensconce { Telegraphic Code

No. 6409
Etched, $7.20 per dozen
Enshrine { Telegraphic Code

No. 776
Etched, $6.00 per dozen
Enrolment { Telegraphic Code

No. 961
Etched, $6.60 per dozen
Exemplary { Telegraphic Code

No. 739
Etched, $6.00 per dozen
Enrich { Telegraphic Code

No. 204
White Acid, $4.20 per dozen
Empirical { Telegraphic Code

No. 607
Etched, $7.80 per dozen
Enjoin { Telegraphic Code

No. 527
Etched, $6.60 per dozen
Evasion { Telegraphic Code

No. 993
Etched, $6.60 per dozen
Existence { Telegraphic Code

No. 984
Etched, $7.80 per dozen
Emphasis { Telegraphic Code

No. 449
White Acid, $4.20 per dozen
Evaporate { Telegraphic Code

No. 702
Etched, $6.00 per dozen
Empanel { Telegraphic Code

No. 756
Etched, $6.60 per dozen
Empaled { Telegraphic Code

No. 215
White Acid, $4.20 per dozen
Enliven { Telegraphic Code

No. 988
Etched, $6.00 per dozen
Exiled { Telegraphic Code

No. 68
Roughed Inside, $4.20 per dozen
Ethical { Telegraphic Code

No. 437
White Acid, $3.60 per dozen
Enlisted { Telegraphic Code

No. 705
Etched, $7.80 per dozen
Examiner { Telegraphic Code

No. 779
Etched, $6.60 per dozen
Exclusion { Telegraphic Code

No. 955
Etched, $6.00 per dozen
Execution { Telegraphic Code

Cameo Glass Vase used for a library lamp of the period with a matching faked cameo-etched shade. Look also for the **Lithopane Bases and shades** which sometimes appeared as gas lights in fine houses. Of course, some collectors would be content just with a true Daisy and Button blue-glass shade or one in Canary Cane. Yes, look for **pattern glass shades** in what is left from this gaslight era. With the light shining through them, they must have made even the darkest day of the Gray 90's Gay!

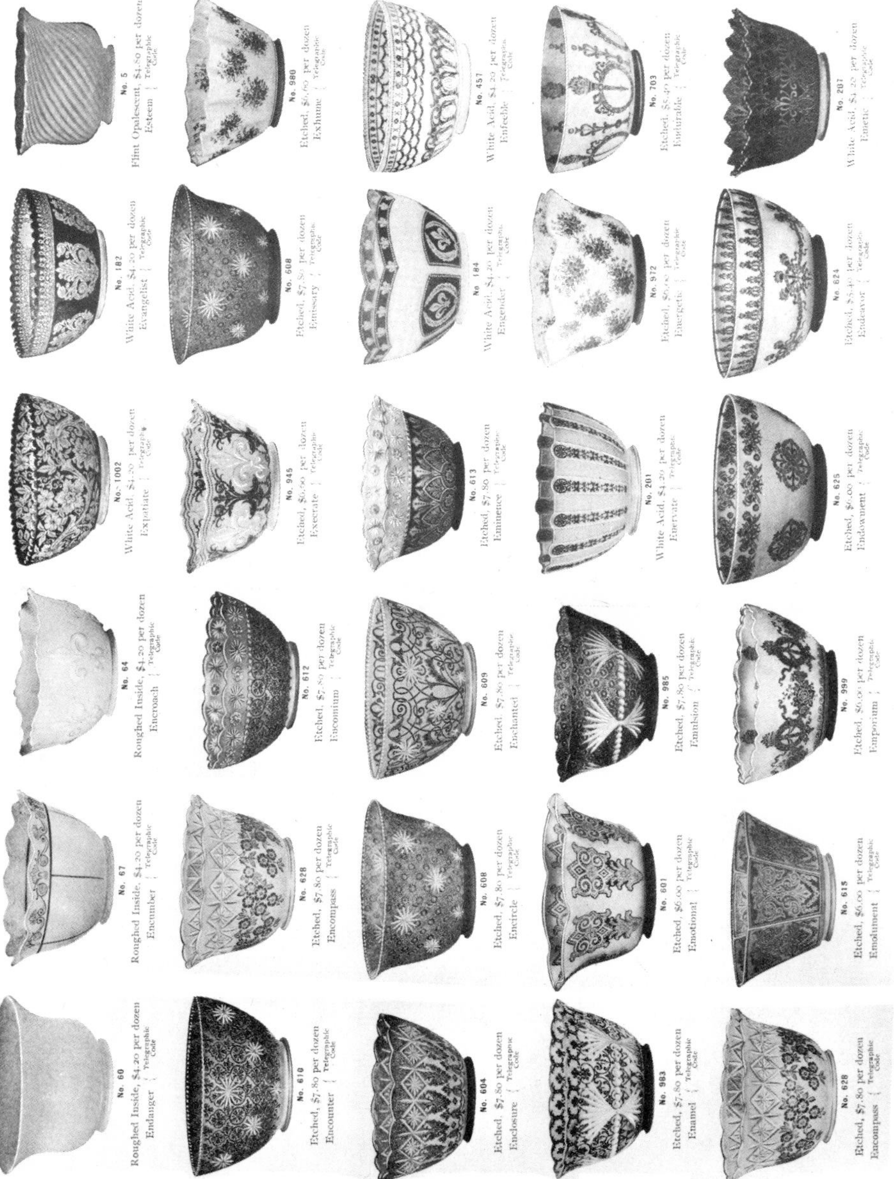

Nº 41

Nº CQ 307

Nº AA 307

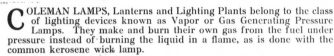

COLEMAN LAMPS, Lanterns and Lighting Plants belong to the class of lighting devices known as Vapor or Gas Generating Pressure Lamps. They make and burn their own gas from the fuel under pressure instead of burning the liquid in a flame, as is done with the common kerosene wick lamp.

Coleman Lamps are made with heavy, tight, metal tanks or founts so that the liquid cannot spill and so that the air pressure will feed the fuel to the burner. At the burner the fuel is converted into vapor and this vapor mixed with air, about 5 parts vapor, 95 parts air, forms a gas that is burned in the mantles, giving an extremely strong, bright, white light.

Mr. W. C. Coleman, inventor of the Gasoline Table Lamp and President of The Coleman Lamp Company. He perfected the match generating burner now used on all Quick-Lite Gas Lamps and Lanterns.

Thus a Coleman Lamp or Lighting System is, in reality, a small or miniature gas plant supplying a light superior to natural or city gas, serving its owner at a very low cost and if he be the proud possessor of a Coleman Lighting Plant he may attach to it a Coleman Stove on which his wife can cook in comfort on the hottest summer days.

Coleman Portable Lamps

Coleman Table Lamps, Lanterns, Portable Chandeliers, Portable Wall or Bracket Lamps, illustrated and described on pages 5 to 31 inclusive, are usually referred to as the Portable Line because each has its own fount for containing the fuel and so can be carried from place to place. This feature has made them popular but for lighting an entire home the complete lighting plants require less care and have the added advantage of making it possible to attach water heaters and burners or stoves for cooking.

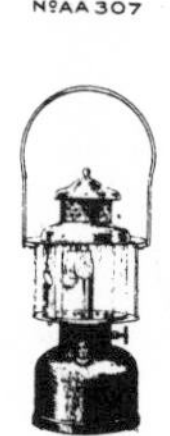

Nº QL 327

Coleman Lighting Plants

A Coleman Lighting Plant consists of a supply tank, the tubing for conducting the fuel to the fixture and the fixture which, in this catalog, includes the shade, or globe, and mantles (See opposite page). Plants can be made up low in price or as expensive as the taste may suggest.

Nº PQ 321

For Homes, Stores, Churches, Schools, Public Halls, Barber Shops and other business houses a Coleman Lighting Plant gives the greatest measure of satisfaction. The care and upkeep require but little time or expense as a tank of ample size will hold enough fuel to last a couple of weeks or even a month. Applying the pressure once a week is usually enough, while the care of the individual fixture has been reduced to the simple process of changing a generator, which, after six months use may become dirty.

A two or three light plant is often sufficient for the actual needs but we recommend plenty of fixtures. They give much better satisfaction than a plant of insufficient size.

Chapter XV

FROM GAS, ACETYLENE AND GASOLINE TO ELECTRICITY

Artificial lighting, especially that for streets and places outside the home, is full of unanswered questions. Why, for instance, did not the Romans with their engineering genius, develop more powerful street lights (including the use of natural gas and electrical effects generally known for an indefinite period back to ancient times). Gas and electricity clearly develop more candle power than oil; and candle power or wattage are measures of how bright a lamp is in connection with the equivalent number of candles. In any event it was not until the Nineteenth century that gas, acetylene and gasoline were sufficiently explored to make their commercial use feasible. Naturally there was great competition to replace the feeble candle and oil flame of the old lamp lighter with something more efficient. The start of public gas lighting dates from London in 1810 and in mid-century had spread to all major cities, including those in America. Most of these lights were piped from a central supply of artificially produced coal-water gas.

We have already reviewed the development of burners which made for more efficient use of the product; but the real competition in the latter part of Victoria's century came from that other upstart—**electricity.** Also at the same time kerosene was being improved for oil lamps in the home, naptha and gasoline were being extracted to produce a fuel which vaporized like gas in the lamp itself. We do not know if this gaseous fluid was used for street lighting but it did result in the **Coleman Gasoline Lantern and Table Models** which are still in use.

Around 1900 W. C. Coleman invented the safe gasoline table lamp with a match-generating burner that far excelled gas lights in brilliance (300 candle power). Requiring only the cheap replacement of its gas generator, this Company went on to produce **quicklite lanterns** and entire home lighting plants which were widely distributed and used in the rural West up to World War II. On accompanying pages we give the full accomplishments of Coleman lamps and lamp parts, all very desirable items for today's new collectors.

Also preceding the mass development of electricity for light, mention should be made of **acetylene** which had a brief vogue in the farm home, far from either a city-gas main or power-lines connected with a city's electric dynamos. Acetylene was a kind of hydro-carbon gas generated by calcium-carbide when decomposed by the action of water. Said to have been discovered by Edmond Davy in 1836, it was not developed until around 1862, when Berthelot piped the resulting vapor into his kitchen to light a simple gas burner. By 1892 a number of enterprising manufac-

No. 25W. CEILING FIXTURE.

A Beautiful Fixture for Dining or Living Room.
Torch Lighting Burner and Chain Pull or Regular Valve.

LIGHT—300 Candle Power.
SHADE—No. 315.
FINISH—Nickel Plate.
FUEL USED—Gasoline

MANTLES—2 No. 41.
FITTER—4⅞ Inches.
LENGTH—48 Inches.
SHIPPING WEIGHT—40 lbs.

CODE WORD—*Palace.*

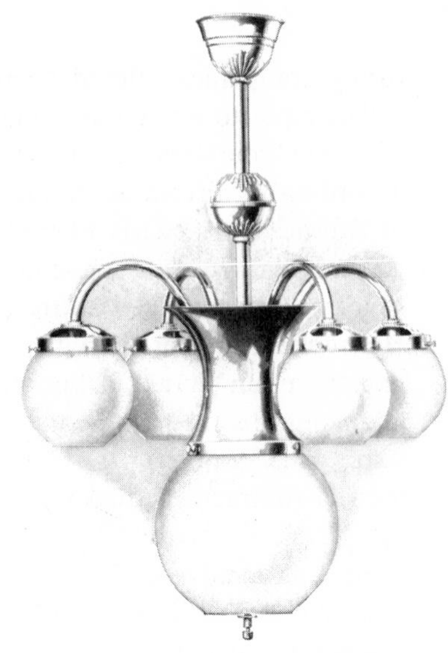

No. 17SA. CEILING CHANDELIER.

Brilliantly Lights a Space 30 Feet in Diameter.
One Burner Serves Entire Fixture. Lights with Floor Torch.

LIGHT—1400 Candle Power.
GLOBES—1 No. 78 and 4 No. 60.
FINISH—Nickel Plate.
FUEL USED—Gasoline

MANTLES—7 No. 41.
FITTER—4⅝-3⅝ Inches.
LENGTH—24 Inches.
SHIPPING WEIGHT—16 lbs.

CODE WORD—*Primer.*

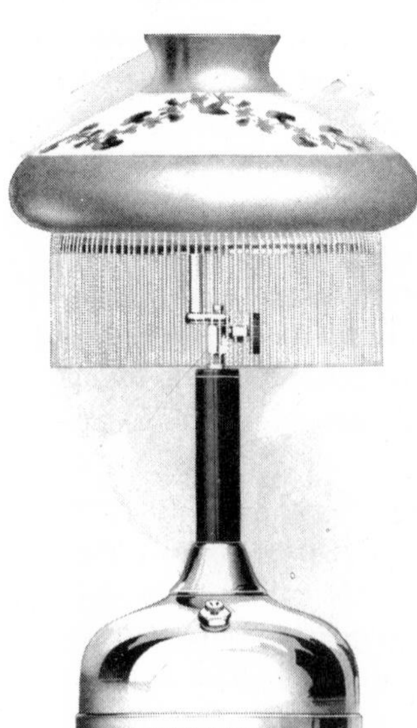

No. CQ314B. QUICK-LITE.

Hand Painted, Straw Color, Vine Green and Red.
Has Match Lighting Burner—No Alcohol Torch Required.

LIGHT—300 Candle Power.
SHADE—Hand Painted Vine.
FINISH—Nickel Plate.
FUEL USED—Gasoline.

DIAM. OF FOUNT—8 Inches.
CAPACITY—3 Pints.
HEIGHT—20 Inches.
SHIPPING WEIGHT—12 lbs.

CODE WORD—*Lifelike.*

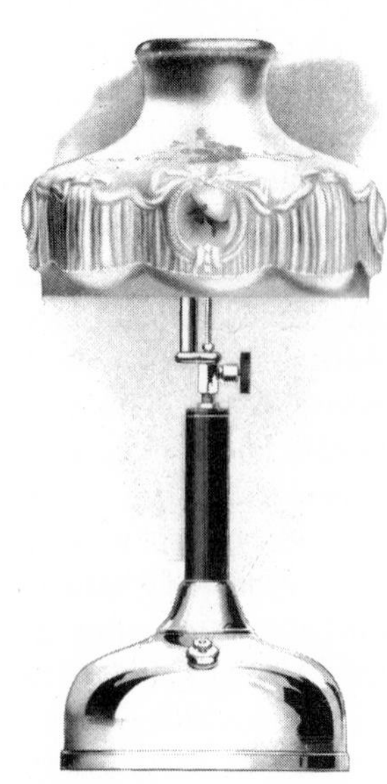

No. CQ318. QUICK-LITE.

Produces a Soft Mellow Light.
Has Match Lighting Burner—No Alcohol Torch Required.

LIGHT—300 Candle Power.
SHADE—Brown and Tan.
FINISH—Nickel Plate.
FUEL USED—Gasoline.

DIAM. OF FOUNT—8 Inches.
CAPACITY—3 Pints.
HEIGHT—20 Inches.
SHIPPING WEIGHT—10 lbs.

CODE WORD—*Liberal.*

turing companies offered "complete home installation with tank in the cellar, pipes to every room and the possibility of non-portable illumination wherever you wish it. Unfortunately, these systems did not always work according to directions. Many farmers were afraid to use them "after one or two blow-ups nearly burned the place down."

Acetylene lighting (in country house installations for which gas was generated more or less on the spot) was soon superceded first by the **Delco Houseplant System,** in which storage batteries were kept charged by a generator run by a gasoline motor. Whenever house lights began to dim, one would have to hurry and charge the batteries again. You can still find some road-shows run by Delco, and the acetylene method is sometimes used in contractor's roadside lights. Bicycle lamps today are usually lighted by electric flashlight batteries. However, in the 1890's (when cycling became a national vogue) most bicycles carried an **acetylene lamp.** These today (along with those made for the early cars) make fine collector items.

Butane was another gaseous fuel used in the late Nineteenth century for illumination (now called 'propane' and used primarily for cooking). Butane (its liquid form vaporizing into gas on release) was first used in places where a coal-gas supply was unobtainable and where the illuminant could not be piped or wired from a distant central source for use in the home. This idea of selling portable gas was anticipated in the mid-Nineteenth century when a company tried to put its manufactured gas into cylinders placed near the house or shop of the consumer and connected to pipes leading to gas jets inside. This enterprise was then a failure. Today, butane and propane gas cylinders mounted outside the house or in-the-ground are big business, as people move away from a large city's source of gas supply. It is, indeed, about the only gas which still has a growing market.

To be complete, the story of **electricity** would take an entire book by itself. We are not here concerned to trace the electrical development as such or enter into the technical details of electric lighting. The story of the lamp could not be told, however, without some reference to this new light-source which by its universality did more to cause the disappearance of primitive oil lighting than anything else. Benjamin Franklin's experiments discovered the secret of nature's electricity and Sir Humphry Davy in 1800 showed how to develop current commercially from volta cells consisting of two unlike metals immersed in an acid solution. As early as 1808 scientists saw the possibility of using electricity for producing light. But the open **carbon-arc light** produced in these laboratories remained there for many years thereafter. Save for a few experimental applications, it was not until 1876 that the first definite electric light appeared outside the laboratory. This was called **Jablochkoff's Candle** and consisted of two carbon-rods placed side by side with an electric spark passing between them to produce the flashing glow. It was tried out for street lighting in Paris and in London (with minimal success due to rapid oxidation of the

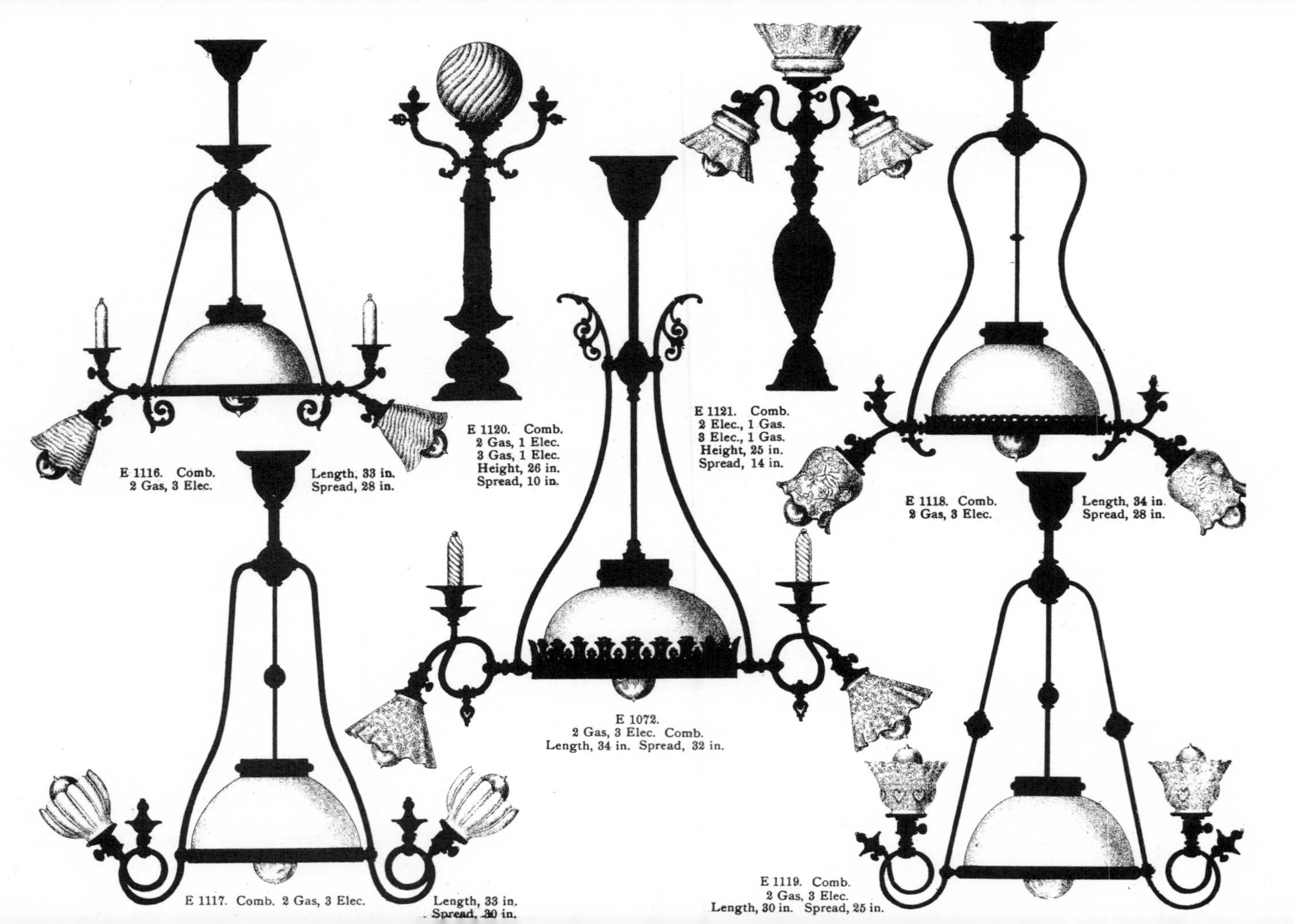

E 1116. Comb.
2 Gas, 3 Elec.
Length, 33 in.
Spread, 28 in.

E 1120. Comb.
2 Gas, 1 Elec.
3 Gas, 1 Elec.
Height, 26 in.
Spread, 10 in.

E 1121. Comb.
2 Elec., 1 Gas.
3 Elec., 1 Gas.
Height, 25 in.
Spread, 14 in.

E 1118. Comb.
2 Gas, 3 Elec.
Length, 34 in.
Spread, 28 in.

E 1072.
2 Gas, 3 Elec. Comb.
Length, 34 in. Spread, 32 in.

E 1117. Comb. 2 Gas, 3 Elec.
Length, 33 in.
Spread, 30 in.

E 1119. Comb.
2 Gas, 3 Elec.
Length, 30 in. Spread, 25 in.

electrodes). In America, Brush invented a more practical arc-lamp than these earlier types. Ordinary household use was, of course, entirely unsatisfactory, largely because of the arm's size and its almost constant need of attention. Brush first lighted the Public Square in Cleveland in this open-to-the-air manner and by 1879 his improved system was so satisfactory, most large communities substituted the carbon-arc lamp for street lighting instead of street lamps burning the often more costly coal-gas.

At the same time, other inventors tackled the problem of producing an incandescent lamp wherein the electric charge would cause a filament to glow in a vacuum. The credit for the first introduction of a practical electric lamp for home was once the subject of keen controversy between England and the United Statse. Both Swan in England and Edison in America were experimenting with a carbon-filament in a vacuum tube which could light-up when an electric current passed through it. It was Edison, however, who produced the first 16-candle power lamp with a carbonized bamboo filament that could stand the strain of repeated onslaughts of current without breaking. **Edison's pear-shaped bulb,** closely approaching the form of the modern incandescent lamp, received worldwide patent rights in 1879. By 1882 Edison had opened the first public electric supply station in New York City and then the race was on to convert the gas mains of the house and street into conductors for the two-way wiring system (positive and negative pole) needed to light a bulb when the generators were running and power flowed through the wires. Later electrical developments which followed include the **Jandus arc lamp** of 1893, a successful closed arc-type lamp.

Despite constant improvement in incandescent lamps, however, the arc lamp was supreme for high-powered lighting until World War I. In 1914 a **gas-filled incandescent lamp** arrived, giving over 2,000 candle-power illumination if needed. Today is the era of luminous gas discharge, the **mercury vapor lamp** of 1900 and **Neon lamp** of 1932. Some of these early electric arc and luminous lamp devices are shown in pictures, but their interest is for the scientist rather than the collector.

FIG. 5

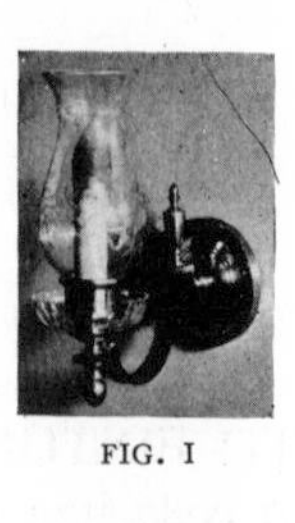
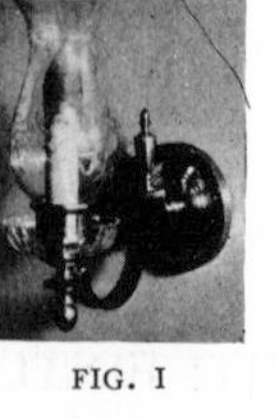

FIG. 1

FIG. 2

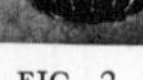

FIG. 3

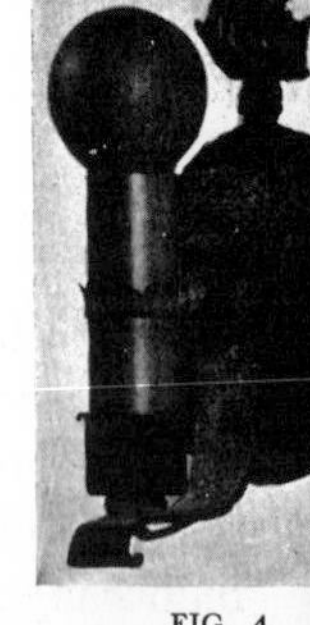

FIG. 4

FIG. 6

FIG. 7

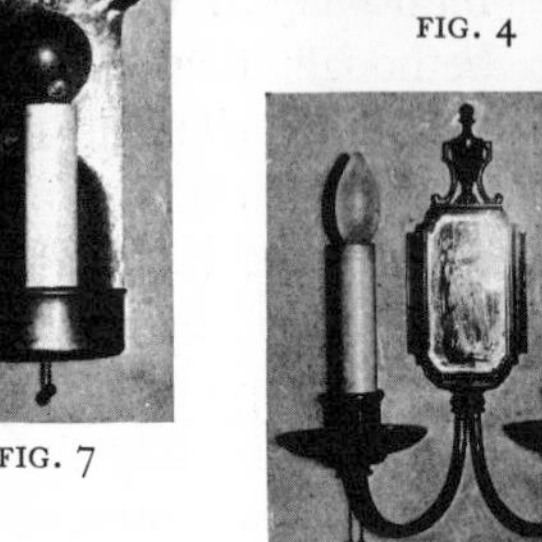

FIG. 8

FIG. 9

FIG. 10

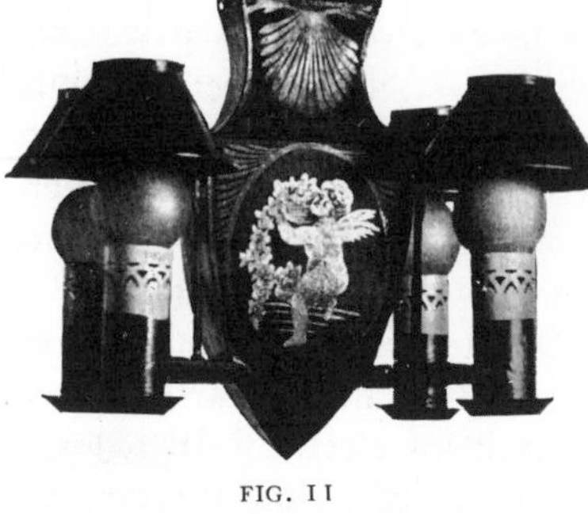

FIG. 11

FIG. 12

FIG. 13

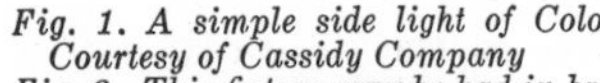

Lighting-Fixtures

Fig. 1. A simple side light of Colonial brass and ebony. Courtesy of Cassidy Company

Fig. 2. This fixture may be had in brass, antique or Colonial finish, or in pewter finish. Courtesy of Cassidy Company

Fig. 3. This fixture like an old candle stand comes in brass, ordinary or antique finish or in antique pewter finish. Courtesy of Cassidy Company

Fig. 4. A fixture of hand-wrought iron with ship in burnt brass. Courtesy of Bigelow, Kennard & Co.

Fig. 5. This lantern comes in several sizes and will fit in almost anywhere. Courtesy of Bigelow, Kennard & Co.

Fig. 6. This sconce is made of hard wrought iron. Courtesy of Bigelow, Kennard & Co.

Fig. 7. A somewhat similar sconce in brass, antique brass or antique pewter finish. Courtesy of Cassidy Company

Fig. 8. An excellent two-light fixture in brass, Colonial or antique finish, or in enamel colors. Courtesy of Cassidy Company

Fig. 9. Similar to No. 4, in hand-wrought iron and burnt brass. Courtesy of Bigelow, Kennard & Co.

Fig. 10. Of the same materials as No. 7. Courtesy of Cassidy Company

Fig. 11. A hanging fixture of red or black painted tin, with gold decorations. Courtesy of Bigelow, Kennard & Co.

Fig. 12. Of brass, antique brass or antique pewter. Courtesy of Cassidy Company

Fig. 13. An inexpensive iron fixture. Courtesy of Bigelow, Kennard & Co.

Fig. 14. A charming lamp of antique brass with a painted tin shade. Courtesy of Bigelow, Kennard & Co.

Fig. 15. A fixture of red or black tin with gold decoration, designed for candle bulb. Courtesy of Bigelow, Kennard & Co.

FIG. 14

FIG. 15

Chapter XVI
EARLY ELECTRIC (CANDLE-LIGHT) FIXTURES

To some it may seem a little premature to start collecting early electric light fixtures. But what an array there is, once you begin to study their development. The first electric house lights were nothing more than a naked bulb hanging by wires from the ceiling. More aesthetically oriented souls bethought themselves to adapt the kerosene parlor lamps of G.W.W. culture by placing an incandescent bulb inside the flowered globes or even in the glass bowl surrounding the old brass oil font. This device not only covered the bulb's nakedness; it enabled one to conceal the ugly wires under a table cover. Many householders had the wires pulled through existing gas piping with the electric socket attached to the now unused gas burner. Naturally the gas company fought back against the electric company's home intrusion with combination fixtures aimed to show that one had better keep the gas in case of electric power failure (not at all uncommon). However, the true start for electric fixture collecting is with those that were specifically designed for the new illuminant. Everyone, of course, wants to collect signed Tiffany lamps in silver, in gold, in copper (though the interest there has been more in the shade than the fixture). Almost equal interest centers in Steuben Art Glass shades. Just look at the variety of table lamps that command attention from old catalog pages! Then turn to the real gem of all (fixture wise),—the candle type socket that was specifically designed for electric light bulbs.

It is one of the anachronisms of technical progress in any field that art enthusiasts of the period will try to affect a throwback to former times. The first automobiles were horseless carriages, complete with dashboard for concealing the radiator. Likewise in the development of electric lighting, many interior decorators and designers sought to ignore contemporary gas and oil fixtures and to give the incandescent bulb the pretentions of even earlier candlelight days. The use of the simulated candle socket (in which the bulbs were first screwed and then covered by hooded candleshades goes back at least to 1900; but reached its peak of artistic development in the 1920's. By that time we find a wide variety of floor and table lamps, ceiling and wall fixtures that attempt to look like a cluster of candles whose flames were concealed by a 'shade' or a 'shield.' Eventually, the electric bulb was perfected which would itself simulate the candle's feeble flame. Only then, of course, could one have the unshaded electrified reproductions of Seventeenth century glass chandeliers and wall sconces. Before that time lies about 25 years of electro-candlestick creations many in solid brass or in copper and now prime collector items.

The author is not sure how this simulation of the candle and candle-

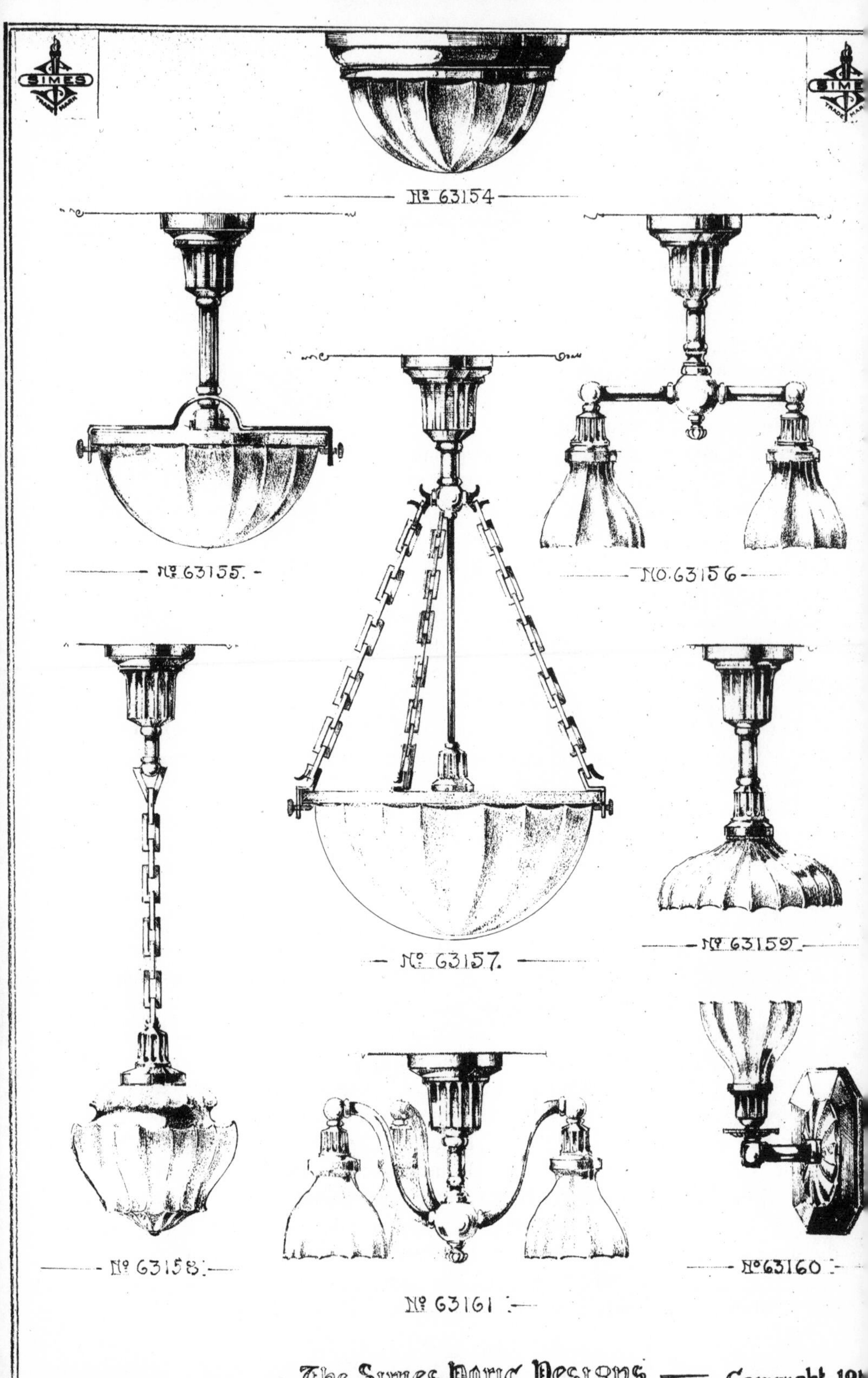
SIMES
TRADE MARK
SIMES
TRADE MARK
No. 63154
No. 63155.
No. 63156
No. 63157.
No. 63159
No. 63158.
No. 63160
No. 63161
Scale. 3". 1 Ft.
The Simes Doric Designs
Copyright 19

Pen drawings from photographs to bring out detail when printed on other than enamel or coated paper

A MAIL ORDER CATALOGUE PAGE

Aladdin Mission Nine Piece Electric Fixture Set $24.80

A beautifully designed set of pure mission type, a very popular design for use in bungalows. Within the last year this style of fixture has come into general use.

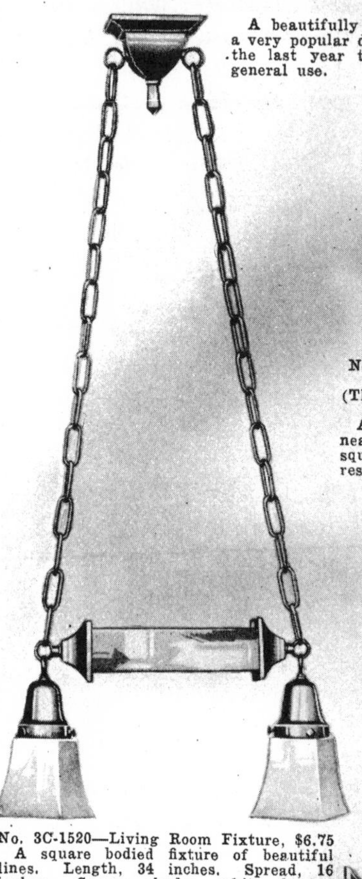

No. 3C-1530—Chamber Fixtures, $1.65 each
(Three of these furnished with each set)
A very practical as well as neat looking fixture with square glass shade to match rest of set.

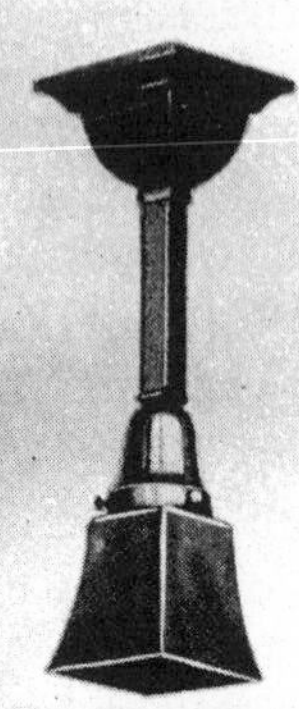

No. 3C-1524—Kitchen Fixture, $1.80
A one-light kitchen fixture made to match the rest of the set.

No. 3C-1528—Hall Fixture, $2.25
Furnished with a closed square ball to match other glassware of set.

No. 3C-1520—Living Room Fixture, $6.75
A square bodied fixture of beautiful lines. Length, 34 inches. Spread, 16 inches. Square shades, white frosted inside.

No. 3C-1522—Dining Room Fixture, $5.75
A beautiful fixture of distinctive design. Massive square body with square glass shades to match rest of set. Length, 34 inches. Spread, 16 inches.

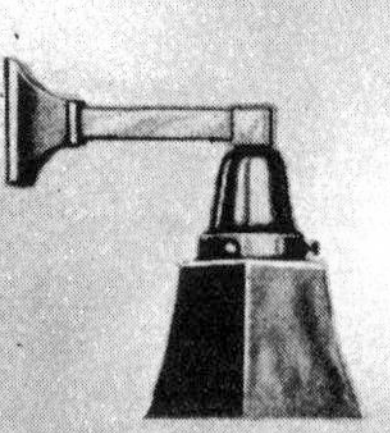

No. 3C-1532—Bathroom Fixture, $1.50

ALL FIXTURES WIRED COMPLETE WITH SOCKETS ASSEMBLED READY TO HANG

No. 3C-1526—Porch Bracket, $2.75
A substantial square fixture made of cast iron.

No. 3C-1534—Nine Piece Mission Set, $24.80

Finished in Brushed Brass, relieved with black, regularly, but can be finished in any standard finish. Living Room fixture may be had in four lights. Also can be furnished in combination if so desired.

stick got started. Presumably those fake wooden candles stuck into candlesticks and sporting little bead-fringed parchment shades (circa 1900) suggested wiring in a small bulb. In any event, a 1926 discussion of decorative lighting in the home on another page pays considerable homage to the simulated candle—a fit counterpoise for today's enthusiasts for the 1920 stained glass table and dining dome lights.

One of the things to remember about early electric fixtures is that whatever shades there were (and at first they were few) tended to throw the light down as a bright and spotty glare rather than as a soft-diffused side-glow or with indirect effects thrown from the ceiling. Just as many early Victorians used unshaded oil and candle ames to prolong their lighted hours, so the late Victorians (enjoying their first incandescent lamps) were content to let the glare hit them directly in the eye.

Consider some of the catalog pages showing early electric fixtures and realize that any such shades were of no advantage to the eyes of the user. Since man cannot see in the dark, he has always been more interested in the light than in its effect on eyesight. This may be the reason why he has placed so much emphasis and attention on the quantity of light—why he requires a night-candle or an electric street light outside before he feels he can safely slumber. Here we have considered the problem of early candle fixtures and the long climb that indicates man's rise from pitch-pine to electricity as aids to self-security. Next to the problem of electric shades and their collecting.

Here are some basic studies of early electric lighting fixtures: Volume 5, No. 1, August 1923-1924 **Trade Journal of the Lighting Industry,** covers all branches of the industry and includes picture of the 'living chandelier' scene in the Passing Show of 1923 at The Winter Garden; Edward N. Riddle Company's Decorative Lighting Fitments shows a, 'New National Polychrome Line'; **Cruset Fixtures** of N.Y.C. cover general illumination; and a series of articles by Robert E. Parrish of Cassidy Co. writes "From Flaming Torch to Twisted Flame" on the architectural and historical importance of the new fixtures.

Related Patent pictures one might want to study include: 'Holder' for illuminating glassware (No. 92,903); Three-in-one Lantern (No. 174,967); Parchment Lampshade (No. 92,676); Art-Glass Table Light (No. 62,916); Silk Electric Shade (No. 62,928); Copper Light-fixture (No. 63,540); Design for Bedlamp (No. 63,807); Reflector Floorlight (No. 80,712); a Cooling and Drying Light-fixture (No. 1,727,708); Lighting Candle Bracket (No. 63,962); Hand-painted glass Boudoir Light (No. 69,231); and patented. Foyer light (with metal figures of Comedy and Tragedy on each side of Ball Shade (No. 62,491).

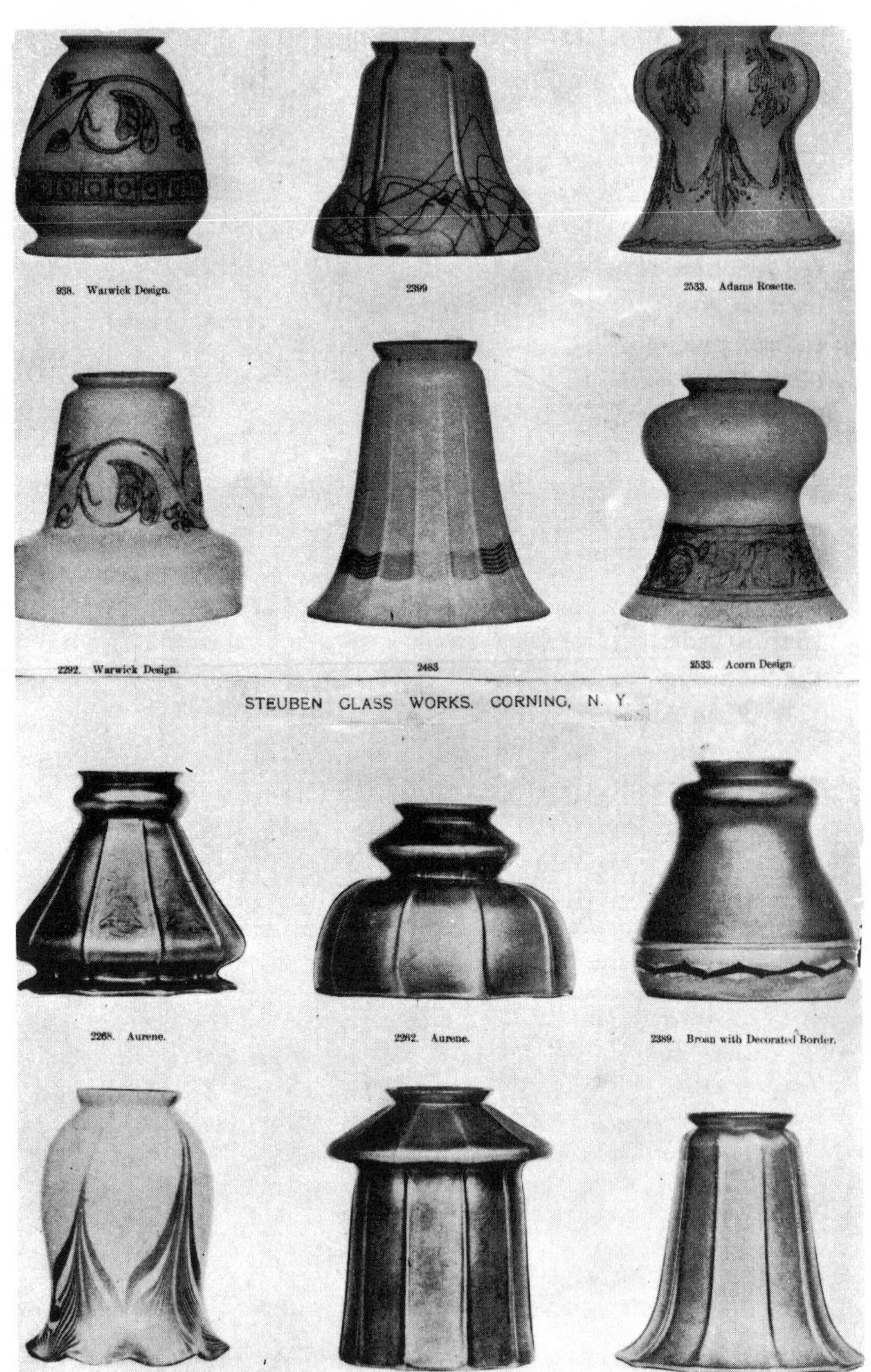

Samples of Collectable Old Lamp Shades.

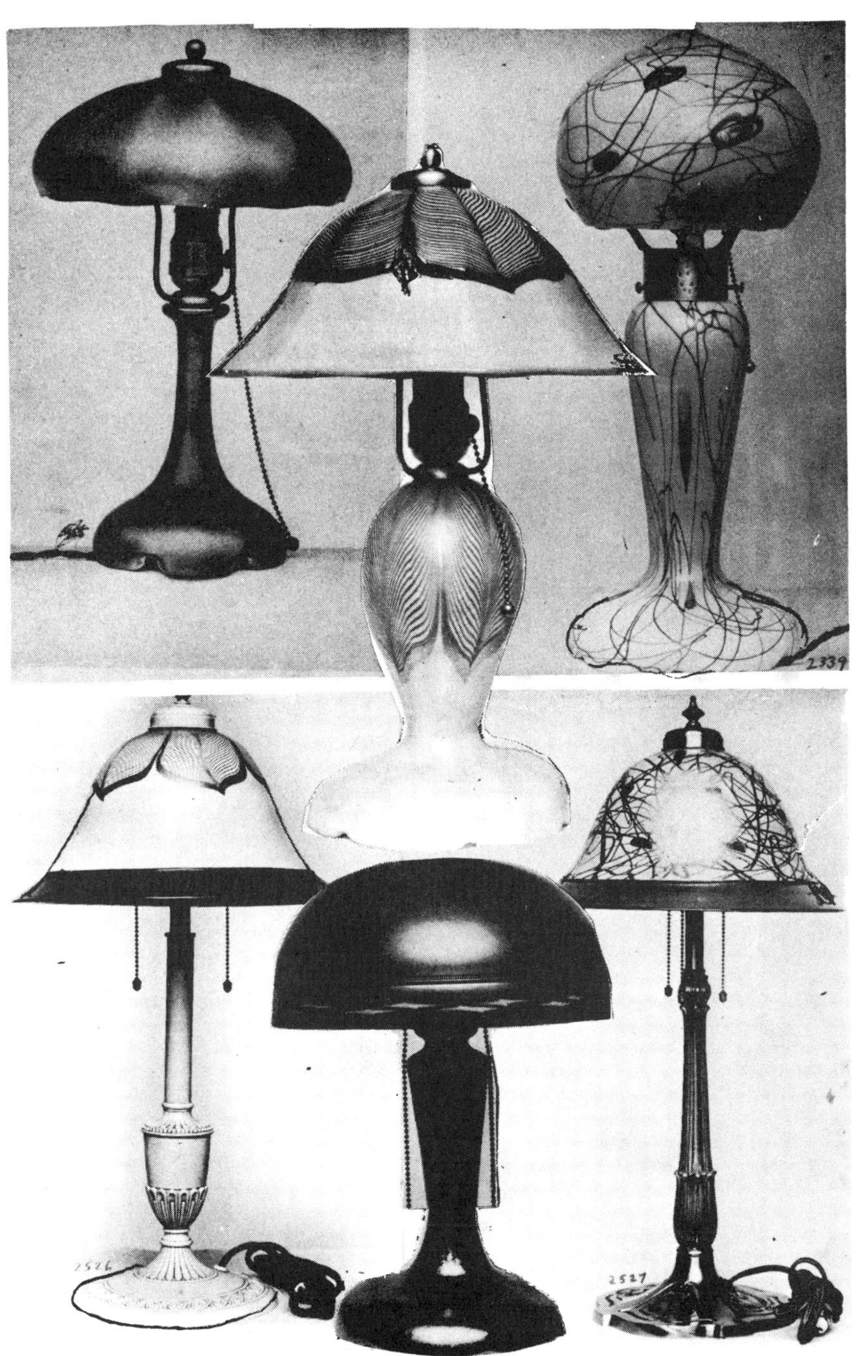

Aurene Lamps.

GLOBES
Protected by Mechanical and Design Patents.
MANUFACTURED BY
Holophane Glass Company,
11 EAST 32d STREET, NEW YORK.
We are the only manufacturers of Scientific Glass Globes in the world.
The Holophane Glass Globes are the only globes on the market that increase the efficient illuminating power of lights. They received the highest awards at all expositions, and have the endorsement of leading gas and electrical experts of the United States and Europe
No other glass globe has received any awards nor can show any endorsements whatever for efficiency.
The Holophane system is not merely a "Globe," but the scientific application of optical laws to a glass article, ensuring definite results not obtained by any other method. They are scientific illuminating appliances that do their work.
Owing to the fierce competition between different kinds of lights, manufacturers and dealers know that it is absolutely essential to show their particular lights to their very best advantage, and they should remember that Holophane Glass Globes, being scientifically and conscientiously worked out secure the greatest efficiency from all lights, both in quality and quantity of illumination.
Other globes may cost less but they are worth less.

Chapter XVII

ELECTRIC LIGHT SHADES; PRESSED, CUT AND ART GLASS

The problem of covers for electric light bulbs has been left to this chapter. But one should recognize (as with gas lighting) their numbers and types are so numerous, a complete checklist will have to await a later book. Many of the pictures shown in this section indicate the correct period shade for different fixtures. Note, for instance, that not all the glass bell shapes (held around a light socket and arranged for screwing in a single incandescent bulb) are of white-milk glass. Some of them are colored; some are etched; some are painted and, of course, many are molded in special patterns reminiscent of pressed glass table forms. All, of course (even the pierced tin, copper, parchment, and leaded stained-glass ones were developed to shield the naked lamp bulb and to increase the decorative effect. How well these early attempts at scientific non-glare illumination succeed is a mute point as indicated below.

Students might well consult "The Lighting Book" (J. L. Stair, Curtis Lighting Co., Chicago, 1930) for a full report on the elimination of harmful glare, first by shades and later by indirect lighting. We reproduce several pages of this development from the time of early downward-reflectors to later concealed upward effects. In between, our attention as collectors will be on the shades' basic shapes and how to use these decoratively as light fixtures or as adapted for vases and bowls.

There are so many different types of glass shades (used to cover a single lamp bulb either hanging down or inverted) that some basic nomenclature must be developed. A growing list of collectors are often more interested in using these for a glass window display than as lighting equipment. Call them just 'many colored globes' or start a checklist according to treatment involved. Here is a suggested beginning.

Class A: la—**White acid-crimpled,** 1b—Colored **acid-crimpled,** 1c—Mixed color **acid-crimpled,** 1d—**Painted acid-crimpled;** 2a—White **acid-Pan** (also b,c,d); 3a—White **Acid-Cone** (also b,c,d); 4a—White **Acid-Squat** (also b,c,d); 5a—**Pressed glass: scalloped top** (also b,c,d); 6a—**Opalescent Flint; Twist;** 7a—**Etched white Crown;** 8a—**Etched white Squat;** 8a—**Etched Cone** (white); and 10a—**Opal fluted top** (white and colored).

Well, there is a start for just one class—excluding special colors and the fact that most come in diameters ranging from 5 to 8 inches. From there on the listing would get even more bizarre: We note **Fluted Top Carcels** and **Rich Glass, Melon and Beaded** (tops: all the colors of the rainbow in different shades from ruby to amberina. In the **etched category** we have: scalloped **Melon Tops, Crescent Panels, Cut and Lily Tops, Silver etched** and **Rich Silvered Glass,** all Class A types according to catalog designations.

5927
4529
5928
5771
5929
5901
5894
5909
5908
6391
6356
6123
5622
5810
4576
5689
5557
5601
6087
6089
6088
6142
6232
6291
6231
6308
6098
6095
5817
6306
6303

5936½ 5937½ 6042½ 5935½

5936 5937 6042 5935

6018½ 6099½ 5904½ 6073½

6018 6099 5904 6073

5944½ 5875½ 5951½ 5947½

5944 5875 5951 5947

5946 5945 5948 5949

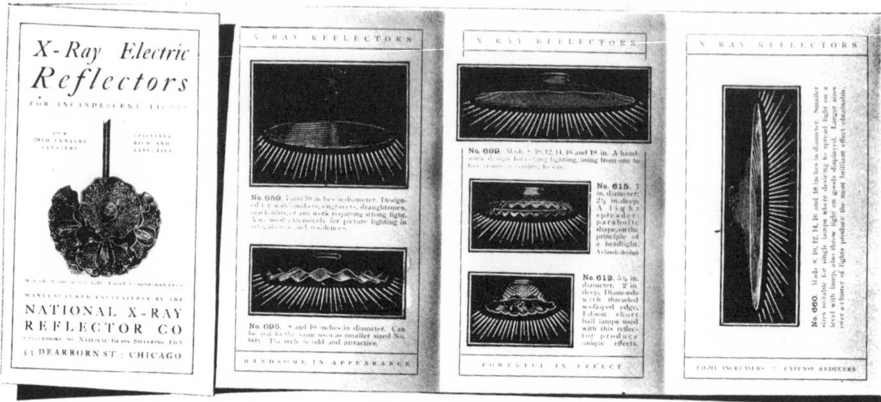

FIGURE 17—This circular was the first published catalog of X-Ray reflectors, issued many years ago by Curtis Lighting, Inc., showing types of "shades" offered to the public for light control. The organization was then known as the National X-Ray Reflector Company.

This courageous suggestion was no idle fancy, but proceeded from a definite conviction of Mr. Augustus D. Curtis, of Chicago, whose many innovations in the field of practical lighting application have resulted in immeasurable good by increasing man's seeing comfort. The chief objection lay in the fact that light, which we possess in abundance, was not adequately controlled; that it was not performing its most potent functions. It is true that in some few restricted fields satisfactory attempts at control had been made as, for example, in optical projection, in the light-house for the seacoast and the control of daylight by means of prisms; but, strange as it may seen, very little had been done to apply fundamental principles of light reflection to the great and increasingly important problems of illumination.

FIGURE 18—An early type of cluster lighting fixture produced by the Curtis organization, utilizing one of the large flat reflectors shown in the illustration above. Now lighting science dictates that each lamp shall have its individual reflector.

As if by some predetermined arrangement at this critical time, Mr. Curtis was approached by a gentleman who had for many months been experimenting with a new reflecting device in a modest laboratory, where the work bench consisted of an old billiard table, and an antique trunk served as a storehouse for his supplies and chemicals. It was Everly L. Haines, the poor but justly proud inventor, who had found as a result of his toil a one-piece silvered glass reflector, of high reflecting properties and permanent quality, for the incandescent lamp. The inventor, who had not the means of broadly marketing his idea, was looking for some one with faith and vision, some one who could visualize as he did the latent possibilities in that innocent looking piece of molded silvered glass. He was not long in the seeking, for it was Mr. Curtis who recognized in this simple device an idea that could be developed into an effective weapon in waging his campaign against glare and wasted light. When a new organization was formed to develop and market this novel device for the control of the radiance from incandescent lamps, it was given the rather imposing name of National X-Ray Reflector Co.

Mr. Curtis, assisted by Mr. Arthur Morgan until the untimely passing of this valued co-worker, organized the details of manufacture, sale and installation with masterful completeness and extraordinary vision. New shapes were designed to multiply the uses and value of the invention, and a ceaseless stream of ideas and suggestions was carefully investigated and tried out. In time the X-Ray reflector reached its present superiority in control and its world-wide demand.

It may be noted, as a matter of record, that the first X-Ray reflectors were used for the lighting of a shop window display in Chicago in 1897. The Washington Shirt Company haberdashery installed them, and so wonderful and unusual were the results that several were used inside of the store as well. The success of this trial led immediately to other installations, until the "Show Window Searchlight," as it came to be called, soon found universal use, and was generally considered as standard for show window lighting.

It is interesting to compare the first published descriptive circular of X-Ray reflectors with the present voluminous catalog and data book of the products of Curtis Lighting, Inc. Before the idea of the concealment of the light source was made a definite and fundamental principle of the business, X-Ray reflectors took on the forms that are shown in Figs. 17, 18 and 19—flat shallow shades more decorative than useful for light control.

While the first applications of the new reflector designs were somewhat crude, as judged by our present standards, they were, nevertheless, revolutionary. The fundamental idea of hiding the lamp began to manifest itself definitely in the new contours. For example, the "Helmet" and the "Beehive," two of the rugged old "musketeers" of the X-Ray brigade, pictured in Fig. 20, show the deep, enveloping style of design that was adopted to hide, as completely as possible, the brilliant filament of the lamp. The "Helmet" was produced for the specific problems encountered in shop window lighting, while the "Beehive" found its widest application in industrial and commercial lighting for factories, garages, printing shops, gymnasiums, etc.

FIGURE 19—A decorative reflector extensively used in the days of the carbon lamp. The sparkle of its silvered surface attracted all eyes.

The most strategic movement in the campaign against the common enemy, "Glare," was made in the discovery and introduction of indirect illumination in October, 1908. It was in the home of Mr. Curtis, in Chicago, that the first public presentation of practical indirect lighting was made before a joint meeting of the Luminaire Studios,

The Helmet

The Pokebonnet

The Beehive

FIGURE 20—These "Three Musketeers" of the X-Ray reflector brigade, popular twenty years ago, fought the early battles for better lighting. They revolutionized lighting for show windows and other applications. The "Poke Bonnet" was the first reflector design to be produced especially for the scientific illumination of shop window displays.

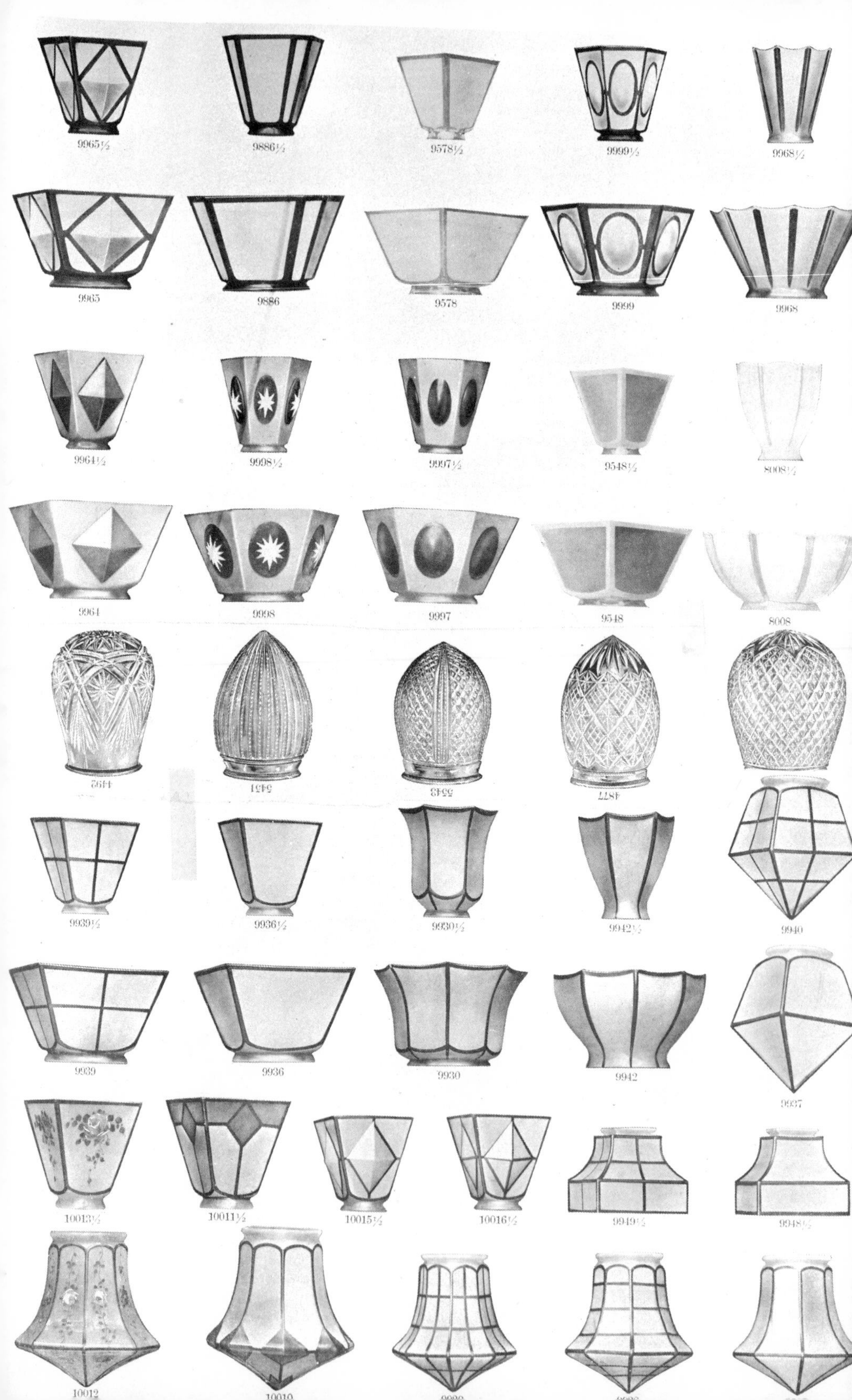
9965½
9886½
9578½
9999½
9968½
9965
9886
9578
9999
9968
9964½
9998½
9997½
9548½
8008½
9964
9998
9997
9548
8008
4492
5431
5543
4877
9939½
9936½
9930½
9942½
9940
9939
9936
9930
9942
9937
10013½
10011½
10015½
10016½
9949½
9948½
10012
10010

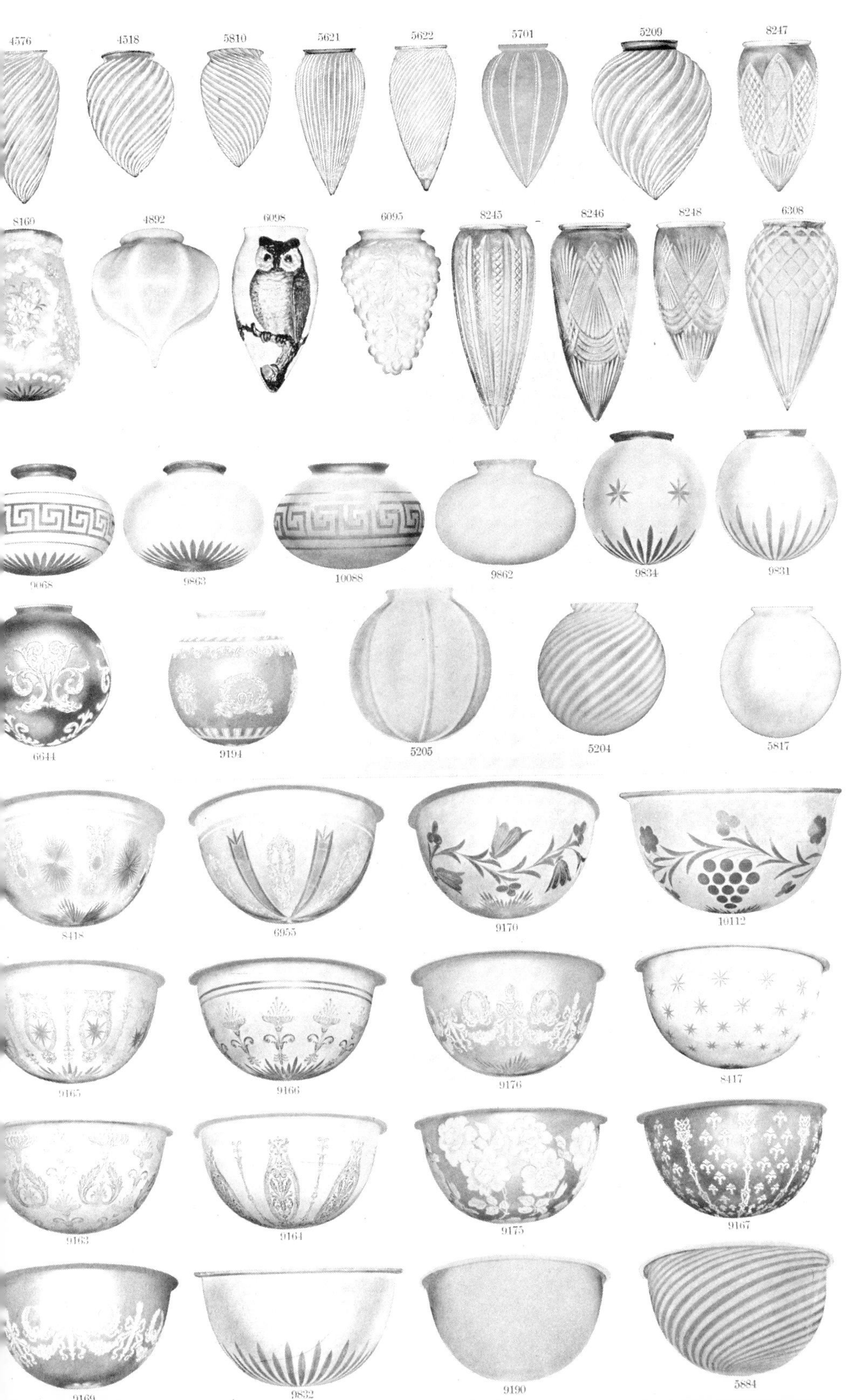
4576
4518
5810
5621
5622
5701
5209
8247
8160
4892
6098
6095
8245
8246
8248
6308
9068
9863
10088
9862
9834
9831
6644
9194
5205
5204
5817
8418
6955
9170
10112
9165
9166
9176
8417
9163
9164
9175
9167
9169
9832
9190
5884

Next would come the **Class B** with **etched** and **roughed** large globes: 1—**electro line-etched globes;** 2—**bevelled tops;** 3—**crystal etched** and 4—and **hand-cut glass** ones. **Class C** would be the **Stalactites** (prize items when done in **art glass by Durand, Steuben** or **Tiffany);** dropped into a tripod holder in the manner of old Egyptian-Roman vases, you can make something very special. **Class D,** would be the **Arch globes** in white opal or occasionally in color. **Class E** would be the **Domes** (a single expanse of blown or pressed glass) for the dome table lamps or dining room fixtures, and finally, **Class F** would be the **Big Ball Shades** for street or even hall lighting.

All of these types are shown or described; but their specific variations are myriad. For instance, some shade companies gave every pattern a name. For the Bauer Co. (Philadelphia) every pattern started with Art, (Art-Enslave, Art-Engulf, etc.). The Phoenix Glass Company had so many different pressed-glass patterns that these were listed by number only. Incidentally, the Phoenix Glass Co. (Pittsburgh, Pa.) was also a member of The Illuminating Glassware Guild. The other nine members were Gillinder Brothers (Port Jervis, N.Y.); Gleason-Tiebout Glass Co. (Brooklyn, N.Y.); H. Northwood Co. (Wheeling, W. Va.); Hocking Glass Co. (Lancaster, O.); Ivanhoe-Regent Works of the General Electric Co. (Cleveland, O.); Jeannette Shade and Novelty Co. (Jeannette, Pa.); Jefferson Glass Co. (Follansbee, W. Va.); Macbeth-Evans Glass Co. (Pittsburgh, Pa.) and United States Glass Co. (Pittsburgh, Pa.). The Gibson Company (Phila. & Pittsburgh) called each shade Great **Ace,** Great **Ball,** etc. Add to these, the fact we haven't yet mentioned the special shade effects made by Tiffany (i.e. **Lily of the Valley** as cover for special thin teardrop lamp bulbs), or the leaded masterpieces of dining domes (dealt with later), and you will see why the collecting of electric light shades is now all the vogue!

We have saved the best collector items of all for the very end; namely the **Art Nouveau Electric Lamp Shades of Signed Art Glass:** Called by their prime authority (Mr. Charles K. Bassett of Buffalo, N.Y.) "Poor Man's Tiffany." It was your author's privilege to introduce Mr. Bassett to the possibilities of such collecting in his book, **Iridescent Glass** (Century House, 1956). Quite different from the pattern glass shades described earlier, these iridescent art-glass shades made by Tiffany, Durand, Quezal and Steuben are in a class by themselves. From samples shown at our American Life Foundation's Study Institute, Mr. Bassett went on to amass a collection of over 800 different ones and to spend the last ten years studying how, where and what was made. Rather than attempt a definite checklist at this time, we reproduce on subsequent pages (courtesy Mr. Bassett) his two published accounts (1961-1964) of what he learned about this fascinating new field of lamp-shade collecting. In a letter to the author dated June, 1967 Mr. Bassett states, "Shades and other pieces of art glass were also made under the trade name of 'Iris' by the Fostoria Glass Specialty Co. (1910-1917). These were unmarked except by a small oval sticker about 3/4" long that bore the name IRIS in bold black letters underneath which, in smaller print, was "Fostoria, O." I made a trip to Fostoria and with the help of a Mrs. Peter was able to identify to my satisfaction a dozen or so shades unmarked, whose source always had troubled me. It would be an endless task to put down in black and white all I have learned about shades in the past ten years." One can only hope that this study will continue; meanwhile smart collectors are trying to corral all remaining examples before prices rise any higher. Whereas a pair of Aurene-type Steuben shades used to be no more than $5 to $10, now they are $25 and are considered prime collector items. How these are converted to make, not only lamp parts, but to use in pairs as vases (on marble plinths or go into bride's basket molded to fill up the bottom of the shade and placed in silver holder) is a subject of a later book. Here we only point out that whether you want these to fix old lights with, or just to put on a glass shelf in your antique window, you have a whole new and important array of antique pattern and art-glass shade types to acquire and to admire. Have fun with it.

Probably the most widely distributed items of the Art Nouveau movement in America in the early 1900s were the blown iridescent glass electric light shades.

Unlike many forms of blown glass articles, such as drinking glasses, vases, and bowls which have been produced for centuries in the same ways they are made today, these shades came in with the domestic electric lighting around 1900 and went out with the Depression in the early 1930's.

That is, these shades were a product limited to the first third of the 20th century. Because of the comparatively limited time they were made, it is hard to get accurate information on the manufacturing procedure or on the glassworks that made them.

We know these shades were made in the glassworks of Louis C. Tiffany of Corona, Long Island; the Steuben Glass Works of Corning, N.Y,; the Quezal Art Glass and Decorating Company of Brooklyn, N.Y., and in the small glassworks of Conrad Vahlsing of Elmhurst, Long Island, an offshoot of Quezal. Vahlsing engraved the shades he made with the script words "Lustre Art" on their bases.

The shades put out by these four glass works were signed — or most of them were. I asked the late Fred Carder if he signed his shades. "We tried to," he said, "but sometimes when we were busy, shades would get out without being signed."

I have taken four Steuben shades from a fixture where they had probably been hanging for 50 years and found two of them bearing the small silvery Steuben mark and the other two showing no trace of any mark at all.

I have heard from several reliable sources that shades were also made by Victor Durand of Vineland, N.J., but were never marked. I believe they were made by the Imperial Glass Company of Bellaire, Ohio, and probably by other glass works in the Ohio and West Virginia areas, but are hard to accurately trace because they were not signed.

There are certain recurring forms of shades and techniques of decoration on unsigned shades that I am sure are not the product of glassworks in the east.

Perhaps 10 percent of the shades in the collection of around 700 I have assembled I believe to be European made. These are never signed but are usually of a thicker and different quality of glass than the shades made in the United States.

A definite mottling of the surface, sometimes faint, sometimes pronounced, seems often to be a part of their intentional decoration. Many are decorated so that they will look their best when lighted, whereas many American shades look better by reflected light than by transmitted light.

Another characteristic of European-made shades is that occasionally you can notice small black flecks of cinder embedded in the glass. This may be due to the glass-makers in Europe using coke-fired furnaces to melt their glass, while in America oil or gas was used.

Some dealers, thru lack of knowledge and for want of a better name, will refer to some of the odder European designs as "unmarked Tiffany" which they are not.

Shades, as with other pieces of glass, were produced as a group effort within the works by small groups known as "companies." According to Fred Carder, the normal composition of a company working on shades would be:

The Gaffer
The Servitor or Decorator
The Blower
The Bit Gatherer
The Carry-in Boy

Their individual efforts would be balanced so that more than a single shade would be in process at the same time.

A "company" would turn out about two dozen decorated or four dozen plain shades in a working day. These sold, at wholesale, for $24 a dozen for the decorated and $12 a dozen for the plain shades. This would make the daily production of a single "company" in the neighborhood of $48.

At the wages paid at that period, small by modern standards, perhaps half of this amount might go to labor and the balance to cover materials, overhead, and profit — a reasonable division.

The most popular type of shade, hence the most often found today was the plain gold iridescent-glass shade of trumpet, vase, or bell shape, sometimes smooth on the outside, and sometimes with longitudinal ribs, often 10 in number.

These ribs would be formed by pressing the molten and partially blown gather in a ribbed mold, then removing it and continuing with the blowing.

—From the collection of Chas. K. Bassett, Buffalo, N. Y.

If decoration was to be applied to the exterior of the shade, the partially blown shade had a thread of molten glass trickled free-hand over the outside by the decorator. Or the partially blown shade, still on the blowiron, was laid in a hand-operated threaded machine, and a thread of molten glass, about the size of a pencil lead, was laid like a screw thread on the cylindrical and partially formed gather.

Just what happened next, in our present state of knowledge is anybody's guess. It depended on the skill and the experience of the gaffer handling the piece.

It may have been first rolled on a steel plate or "marver" to incorporate the threads into the body of the shade and then hooked with a small hand-hook, slightly larger than a button-hook into a feather pattern or other desired design. Or it may have been hooked first, and then rolled. Perhaps a combination of these two methods was used.

Fred Carder told me that all the patterns were produced either by hooking, or by lightly squeezing the threaded gather in a mold and either slightly twisting it or pushing or pulling it.

There are some of the rarer netted patterns that it is very hard to understand just how they were made. Perhaps we shall know some day. It is my hope that we shall.

I believe there were many touches at this particular point that depended on the manual dexterity of the gaffer, and I believe further, that if a gaffer was able to turn out a particularly pleasing design, it was more or less a closely guarded trade secret, and not written down in any book.

The shade was then further blown, the outer end cut off, and the base flange formed. This flange, in the standard shade, was 2¼ inches in diameter.

It would seem that the close tolerances necessary for this base would indicate that the base would be formed by twisting it in a hinged mold of some sort. But several old glass-workers have insisted that it was formed by eye, and with the ordinary hand-forming tools.

This formed end was then stuck on to a gob of molten glass on the end of a ponty iron held by the servitor. The shape was then trimmed at the outer or blowiron end and shaped to the desired form.

If the outer edge was to be ruffled or crimped it was pressed down on a crimping-form or crimper. I The carry-in boy would then carry the shade to the tempering lahr where it was slowly cooled to remove internal stresses in the glass.

When finally cooled the shade would have the base ground to remove irregularities and it would be sprayed with or dipped in an acid solution to give both the outer and inner surfaces a matte finish.

One of the rarest and most individual of the feather designs is known as "the hooked feather" in which the outer points of the feathers are hooked with a bold swirl.

Frank Blake of Painted Post, N.Y., now one of the mixmasters at the Corning Glass Co., and whose father was a glass-worker before him at the now defunct Sinclair Glass Works of Bath, N.Y., tells me that older glass-workers say this hooked feather pattern, in its different variations, was done in its greatest perfection by the master glass-worker Emil Larson.

Blake says that the old Steuben Glass Works was not satisfied with their trials to produce a satisfactory hooked feather and that Emil Larson was hired to come to Corning and teach their gaffers the knack of making it. This did not work out.

Larson told me the same thing. It seemed to take an extreme manual dexterity that he only could produce.

There was another design that seemed to be Larson's own where the threads were hooked in an all-over design of hooked swirls. Larson refers to this as his "King Tut" pattern. This pattern is often seen on vases made by Larson when he was working for Victor Durand of Vineland.

Emil Larson, now in his middle 80's, is retired and lives in St. Petersburg, Fla. I have talked with him twice in the past two years and he confirms the hooked feather story. He told me that his services were most eagerly sought after by the different glassworks and that he was always "paid above the scale."

He also mentioned that, to his knowledge, for at least two years and perhaps more, the Quezal Art Glass and Decorating Company made only shades.

I have worked with mechanics all of the 44 years of my active business life and know, thru working with them, how a mechanic's hands should be shaped. I consider Larson to have the finest pair that I have ever seen, large and beautifully formed. I can readily believe that anything that took skill, he could do.

Originality of Conception and Execution endow the productions of the TIFFANY STVDIOS with an artistic individuality which makes them particularly appropriate for

Holiday and Wedding Gifts

The stock now assembled in our studio show-rooms includes *exclusive productions* in Lamps and Electroliers, Favrile Glass in a variety of forms, together with many attractive articles suitable for desk furnishings or boudoir appointments

Individual photographs sent when desired. Correspondence invited
Show-rooms open to visitors

TIFFANY STUDIOS, 333 to 341 FOURTH AVE., NEW YORK
ONE SQUARE EAST OF MADISON SQUARE

Chapter XVIII

ARTS AND CRAFTS AND ART NOUVEAU TABLE LAMPS

We have previously mentioned the prominence of art movements in the development of home lighting. Here attention centers in that brief period between the end of Victoria's era and the coming of our first World War. Often called Edwardian to place it in a time sequence, it was actually the flowering of two quite distinct decorative trends each of diverse backgrounds and intents. As they affected the use of electric lamps in the home, we describe first those of Art Nouveau fame, followed by those in the tradition of the Arts & Crafts Movement.

Art Nouveau lamps, of which those of L. C. Tiffany sparked a host of imitators, had glass shades which utilized his iridescent or favrile glass, combined with table lamp bases made of copper. The distinguishing feature of both base and shade was the use of naturalistic flower and leaf forms, designed in such a way as to suggest tulip vases, lily of valley drop lights or twining ivy. Another distinguishing feature of the Art Nouveau is the wavy convoluted line (sometimes called the Whiplash effect). Pictures of such lamps which follow, reveal some of the most-sought after and costly lamps wanted by present day collectors. It is nothing to demand $250, or $300 for a signed Tiffany, three drop Lily of the Valley table lamp or a four light lamp which has a copper candle base with a small blue iridescent hand-blown dome apeing the petals of a rose. Of course, pieces of this iridized and stained glass fragments were often combined to make leaded domes and chandeliers but that development comes in the next chapter. Here we show the table lights (some with Stuben, Durand Quezal art glass shades with special designed bases). These were high style for the 1900-1920 decade and are now quite gone from the scene.

As for the Arts & Crafts Lamps of this same period, we are especially indebted to the reports from Gustav Stickley's **Craftsmen Magazine** (1900-1916) and the movement reported thereon in THE FORGOTTEN REBEL (Century House); also **American Life Collector,** Vol. 4 and Vol. 5.

The Arts and Crafts Movement in America is usually identified with **Mission Style** Furniture and electric **hanging lanterns,** with Pierced-Copper shades or Art-glass side-panels, supposedly based upon the interior fittings of early Spanish Missions of California. This Boxy-treatment of decorative household articles came, actually, from the Nineteenth century **Gothic Revival** led by William Morris. The association of such work with the term 'Mission' is a gross mis-nomer! Working to escape the 'commercial monstrosities of the Industrial Revolution,' Morris preached a return to hand-craftsmanship and backed this up with simple designs and beautiful objects built therefrom. Not until Morris' death in 1896, however, did his

The Craftsman Workshops

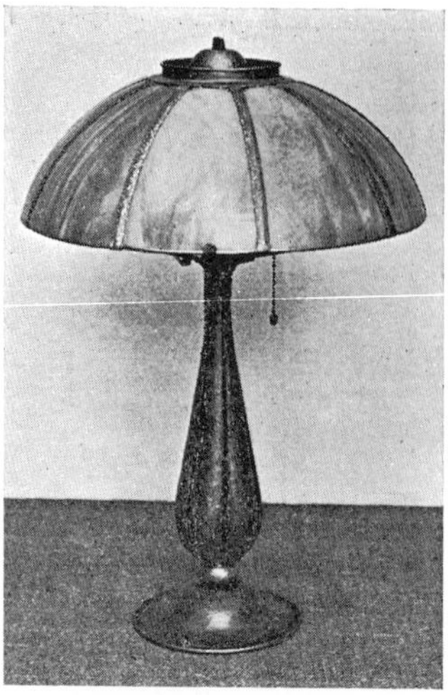

No. 262, Electric Portable

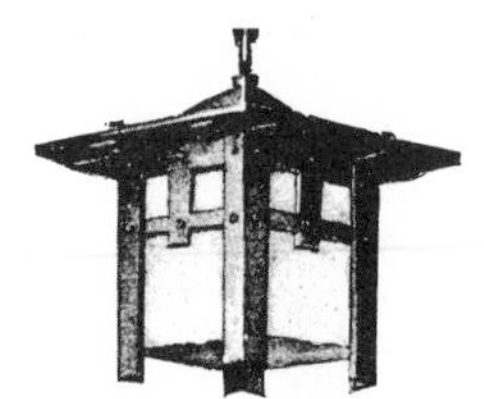

No. 673

No. 294, Oil Lamp

No. 205, Electric Lantern

Copper in natural,
or vert antique finish,
produced
without aid of lacquers,
and growing finer
with age

No. 293, Oil Lamp

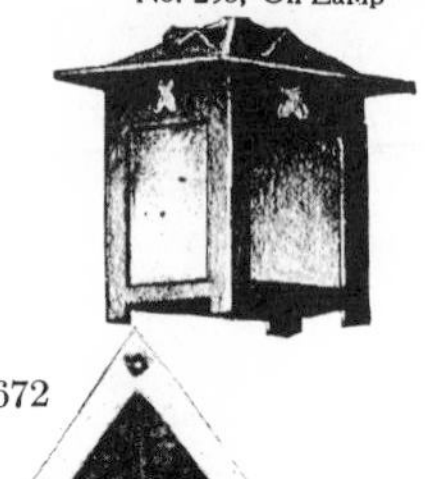

No. 672

No. 229
DIAMOND SHAPED ELECTRIC SIDE LIGHT

disciples put the arts and crafts movement into truely modern orbit. . . . Led by such well-known figures as Frank Lloyd Wright and Gustav Stickley, America launched its Prairie School of Architecture and developed the so-called 1900 Mission Style of home decoration. Such American products were in direct opposition to the French Art-Nouveau contortions of the same period, and always stressed **functionalism** in design. For instance, "a lamp should look like a lantern made to shed light and not some Tulip flower form bent on imitating nature. . . ."

A look at the special catalog pages reproduced herein is ample evidence of the two different types of treatment available to collectors in this field. Rightly enough, the major stronghold of the Arts and Crafts Movement was located in the West rather than along the Eastern Seaboard. In fact, there is even poetic justification for having this style become known as **Spanish Colonial** and set in sharp contrast with the Frenchified Art-Lamps which at first had few takers.

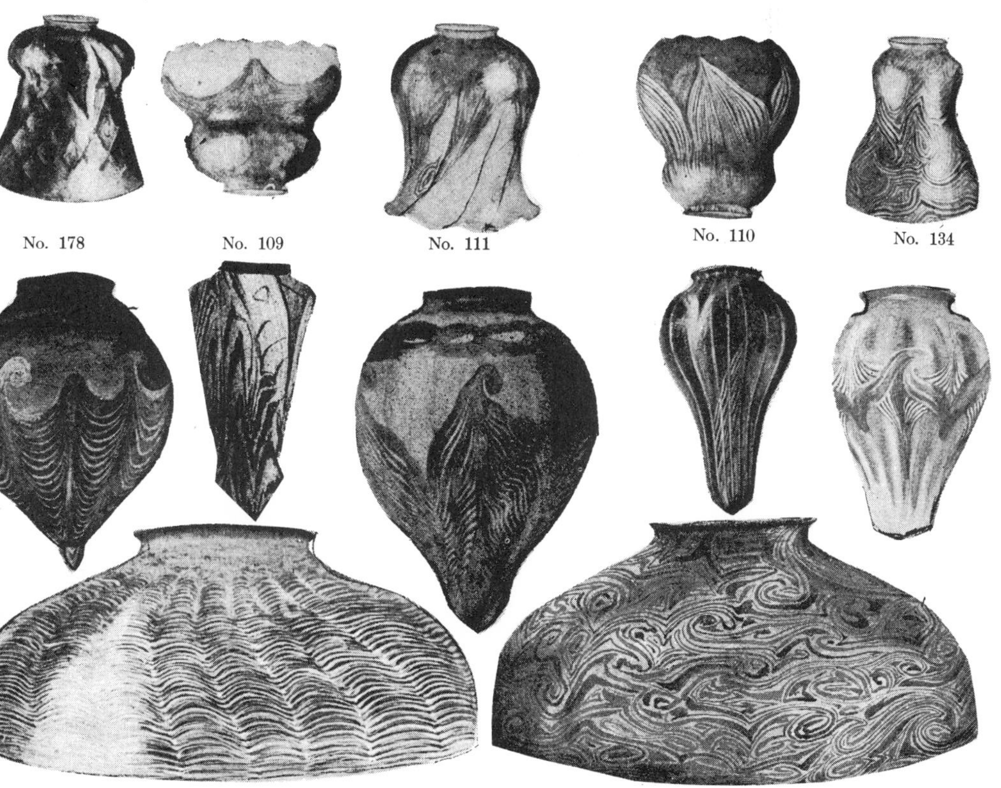

FFANY FAVRILE GLASS DOME SHADES STALACTITES FOR ELECTRIC LIGHTING

DOMES

Special **$8.49** Complete

10K6040 Beautiful Large Mission Style Hexagonal Electric Chandelier that hangs on an extra heavy brass plated chain. Has a large 22-inch hexagonal dome of solid brass in English brushed finish, lacquered to prevent tarnishing. The panels are mottled green glass. Apron sides are 3½ inches deep, with 4-inch bead fringe that matches the panels. It hangs 56 inches from the ceiling, on a square brass canopy. The glass panels are easily taken out for cleaning and should any become broken, new ones can be obtained at any time. Comes completely wired, with one pull chain socket. Shipping weight, 45 pounds.
Price, complete.................... **$8.49**

"Modern Art"—Full ht. 56 in., 22 in. hexagon shade, cast frame and crown, removable amber art glass panels, ornamental casting. 1 in case, about 70 lbs.

C3234 — **Electric.** Wired, complete with pull chain socket. Each, **$7.95**

C3235—**Gas.** Brass stem, complete with burner, mantle and globe. Each **$7.95**

Special **$5.25** Complete

10K6041 Large Electric Dinging Room Chandelier, with 16-inch hexagonal dome made of solid brass, brushed finish and lacquered to prevent tarnishing. Has removable green glass panels and 3-inch apron, with 4-inch glass bead fringe to match. It hangs 42 inches from the ceiling on a heavy brass plated chain. Comes completely wired and fitted with one pull chain socket. The panels are easily removed and new ones can be obtained at any time in case any should become broken. For a low priced electric dining room chandelier you cannot possibly find a better value nor could you make a more satisfactory selection than this beautiful hexagonal dome. Shpg. wt., 35 lbs. Price. complete.. **$5.25**

(A more complete work of varieties is promised later.)

Each **$14.85**

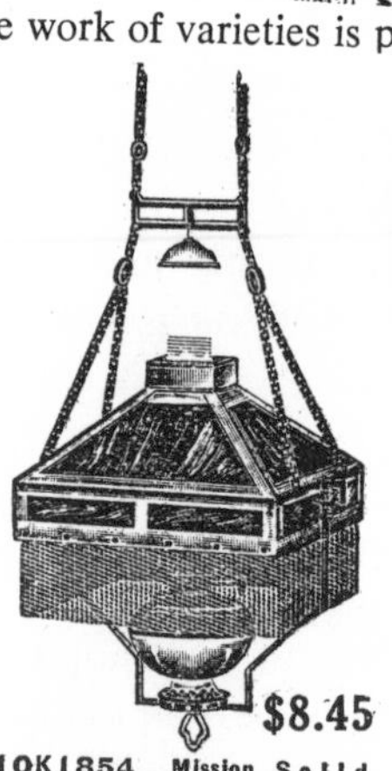

$8.45

10K1854 Mission Solid Brass Extension Lamp with Green Glass Shade. Full fire

Each **$16.50**

ELECTRIC PORTABLE

Electric and Gas—Ht. 19 in., fumed oak finish, 12 in. amber art glass shade, 2 in. skirt, square base and column. 1 in shipping carton, 10 lbs.

C3182—Electric.. } Each
C3183—Gas....... } **$3.25**

C3191—Ht. 22⅛ in., spun brass base and column, 16 in. leaded amber art glass shade, ruby insets, 2 pull chain sockets. 1 in case, 45 lbs.
Each, **$8.00**

C3111 — Ht. 19 in., spun brass base, cast reeded column, 12 in., etched glass shade, hand painted summer landscapes, brass cap, parallel silk cord, Benjamin plug, key socket. 1 in case, 25 lbs......Each, **$3.50**

Solid Brass Frame, Brush Finish, 22-inch Hexagon Shade with Green Glass Panels

$8.45

10K6055 Oil Chandelier, with 22-inch hexagon dome. Made of solid brass in English brushed finish, lacquered to prevent tarnishing. Panels are mottled green opalescent glass. The apron sides are 3½ inches deep, with mottled red, green and am[ber] glass, and a 4-inch glass bead fringe to match the pan[els]. Hangs 56 inches from ceiling by a square canopy [and] heavy chain. Comes complete with center draft bur[ner,] large fount, wick and chimney. A very high class la[mp,] a splendid value at the price. Shpg. wt., 45 lbs.
Price, complete............................ **$8.4[5]**

Chapter XIX

STAINED GLASS SHADES AND LEADED DOMES

Here are some more 1910-1920 methods for enhancing the decorative effect of electric home lighting. Stained glass is somewhat allied to the art glass shades of the preceding chapter, but of different construction. Bits of colored stained glass (such as are found in church windows) were assembled to make light domes which could be attached to both ceiling and floor fixtures so that a diffused light would show through the design while the major light effect would be thrown on the dining table below. The author recalls many a house wrecking in the 1930's and 1940's when these dining room lights would be thrown on the auction block for only a dollar. Today, however, any that are still in perfect condition would bring a price of $100 and up; (so fairs the fashions in decorative art styles from decade to decade). Space permits only a sample showing of types,—the study of how they were made (being equally important); the main thing that distinguishes a stained glass lighting dome is the leading of individual pieces and colors to make an artistic effect.

The term **stained glass** is generally understood to refer only to glass windows that have been colored by such methods as the fusion of metallic oxides into bits of glass, the pieces then being cut and joined together by leading to produce some Biblical picture as viewed from the inside of a church looking out. The origin of stained glass effects was probably the Near-East and is of great antiquity. The art of producing stained glass pictures naturally spread to Italy with the Venetian artists and glass makers as its first masters. The technique of holding these translucent bits and pieces of glass together by lead is the simplest conception of its techniques. Actually, other considerations come into play in the design and creation of a stained glass window or light-dome as a work of art. Lead for a top stained glass worker was not merely a connecting medium, but played its own part in the development of the total design. Thus lead outlines the main constituents of a design whether people or flowers and gives definition and rhythm to its masses of color. For many centuries after 1,000 A.D. stained glass artists worked full time turning a cartoon or first drawing prepared by cleric illuminators into a stained glass religious study. Secular subjects began to emerge in the Nineteenth century; the urge to decorate the home as well as the church was brought on largely by William Morris and Ruskin. Their Gothic Arts and Craft Revival (came as an offspring of the Romantic Movement of the early Nineteenth century) and was not without its effect upon decorative style home lighting. Rebelling against the sterile formula of commercialized colored church windows (with factories springing up all over Europe) the pre-Raphaelites and William Morris

Tiffany Glass Shades
and Pottery Bases.
TIFFANY
GLASS

revolted to make the feeling of design again a vital force in the home.

Now for the first time artists, like Burne-Jones began to design windows not only for church but also for the home study. In his appreciation of the Gothic, Morris evolved a style and invented a technique of home-leaded, glass, window and lamp effects appropriate to his age. Sacred stained glass windows were included in the first exhibition of his Company in 1862; but as time went on, his company made a great deal of stained glass for secular purposes. The choice of this domestic (profane) leaded glass involved subjects of a romantic and stylized nature. By 1890 the whole movement had itself become highly commercialized. From leaded glass windows for every downstairs room in the late Victorian's gingerbread castle, mass factory production began for light domes which were to be used over the dining table. Individual craftsmanship gave way to throwing heterogeneous pieces of stained glass into frames without any pretension of design beyond what some called "crazy quilt." Certainly the army of leadsmen, who put such pieces together, must have worked for a pittance, as original costs were low and great quantities available. Not art but garishness is found in many of the old dining lamp domes. Some that remain are very individual and artistic, hence greatly desired. As for those that are damaged, (with pieces which are lost or dropped out), just try to find a leaded glass repairman and you will realize this craft is now gone.

In the brief space that remains, however, we indicate, what the technique involves and also note that for those who can't find an old stained glass light shade at a reasonable price, it is possible to buy a kit of such pieces along with a rope of lead and instructions for how-to-do-it-yourself. These small imperfect reproductions of what were once so plentiful in the average American home, can be had disassembled for $35.00. Want to try it?

To assemble stained glass pieces to form a window pane, or a rounded dome, the pieces have to be first cut and then laid out together much as one would work on a jig-saw puzzle. To shape a piece of glass to an outline requiring a special design (say a bunch of purple grapes surrounded by green foliage) one would cut a piece of purple glass for each grape, etc. using a hot grozing iron,—a flat notched piece somewhat like a 'spanner.' After cutting out your grapes, and leaves the next step would be the leading. This was, and still is, done by means of a strip of lead cast in sections like the letter 'H.' Next these lead strips would be cut to the required lengths and shaped, then put around the individual glass pieces (your purple grapes and green leaves) where they would be soldered together at the points of junction. Finally the whole mass would be raised up from the table or form you were working over and cement or putty forced in between the lead and the glass. Sounds simple doesn't it? Well, try even to make a repair of some piece yourself then see if you want to create your grape lamp shade or pay an unbecomingly high price to get one of the original 1910 darlings that have somehow survived.

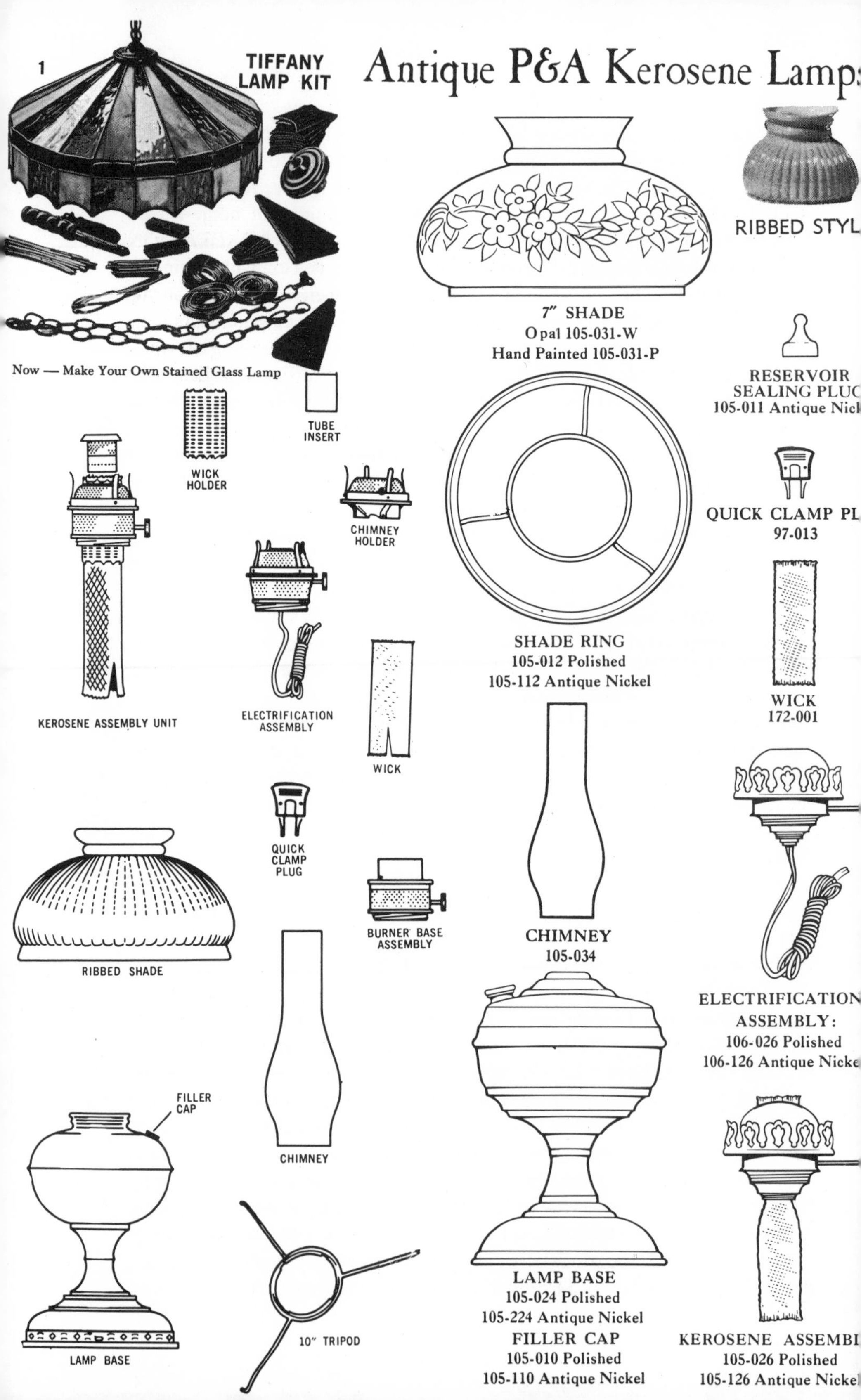
Antique P&A Kerosene Lamps
1
TIFFANY LAMP KIT
Now — Make Your Own Stained Glass Lamp
7" SHADE
Opal 105-031-W
Hand Painted 105-031-P
RIBBED STYL
RESERVOIR SEALING PLUC
105-011 Antique Nick
TUBE INSERT
WICK HOLDER
CHIMNEY HOLDER
KEROSENE ASSEMBLY UNIT
ELECTRIFICATION ASSEMBLY
WICK
SHADE RING
105-012 Polished
105-112 Antique Nickel
QUICK CLAMP PL
97-013
WICK
172-001
QUICK CLAMP PLUG
BURNER BASE ASSEMBLY
RIBBED SHADE
CHIMNEY
CHIMNEY
105-034
ELECTRIFICATION ASSEMBLY:
106-026 Polished
106-126 Antique Nicke
FILLER CAP
LAMP BASE
10" TRIPOD
LAMP BASE
105-024 Polished
105-224 Antique Nickel
FILLER CAP
105-010 Polished
105-110 Antique Nickel
KEROSENE ASSEMBI
105-026 Polished
105-126 Antique Nickel

Chapter XX

USING OLD LAMP PARTS: REASSEMBLY AND ADAPTATION

With the modern desire always to have only the newest gadgets in the home, it is not surprising so many lamps from Victoria's Era went on the trash pile several decades ago. However, the junk pickers or sanitation men of large cities could always realize a small sum for anything of brass, copper or other metal that they salvaged from the discard. When such 'junk' is not immediately consigned to a blast furnace, local scrap piles and rummage sales have long been the happy hunting ground of collectors seeking old lamp parts. Seldom, of course, is a complete brass Rochester Burner found in such discards, unless its bowl is bashed almost beyond recognition. On the other hand, gas and electric fixtures seem to have fared better. Not uncommonly, the picker comes upon something which was obviously once a part of a bygone lighting device, but has no idea of what to do with it, restoration-wise. It is to this purpose that our final chapter is dedicated.

Of course, every lamp collector always dreams of finding complete intact **G.W.W. oil lamps** or early **gas chandeliers** living around in an old attic waiting to be rediscovered and put to use. Unfortunately, such pickings are now few and far between. Therefore the junkman or resale rummage shop is a major source of supply for those who neither care nor can afford the completely restored specimens hanging in our deluxe antique shops. This resulted in a whole new cult of fix-it-yourself restorers adapters.

The author, who was an early member of this fraternity, made it a rule never to turn down an obvious old lamp part even though he had no idea what was lacking or how it could be used. In his workshop (only a tiny sample of which is here shown), he has long tried to unravel the secrets of what parts went together or what was absolutely lacking to make an authentic reassembly of a particular type of fixture. Such pursuits were greatly aided by pictures in original lamp catalogs from the **Library of the American Life Foundation & Study Institute.** In fact, pages are here reproduced in great profusion to help others see what would be a correct period connection rather than the fake fixups that some pass off as antiques. Over the past 30 years which have intervened since the author first undertook to reassemble scattered old lamps for rebirth and decorative use in his home and elsewhere, a small army of other adapters has sprung up. They form a kind of club! In recognition of such interest, a group of such enthusiasts and museum experts came here as members of a special seminar to study the problems and pricings involved in **old lamp collecting.** With the present book for general guide-lines, **Study Guide No. 3** (American Life Foundation, Watkins Glen, N. Y. $4.50 gives curent values) also

WIRED OIL LAMP CONVERTERS & ADAPTERS

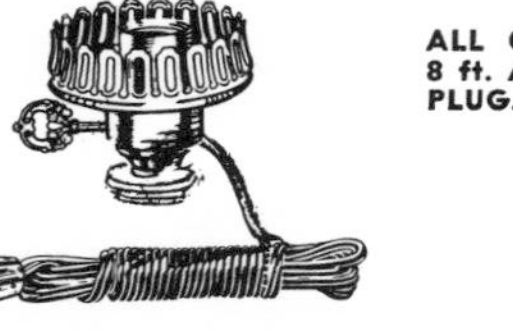
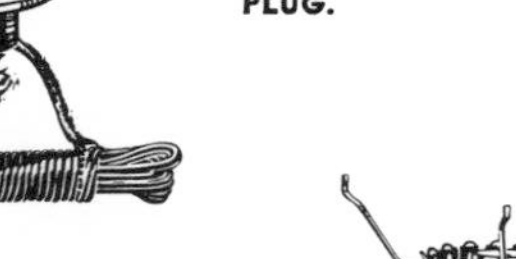

ALL CONVERTERS WIRED WITH 8 ft. APPROVED WIRE & MOLDED PLUG.

Wired Oil Lamp Converter

No. 721 —No. 1 Adapter 2⅝″ Holder
No. 721½—No. 1 Adapter 3 ″ Holder
No. 722 —No. 2 Adapter 2⅝″ Holder
No. 723 —No. 2 Adapter 3 ″ Holder
No. 723A —No. 3 Adapter 2⅝″ Holder
No. 723B —No. 3 Adapter 3 ″ Holder

NOTE: OIL LAMP SIZES

No. 1 Fits ⅞″ Opening
No. 2 Fits 1¼″ Opening
No. 3 Fits 1¾″ Opening

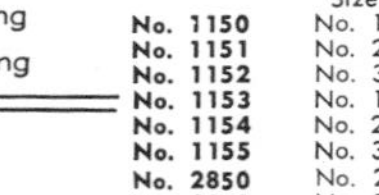
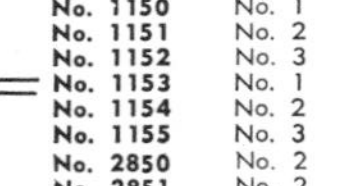

Wired Oil Lamp Converter

Cata. No.	Adapter Size	Chimney Size	Tripod Size
No. 1150	No. 1	2⅝″	7″
No. 1151	No. 2	2⅝″	7″
No. 1152	No. 3	2⅝″	7″
No. 1153	No. 1	2⅝″	10″
No. 1154	No. 2	2⅝″	10″
No. 1155	No. 3	2⅝″	10″
No. 2850	No. 2	3 ″	10″
No. 2851	No. 2	3 ″	14″

Wired Oil Lamp Converter

Cata. No.	Adapter Size	Chimney Size	Ring Size
No. 770	No. 1	2⅝″	4″
No. 771	No. 2	2⅝″	4″
No. 772	No. 3	2⅝″	4″
No. 773	No. 1	3 ″	4″
No. 774	No. 2	3 ″	4″
No. 775	No. 3	3 ″	4″

NOTE: OIL LAMP SIZES

No. 1 Fits ⅞″ Opening
No. 2 Fits 1¼″ Opening
No. 3 Fits 1¾″ Opening

Wired Oil Lamp Converter

Cata. No.	Adapter Size	Chimney Size	Ring Size
No. 1156	No. 1	2⅝″	7″
No. 1157	No. 2	2⅝″	7″
No. 1158	No. 3	2⅝″	7″
No. 1159	No. 1	2⅝″	10″
No. 1160	No. 2	2⅝″	10″
No. 1161	No. 3	2⅝″	10″
No. 2852	No. 2	3 ″	10″
No. 2853	No. 2	3 ″	14″

CANDLESTICK AND BOTTLE ADAPTER

No. 765—¾″
No. 765½—⅞″
No. 766—1″
No. 766½—1⅛″
No. 767—1¼″

White Corrugated Rubber

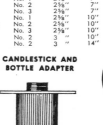

No. 1868
1½″xSlip ⅛ IP
Solid Brass Washers
(Same as used in the above adapters)

Cata. No.	Adapter Size	Chimney Size	Ring Size
No. 789	No. 1	2⅝″	7″
No. 790	No. 2	2⅝″	7″
No. 791	No. 3	2⅝″	7″
No. 792	No. 1	3 ″	7″
No. 793	No. 2	3 ″	7″
No. 794	No. 3	3 ″	7″
No. 795	No. 1	2⅝″	10″
No. 796	No. 2	2⅝″	10″
No. 797	No. 3	2⅝″	10″
No. 798	No. 1	3 ″	10″
No. 799	No. 2	3 ″	10″
No. 799A	No. 3	3 ″	10″

ALL CONVERTERS WIRED WITH 8 ft. APPROVED WIRE AND MOLDED PLUG.

WIRED OIL LAMP CONVERTERS AND ADAPTERS

WIRED OIL LAMP CONVERTER

No. 1175 Combination No. 1 and No. 2 Adapter Takes a 3″ Chimney
No. 1176 No. 3 Adapter

Our No. 1175 converter is made from the original brass burner . . . Therefore there is nothing to do but replace old burner with proper size converter — by doing this lamps will retain their original beauty . . . All converters wired with white approved cord and molded plug.

WIRED OIL LAMP CONVERTER

3″ CHIMNEY HOLDER &
4″ BALL SHADE HOLDER

No. 1177—#1 Adapter
No. 1178—#2 Adapter
No. 1179—#3 Adapter

Wired Oil Lamp Converter

1⅝″ Chimney Holder
4″ Student Shade Holder
No. 1180—#1 Adapter
No. 1181—#2 Adapter

WIRED OIL LAMP CONVERTER

No. 1182—#1 Adapter
2⅛″ Chimney Holder
No. 1183—#2 Adapter
2⅛″ Chimney Holder
Holds No. 1514 Chimney

Wired Oil Lamp Converter

Cata No.	Adapter Size	Chimney Size	RING Size
No. 1184	#1	2⅛″	6″
No. 1185	#2	2⅛″	6″

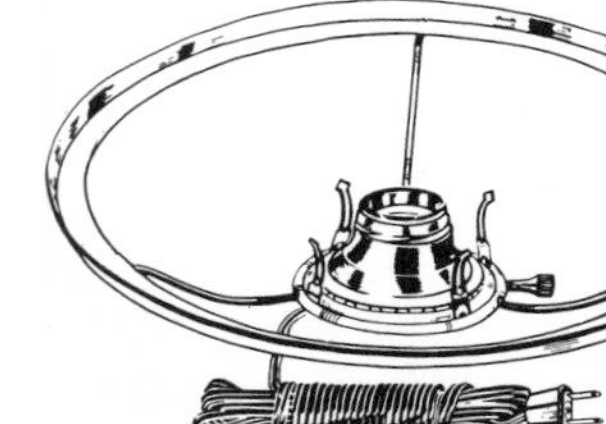

WIRE OIL LAMP CONVERTER

CATA. No.	Adapter Size	Chimney Size	Ring Size
No. 1162	#1	3″	10″
No. 1163	#2	3″	10″
No. 1164	#3	3″	10″
No. 1165	#1	3″	7″
No. 1166	#2	3″	7″
No. 1167	#3	3″	7″

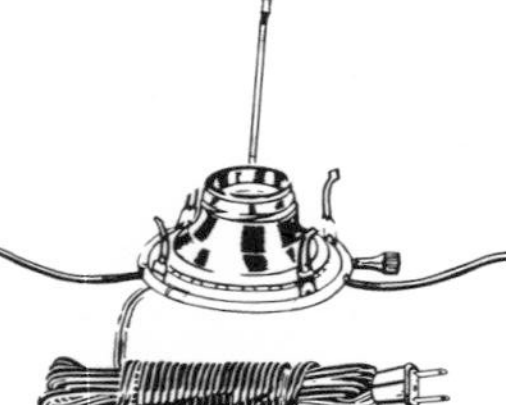

WIRED OIL LAMP CONVERTER

CATA. No.	Adapter Size	Chimney Size	Tripod Size
No. 1168	#1	3″	10″
No. 1169	#2	3″	10″
No. 1170	#3	3″	10″
No. 1171	#1	3″	7″
No. 1172	#2	3″	7″
No. 1173	#3	3″	7″

BALL SHADES

No. 594

Plain Opal Ball Shade

Can be fired up to 1000 degrees. Stocked in the sizes listed below.

Note: State Ball Size When Ordering

Ball Size	Fitter	Height	Top Opening
3″	1⅞″	3½″	1¼″
4″	2″	4″	1¾″
5″	2¾″	5¾″	1⅞″
6″	3¼″	5½″	3″
7″	4″	6½″	3″
7¼″	4″	6″	3″
8″	4″	7¾″	3⅛″
9″	4″	8½″	3⅛″
10″	4″	10″	3⅛″
11″	4″	11″	3¼″
12″	4″	12″	3⅛″
14″	5″	14″	3¾″

NEW SATIN WHITE OPAL BRISTOL BALL SHADES

No. **2908**— 8″ Ball x 4″ Fitter
No. **2909**— 9″ Ball x 4″ Fitter
No. **2910**—10″ Ball x 4″ Fitter

FROSTED SHADES WITH CUT GRAPES AND LEAVES

No. **1569**— 8″ Ball 4″ Fitter
No. **1570**— 9″ Ball 4″ Fitter
No. **1571**—10″ Ball 4″ Fitter

HOBNAIL OPAL (WHITE) BALL SHADES

No. **2223**— 6″ Ball 4″ Fitter
No. **2224**— 8″ Ball 4″ Fitter
No. **2225**—10″ Ball 4″ Fitter

No. 597

Hand Decorated Ball Shade

Decorated front and back with red roses and green leaves. Tinted pink top and bottom. All colors fired on.

STOCKED IN THE SIZES LISTED BELOW

Ball Size	Fitter	Height	Top Opening
3″	1⅞″	3½″	1¼″
4″	2″	4″	1¾″
5″	2¾″	5¾″	1⅞″
6″	3¼″	5½″	3″
7″	4″	6½″	3″
7¼″	4″	6″	3″
8″	4″	7¾″	3⅛″
9″	4″	8½″	3⅛″
10″	4″	10″	3⅛″
11″	4″	11″	3¼″
12″	4″	12″	3⅛″
14″	5″	14″	3¾″

RUBY AND AMBER THUMBPRINT OPTIC BALL SHADES

No. **2918A**— 8″ Amber 4″ Fitter
No. **2918R**— 8″ Ruby 4″ Fitter
No. **2919A**— 9″ Amber 4″ Fitter
No. **2919R**— 9″ Ruby 4″ Fitter
No. **2920A**—10″ Amber 4″ Fitter
No. **2920R**—10″ Ruby 4″ Fitter

No. 1050—A. & B.

No. 1050-A
Diam. 5½ — Height 6¼″ — Fitter 2¾″

No. 1050-B
Diam. 7″ — Height 7½″ — Fitter 3⅛″

No. 596

Hand Decorated Ball Shade

	Diam.	Height	Fitter
596-A	5½″	6¼″	2¾″
596-B	7″	7½″	3⅛″
596-C	7″	9½″	3⅛″
596-D	8″	10¼″	4″

No. 1050—C. & D.

No. 1050-C
Diam. 7″ — Height 9½″ — Fitter 3⅛″

No. 1050-D
Diam. 8″ — Height 10¼″ — Fitter 4″

FROSTED SHADES

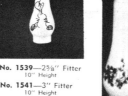

No 1535

Satin Frosted with Grape Pattern
Height 7″ fitter 3″

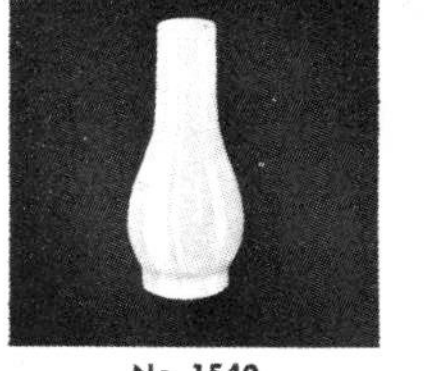

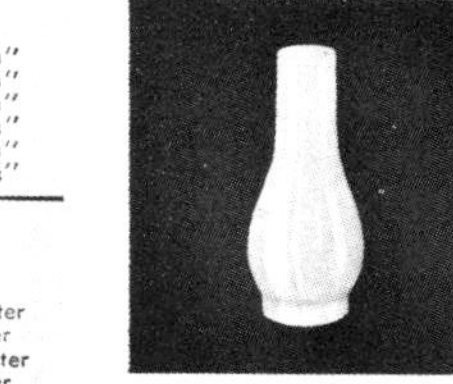

No. 1540
Plain Opal Chimney
2⅝″ Fitter—10″ Height

No. 1542
3″ Fitter—10″ Height

No. 1539—2⅝″ Fitter
10″ Height

No. 1541—3″ Fitter
10″ Height

Green Ivy Fired-On.
Hand Decorated Colors

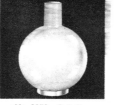

QUALITY (Fired on Colors) STUDENT SHADES

No. 2235—Hanging Lamp Shade

No. 2346—OPAL SHADE
6¾″ Fitter
4½″ Top
5¾″ High

RIBBED STYLE
No. 582—10″ Fitter

Colors

White (Opal)	Red
Apple Green	Rose
Dark Green	Yellow

Crown on Top

Use Our No. 1695

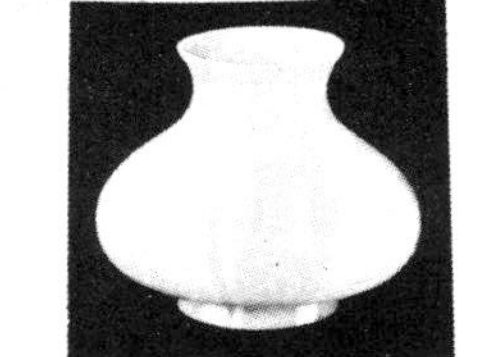

No. 1576—Plain Opal
Fitter 3¼″
Height 5½″
Diameter 6″

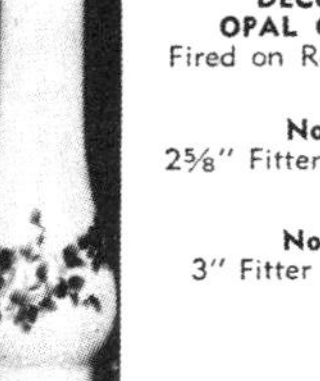

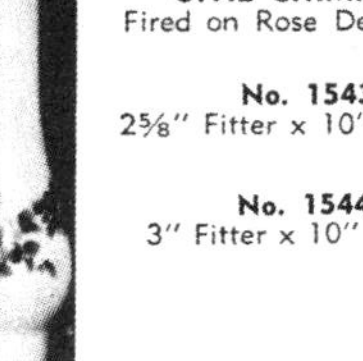

DECORATED OPAL CHIMNEYS
Fired on Rose Decoration

No. 1543
2⅝″ Fitter x 10″ Height

No. 1544
3″ Fitter x 10″ Height

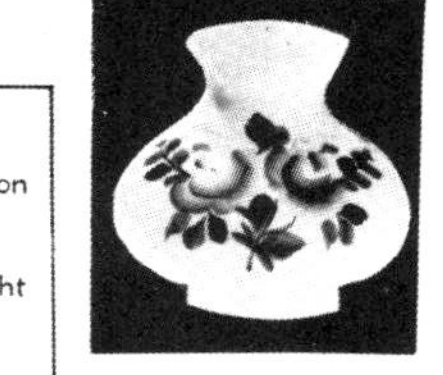

No. 1575—3¼″ Fitter
Height 5½″
Diameter 6″
Fired-On Hand
Decorated Colors
Red Roses — Green Leaves
with a Touch of Blue

Dr. Freeman in his Old Lamp Shop.

A section of Dr. Freeman's Old Lamp Shop.

becomes its value guide.

No attempt is made in the pages which follow to indicate precisely which examples of lamp and lamp parts are **reproductions** from original molds and which are new conceptions (especially in glass shade effects) of questionable authenticity. An observant student can tell at a glance that many a very fine electrified reproduction of a ruby or amberina oil hanging lamp does not have the softness or patina of the real thing. This is not to depreciate the use of reproduction parts to fill out on shade or bowl, smoke-bell, runner or chain lost in the ravages of time. We are indeed fortunate that there are several wholesale manufacturers (like the Dorset Division of the Williams Company at Thomaston, Conn.) who still supply many of the old Plume & Atwood, Miller and other old lamp parts seen in original catalog pages. Any reassembler who lacks a ring to hold a ball shade or who wants a particular kind of chimney to finish out something he has soldered together from the junkpile will need to consult the antique magazine ads of retailers in this field. This book provides your key to authenticity and what not to do. Guard it well.

As for the even greater fun of trying to make entirely new adaptations from lamp parts originally intended for other usage (i.e. gas ceiling fixtures turned into **torchiers,** oil or electric table lamps turned into wall brackets or vice-verse), the limits are only set by a tinker's ingenuity. Some so-called lamp adaptations are bizarre beyond words, others are true artistic creations.

Few men have been as ingenious in putting old lamp parts together and actually creating their own missing links as Clair E. Myers of York, Pennsylvania. His enthusiastic letter (on learning about the author's new issue of this book) is reproduced, along with a sample of his adaptive workmanship. This may inspire other master **fix-its** to using the butane torch, soldering iron and tin-snips to see what can be made of odd lamp parts that are crying out for rebirth and new decorative utility. Yes, some of these **home-talent creations** will be laughable in the eyes of the experts; but none will deny such collector-adaptors their fun. Furthermore, with this book, one will be more likely to produce an artistic and period-centered achievement than to produce a complete dud. "Dear Dr. Freeman, I have been collecting lamps and parts since I was 12-14 years old and then I would restore them and sell them. From 1950 to 1965 I worked and restored Brass car lights and radiators—all museum quality (some were for Ford display at World's Fair). I make wall brackets out of Rochesters."

Here is a picture of a hall lamp I made for $75.00. The bottom glass is about 125 years old. Your own collection must be fabulous; but I understand it is shown only to large study groups who have arranged in advance for a paid tour. Perhaps you can use some of my old lamp adaptations (in the seminar) if I can get them together again. Best Regards, Clair E. Myers"

Epilogue: The Light of Home

Concern in earlier chapters with the nature and use of bygone lighting devices has often led to neglect of social history. Hence, this epilogue. Our Victorian grandparents, to whom this book is dedicated, understood very well **the light of home** as the symbol of family togetherness. Whatever its source (candles, kerosene, gas or electricity), this was the beacon towards which the weary relative or friend turned his steps to escape the outer darkness and dank. More than just as 'escape,' the well-lighted home gave its family a sense of economic security, solidarity and inner peace. Even today, those who scoff loudest about "Victorian Sentimentality'' and call its close family ties "a decadent sub-culture" are themselves envious of that **light of home.**

True, times have changed; modern parents don't hold children so tight, accept the fact they must be off and on their own (often separated by whole continents in time or space). The large Victorian family house is gone; 'Dad' and 'Mom' now live in a trailer park or have a tiny city flat. Grown children often sleep-around, have no place of their own.

Where now is the **light of home** for relatives so widely dispersed? What chance for a symbol that all should keep the home fires burning? Well, as a psychologist and collector, the author finds this human trait can be preserved through the **gift of family lamps.** Everyone can take a special lamp with him whenever he moves or leaves a home; and this (symbolically regarded) can be the tie-that-binds. Children do not throw off the ties of home just for 'the devil-of-it,' often its a necessity to work elsewhere.

There is always a **persistence of aggregates** (always some part of a home's togetherness that is never forgotten). In one family (the author's in fact) Grandparents and Great-grandparents down to the newest member of the clan will always be remembered by some family table light they worked or studied by. When the young left home there was given to each one a **family lamp;** then, as death shortened the circle, children were given grandpa's, grandma's, dad's or mother's family lamp. This became a sort of 'legacy'; one could take it away with him and so light a new home. Just as grandmother's legacy for a neighboring family survived through countless generations by hollyhocks grown from seeds originally in her garden, so in this collector's family, the gift of a lamp has helped to keep up the chain of affectionate association with the **home-place** even when it is gone.

Call this **Victorian Sentimentality** or what you will; here is one group, widely separated in space and interests, whose only sure-fire connection with some common past is **the lamp of home.** Lighted, it stands for personal integrity and solidarity in a topsy-turvy world. What is more, the glow conveys something to even those who are neither kith nor kin. Certainly the symbolism of the lamp transcends this unique family interest. It is found in many religious and social customs as well. In fact, if more people would leave a home lamp beckoning throughout the entire dark night, this might (in the course of time) once again make everyone light and gay the whole world over and express a great Victorian philosophy.

BIBLIOGRAPHY

Books

Adry, Eg. *Unsiecle d'e'clairace,* 1824-1924 (1925).

Allemagne, H. *Historie du luminaire depuis l'epoque romaine,* (Paris, 1891). *Musee du luminaire,* (Paris, 1900).

Allen, Ruth C. *How to Make Lampshades* (Pelham, N.Y. 1928).

Allphin, Willard. *Primer of Lamps and Lighting* (Chilton Co., 1959).

Barrows, B. H. *The Evolution of Artificial Light: From a Pine Knot to the Pentsch Light* (Omaha, Neb., 1893).

Benesch, L. *Lighting Candelabra, Chandeliers, Lamps, Art Objects* (1905). *A Revue of the Development of the Lighting Fixture: From Middle Ages to the Middle of the Nineteenth Century* (1933). *Old Lamps of Central Europe and Other Lighting Devices* (1963).

Bell, Louis. *Art of Illumination* (McGraw Hill, 1902).

Block, Werner. *Vom Kienspan vis Zum kunstlicken* (1925).

Bolton, Henry. *Legends of Sepulchral and Perpetual Lamps* (London, 1879).

Bowles, John D. *Acetylene for Lighting Country Homes* (Mo., 1910).

British Engineering Standards Assoc. *British Standards Specifications for Oil Lamps for Use on Ships* (London, 1922).

Broneer, O. T. *Terracotta Lamps* (Cambridge, Mass. (1930).

Caldwell, F. C. *Modern Lighting* (MacMillan Co., 1930).

Christopher, F. *Lampshade Making* (Dover Pubication, N.Y., 1952, 1953)

Cravath, J. R. and Lansing, V. R. *Practical Illumination* (McGraw, 1907).

Cudworth, Wm. *Antique Lamps—A Dissertation on Antique Terracotta Lamps* (London, 1893).

Dow, J. S. *Light in Daily Life* (London, 1939).

Dragoo, A. *Wire Lamp Shade Frames and How to Make* (Milwaukee, Wis., 1922).

Dryad Handicrafts. *Small Electric Light Shades and Candleshades* (Leicester, 1932).

Earle, O. *Lampshades: How to Make Them* (Dodd, Mead & Co., 1921).

Eaton, Jeanette. *The Story of Light Pictures by Max Schwartz* (Harper, 1928).

Freeman, Dr. Larry *Light on Old Lamps* (Century House, 1944).

General Electric Co. *Lighting of Hotels, Cafes and Clubs* (Schenectady, N.Y., 1911).

Gerhard, Wm. P. *Artificial Illumination* (N.Y., 1893).

Great Britain Patent Office, *Patents for Inventions* (London, 1871). *Works on Peat Destructive Distellation, Artificial Lighing, Mineral Oils and Waxes, Gas Lighting and Acetylene* (London, 1911).

Holophane Co., Inc. *Some Practical Hints on Lighting and Illumination* (N.Y., 1900).

General Electric Co. *Hotel Lighting* (Cleveland, 1925).

Hough, Walter. *The Lamp of the Eskimo* (Washington, 1896, 1898). *The Origin and Range of the Eskimo Lamp* (Washington, 1898).

Jonesbury, J. *Lamp Primer or Lamp Light and Lamps and How to Care for Them* (Harrop Co., 1893).

Kielland, T. B. *Chandeliers: English Summary on Glass Chandeliers* (1950).

Kunerth, W. *Lighting for Country Homes and Village Communities* (Ames, Ia., 1919).

Lewes, V. *Acetylene Handbook for Student and Manufacture* (MacMillan, 1900).

Little, Ruth. *Old Lamps & New; Restoring & Decorating* (Lubbock, Texas, 1964).

Luckiesh, M. *Lighting Fixtures and Lighting Effects* (McGraw-Hill, 1925). *The New Science of Lighting Cleveland: Incandescent* (1934).

MacSwiggan, A. E. *Fairy Lamps: Evening's Glow of Yesteryear* (Fountainhead, 1962).

Menke, H. *28 Table Lamp Projects* (McKnight Co., 1953).

Millspaugh, L. *Kerosene Accidents: How to Prevent Them* (MacDonald, 1874).

Mitchell, R. *The Study Book of Lamps and Candles* (London, 1960).

N.Y. Public Library. *List of Works Relating to Ilumination* (N.Y., 1908).

O'Dea, W. T. *The Social History of Lighting* (London, 1958).

Palestrant, S. S. *Lamps and Lampshade Making* (N.Y. Homecrafts, 1951).

Powell, A. L. *Marble: Aid to Lighting and Lamps* (N.Y., 1937).

Robins, F. W. *The Story of the Lamp and the Candle* (London, 1939).

Rourke, M. *Lampshades* (New Rochelle, N.Y., 1960).

Sharples, P. M. *Lampshade Making* (London Bell, 1966).

Southland, S. E. *Catalogue and Wholesale Price List of Jone's Improved Patent Lamps for Burning the Various hydro Carbon Oils* (Phila., 1859).

Stair, J. L. *The Lighting Book* (Chicago, 1930).

Sturrock, W. *Light Sources of the Past and Present* (Cleveland, 1952).

Thwing, L. L. *Lamp Oils and Other Illuminats* (Boston, 1932). *A Dictionary of Old Lamps and Other Lighting Devices* (Cambridge, 1952). *Flickering Flames* (C. E. Tuttle Co., 1958).

Tibbetts, D. F. *Clarke's Fairy Lamps* (Mission Press, 1951).

U.S. Quartermaster's Dept. *Lamps and Mineral Oil for the Army* (Wash., 1884).

Walters, H. B. *Catalogue of Greek and Roman Lamps in British Museum* (1914).

Periodicals and Journal Reports

Adams, J. C. "Lamps & Shades in Metal & Art Glass," *Popular Mechanic* (1911).

American Architect. "Modern Interior Lighting" (Nov., 1934).

Ackerley R. "An Introduction to the Science of Artificial Lighting," *Architecture and Building Series* (1948). *Lamp Buyer's Journal* (1926). *Lamp Manufacturer* (1932). *Lamplight* (Aug.-Dec., 1932). *Lamps* (Mar., 1924; Oct., 1933). *Scientific American* (articles from) I,xx (1859); "Drake's Improved Lamp," Ixvii (1859); "Marsh's Improved Gas Apparatus," I,xiv (1859); "Combination Lamp and Match Box," II,iv (1860); "Shaw's Shade-Supporters or Shade Clasps for Lamps," II,xiii (1860); "Green's Gas Lamp," II,xiv (1860); "Thompson's Regulating Gas Burner," II,xxi (1860); "Gas Burner Lamps," III,i (1860); "Guthrie's Improved Lamp," III,x (1860); "Humphrey's Mica Chimney for Lamps," III,v (1860); "Jone's Burner for Coal-Oil," III,iii (1860); "Dethridge's Oval Lamp Chimney," V,xvii (1861); "Marsden and Burrel's Camp Candelstick," VI,i (1862); "Scheeper's Lamp Attachment for Carriages," VI,i (1862); "Platt & Rosecran's Star Burner," VI,ii (1862); Monier's Gas Burner," VI,xiii (1862); "Jacob's Mode of Securing Chimneys to Lamps," VI,xxvi (1862); "Irwin's Lamp & Lantern," VII,iii (1862); "Fish's Lamp Heating Attachment," VII,iv (1862); "Mencci's Kerosene Lamp," VII,xii (1862); "Rebbeck and Davie's Lamp Burner," VII,xv (1862); "Vidal's Rock-Oil Lamp," VII,xvi (1862); "Hodgson's Chimney Fastner and Holder," VII,xiii (1862); "Brown's Lamp Chimney," VII,xv (1862); "Baker's Improved Lamp Attachment," VIII,iii, (1863); "Tisdel's and Nash's Patent Lamp Burner," VIII,xv (1863); "Seaman's Patent Reservoir," IX,v (1863); "Millar's Patent Lamp Chimney," IX,xiv (1863); "Colbum's Lamp Filler," IX,xxi (1863); "Day's Kerosene Lamp," IX,xxv (1863); "Fish's Heating Apparatus for Kerosene Lamps," X,v (1864); Straszer's Improved Lantern," X,viii (1864); "Union Lamp," XI,xx (1864); "Cornelius & Baker's Electric Bracket," XI,xxi (1864); "Colburn's Bracket Lamp Chimney," X,xxii (1864).

Atkinson, J. R. *Journal of the Scottish Societies of Antiquaries* (1910).

Curle, A. D. "Domestic Candlesticks from the 14th to the 18th Century," *Proceedings of the Society of Antiquaries of Scotland* (1900).

Hocart, J. C. Paper, *Proceedings of the Gurnsey Society of Natural Science* (1908).

Illustrated London News, The. Various issues. 1900-1930.

Journal of Egyptian Archaeology, (Apr. 1924, Nov. 1931).

Quarterly of the Dept. of Antiquities in Palestine, (Vol. V, Nos. 1 & 2).

Reliquary & Illustrated Archaeologist, The. Various papers (1900).

Report of the Research Committee of the Society of Antiquaries on Uriconium.

Rushford, Dr. "Pan Lamps of Pennsylvania," *Hobbies* (Sept. 1937).

Watkins. "Lamps of Colonial America," *Antiques* (Oct. 1937).

Woolley, Sir L. *Reports on the Ur Excavations* (1933-4).

Smith, Wm. L. "Shades & Globes for Electric Lights,"*Technology Quarterly* (Vol. 13).

"The Lamp," *Standard Oil Company* (1957 for 75th Anniv. of Jersey Standard).

"Salesman's Lamp Handbook," (Series No. 1) *Westinghouse Electric Corp.* (1930).

Note: Glossary Price Guide, etc. to lamps in this book appears in Study Guide No. 3, Century House, Watkins Glen, N. Y. ($4.50)